TRUE CRIMES

TRUE CRIMES

KILLING FOR LOVE

igloo

igloo

Published in 2011

by Igloo Books Ltd
Cottage Farm
Sywell
NN6 0BJ

www.igloo-books.com

M044 0311
10 9 8 7 6 5 4 3 2 1

ISBN: 978-0-85734-793-0

Printed and manufactured in China

Contents

Contents

Introduction

Crimes of Passion are not cold, premeditated acts, carefully planned by a killer who takes pleasure from the very act of violence. A crime of passion is committed in the heat of the moment, sometimes, almost unwillingly, as an act of desperation.

Jealousy, love, hate – whether nurtured over many years, or a spur of the moment loss of control – high emotions are the triggers to this type of murder. Crimes of passion are almost always committed by people who know their victims; in fact, they are committed because the murderers know their victims.

Crimes of passion murderers may not be in complete control of their actions, and may not be in control of their emotions, at the time they commit their crime. They may not be completely aware of what they are actually doing, and may suffer extreme remorse when they become aware of what they have done.

People we see everyday – in a supermarket, an office or even next door to us – anyone might be pushed a little too far in an argument with a friend, lover, wife or husband, and suddenly turn into a person capable of committing a crime of passion.

We are fascinated by crimes of passion because they reveal what some people are capable of doing to those they care about. Crimes of passion are moments of extreme emotion and, because of this, they offer an insight into our own minds.

Crimes of passion have been committed as far back in time as there were people to tell the stories. Jean Harris was driven by jealousy to kill her long-time lover; Ruth Ellis was hanged for shooting her lover; Thomas Keir killed both his first and second wives because of crazed jealousy.

Whatever the motive, crimes of passion are intriguing, portraying people's deepest motives and emotions.

BELOW: Italian veterinarian Renzo Ferrari (top, center) sitting in the defendants box before a Court of Assizes judge and a jury in Imperia on the Italian Riviera, during his trial for the killing of Tranquillo Allevi with strychnine in a bottle of bitter in 1962.

ABOVE: Nannie Doss, shown here soon after her confinement at the Oklahoma penitentiary in 1955. She had admitted to killing four of her husbands with rat poison.

ABOVE: Edward Allaway (center) being led into Orange County courthouse. Allaway was convinced that his wife Bonnie was sleeping around and his jealous rage led him to kill seven people at California State University.

ABOVE: Winnie Ruth Judd sitting in a Phoenix courtroom in 1932. Judd spent 40 years in a mental hospital for killing her two roommates in a jealous rage fuelled by her belief that they were sleeping with her boyfriends.

ABOVE: Brian Tevendale (right), who was jailed for life along with Sheila Garvie for the murder of her wealthy farmer husband.

ABOVE: Denise Labbe, in the custody of two Gendarmes, arriving at Blois Court House in Blois, France, to stand trial for the murder of her 2-year-old daughter Catherine. Labbe drowned the child to prove her love for Jacques Al Garron, who urged her to kill Catherine because she was born of a previous love affair.

ABOVE: Ruth Ellis, who was convicted of the murder of her lover, David Blakely, and hanged at Holloway Prison, becoming the last woman to receive the death penalty in Britain.

Millicent Adams

The case of Millicent Adams is a classic example of what can happen when a woman in love is treated with contempt by her lover. What is unusual about it is that even though Millicent freely admitted killing Axel Schmidt, her sentence was as light as the court could possibly impose while still seeming to punish her.

The daughter of a wealthy and respected Philadelphia family, the misfortunes of Millicent Adams began at Bryn Mawr University in the early 1960s where she met and fell in love with fellow student Axel Schmidt. Although he was studying to be an engineer, it occurred to Schmidt that a faster route to the wealth and the glittering social life he dreamed of might be through marriage, and he tirelessly courted Millicent until another girl came along whose family was even more wealthy and prominent than hers. With richer pickings on offer, Schmidt quickly dumped Millicent. As she later told police, she had been so hurt that she just wanted to kill herself.

BELOW: A Smith And Wesson Ladysmith .22 revolver, similar to the one used by Millicent Adams.

In preparation for her suicide Millicent bought a large St. Bernard dog, then took it to an unused room in her parents' mansion and shot it with a .22 caliber Smith & Wesson pistol. She explained during questioning that she wanted to be sure that it worked when she turned it upon herself. But it wasn't Millicent that ended up dead. With the promise of farewell sex in the air, she lured Schmidt to her home and after inviting him into her bed fired a single bullet and killed him. If she had been thinking about suicide before, she seemed to have forgotten about it now, for she didn't shoot herself after all. It may have been the knowledge that she was carrying Schmidt's child which stopped her pulling the trigger.

At her trial, Millicent's defense argued that she had acted in a moment of insanity caused by her lover's cold treatment of her. The court agreed that she should be allowed to plead guilty to manslaughter and not murder and, when she was pronounced guilty, gave her a ten-year probational sentence on condition that she admitted herself to a mental health institution.

Millicent gave birth to a baby daughter, Lisa, soon after. The child was taken away from Millicent though she was still given regular access. After three years under the care of mental health doctors, Millicent was deemed to be rehabilitated and released from detention. Disowned by her parents, Millicent Adams moved to build a new life on the West Coast.

Antonio Agostini

The case that became infamous as the "Pyjama Girl" murder was surrounded by mystery and took Australian police nearly 10 years to solve. The jealous husband, who eventually served time for Linda Agostini's death never fully revealed what happened that day, but it seems likely his passions were inflamed by her cheating and he set out to bring a murderous end to his unhappy marriage.

Italian immigrant Antonio Agostini married Linda Platt in 1930, and the couple settled in Melbourne, Australia. But their marriage wasn't a partnership of mutual support. Agostini worked at odd jobs to raise money, while Linda spent her days drinking and entertaining a string of lovers until suddenly, she disappeared. The last time anyone saw Linda Agostini alive was at her home in August 1934.

When asked about his missing wife, Agostini said that she had run away with one of her boyfriends, but before long a farmer discovered the body of a woman in a culvert between Melbourne and Sydney. She had been savagely beaten in her last moments before being shot through the head, then the corpse had been burned. Little was left to identify her from save the yellow silk pyjamas she had been wearing.

BELOW: Linda Agostini was born in Forest Hill, London, in 1905. She moved to New Zealand at the age of 19 after a failed romance. In 1927, Platt moved on again to Sydney, Australia.

At first, police believed the body to be that of Mrs Anna Philomena Coots who had gone missing at the same time. Even Linda's mother could not confirm the mutilated body was that of her daughter but she wasn't told about the pyjamas that later proved to be a crucial piece of evidence. The case was closed and might have remained so were it not for a policeman whose wife had been a friend of Linda's. He was certain that the body was hers and set about trying to prove it. Finally, Linda's mother was shown a photograph of the pyjamas the murdered woman had been wearing and identified them as a set that she had given to Linda as a wedding gift. She also told police again that Agostini had mistreated her daughter. Linda was identified through dental records, and Agostini was arrested in 1944.

Under interrogation, he admitted to killing his wife 10 years earlier, but said it was not intentional. He told police that he and Linda had both got drunk on August 28, 1934, and that she had accused him of having an affair with a woman at the restaurant where he worked. Agostini said Linda had been drunkenly waving a gun around and when it went off by accident she had been shot. It was obviously a tissue of lies. Further examination of Linda's body revealed that her brutal head wounds had been inflicted before she was shot and that it one of these was that killed her, not a bullet. Incredibly, Agostini also maintained that he had no idea how her body had come to be burned and suggested that someone else must have stumbled across her corpse and set fire to it.

Agostini went on trial on June 9, 1944, charged with his wife's murder. But the charge was reduced to manslaughter, and he was sentenced to six years' hard labor. He was released in 1950 and returned to Italy.

Edward Charles Allaway

Edward Allaway had long shown all the symptoms of paranoia schizophrenia, but he was a quiet man who kept himself to himself and few suspected how deep his psychological problems ran except the women he was married to. But when his second wife left him, his weak grip on sanity broke and he went on a killing spree that left nine people dead.

Allaway was diagnosed as a paranoid schizophrenic during his first marriage to a woman named Carol and though he once received a month-long course of electric-shock therapy it did little to help. The delusions continued and were particularly vivid. Carol, he thought, was not only sleeping around but posing for pornographic photos behind his back. The fact that she remarried within days of the couple's divorce being finalized did nothing to stem his suspicions or alleviate his mental condition.

Nevertheless, Allaway married again within a few months of moving south to Orange County, California, in 1973, and he and his new wife Bonnie took a long, cross-country camping trip, living a hand-to-mouth existence and taking work wherever they could find it. Eventually, they returned to Orange County and Allaway's sister managed to secure her brother a custodial job in the library of California State University, Fullerton.

All of Allaway's old symptoms were by now beginning to re-assert themselves, and were chillingly similar to those he had had before. Like with his first marriage, Allaway was certain that Bonnie had begun sleeping with other men and also that she was appearing in pornographic films made by employees of the library where he worked. He also began verbally abusing his co-workers as well as becoming increasingly prejudiced toward African and Hispanic Americans. At home his violent streak became more pronounced. He was insanely jealous and threatened to slash Bonnie's face with a pen knife if he caught her cheating. It was more than she could bear. Bonnie left.

ABOVE: A memorial grove of seven pine trees that honors the seven people killed by Edward Allaway on July 12, 1976, in the library of California State University.

In a towering rage of jealousy, Allaway snapped. But where a more sane man might have tried to take revenge on his wife, he just wanted to inflict some of the pain he was feeling, indiscriminately. On July 12, 1976, 37-year-old Edward Allaway walked into the library at California State University armed with a .22 caliber rifle and fired. As he roamed the halls, the psychotic gunman shot nine people, killing seven. He then drove to the nearby hotel where his wife worked, called the police, and quietly surrendered.

In 1977, Allaway was convicted of murder, but found not guilty by reason of insanity. Although there was an attempt in 2001 to reintroduce him to society, it was overruled by a judge in 2003 who said that Allaway should not be released from the Patton State Hospital in San Bernardino County.

Anibal Almodovar

A serial womanize who was quick to anger, Anibal Almodovar became so furious at his new wife's insistence that he give up his wayward sexual lifestyle that he killed her just weeks after the wedding. Unfortunately for him, he did not stop to consider that it might not just be witnesses that could place him at the scene of the murder. The evidence that convicted him came from somewhere no one would have suspected.

An extremely handsome man and former sailor, 25-year-old Puerto Rican Anibal Almodovar was working as a porter in New York City when he met a waitress in a Manhattan bar and married her. Two years younger than her new husband and strikingly pretty herself, Louise Almodovar assumed that as a married man her husband would give up the one-night stands

BELOW: An aerial view of Central Park, where Anibal Almodovar dumped the body of his wife Louise.

and frequent flings he had been so used to enjoying. But she was wrong. The couple hadn't been married more than a few weeks when it became apparent to her that Almodovar was still pursuing the same lifestyle; he made few efforts to hide the fact from his wife. She protested and a violent argument broke out, after which Almodovar stormed out of the apartment.

Unwilling to give up on her marriage so quickly, Louise later called him at a local bar and asked to meet so they might try and resolve their problems more calmly. He agreed and told her that he would see her in Central Park. Louise's body was found among tall grass in the famous park on November 2, 1942. The ripped sleeve of her jacket suggested that she had struggled furiously, and the chief medical examiner concluded that she had been throttled by a killer who had placed two fingers from each hand on her windpipe.

Unable to identify the corpse and assuming that it was a random killing committed by one of the many dubious characters that could be found in Central park at night, the police department was initially at a loss. But when reports of a missing woman whose husband was a known cheat and violent bully came in, they scented a murderer.

Almodovar was brought in for questioning and his clothes taken away for examination. The seeds found in the turn-ups of his trousers would later prove crucial in convicting him of his wife's murder.

At first, Almodovar made a full confession, telling police he had lost control when Louise nagged him about seeing other women. He said he had strangled her and left the scene. However, when the case came to trial, on February 24, 1943, he retracted the confession. The police, he said, had forced it out of him under duress. Now he maintained that he had nothing to do with Louise's death.

Unfortunately for him, the seeds that had been found in his trousers were from rare plants growing at the murder scene. They had been planted there as a nursery experiment and could not be found anywhere else in New York. What's more, as a professor of biology and botany explained to the court, as the seeds found on Almodovar's trousers only matured within a week of the murder, the evidence placed Almodovar at site on the night Louise was killed. Anibal Almodovar's was the first case in US legal history to rely on botanical evidence to get a conviction. He was found guilty and sentenced to death in the electric chair.

Tracie Andrews

A former boyfriend would later recall, "When Tracie gets angry her eyes go wild," and the parents of her victim have spoken of their fear that she will kill again if ever released. For Tracie, it seems that rage is never far from the surface and if roused to passion she can be deadly, as Lee Harvey found out.

The relationship of barmaid and former model Tracie Andrews and her fiancé Lee Harvey was a stormy one. Both had tempers and—as neighbors would later tell the police—often had violent arguments. The row they had while driving to their home in Alvechurch near Worcester, England, on December 1, 1996, was no different from the rest, except in the way it ended. Tracie's uncontrollable temper finally snapped completely and, in a frenzy of rage, she pulled a knife and stabbed Harvey 15 times.

Two days later, she appeared at a press conference appealing for information about Harvey's killer. She told the cameras and waiting reporters that Harvey had been the victim of a road rage attack by a man with "staring eyes." Her story was that a "tatty" Ford Sierra had followed them flashing its lights, before drawing level when they stopped. The driver then got out and knifed Harvey. The police described the attack as "particularly vicious" and the killing was highly publicized in the national press.

single member of the public had come forward. All the evidence pointed to the killer being closer at hand.

Even after she had been charged and released on bail, Tracie maintained her story, but she could not stop the truth seeping out. At her trial the jury heard that Harvey had been obsessively jealous over her and accused her of seeing other men. The neighbors told their own stories of screaming rows.

Tracie Andrews was found guilty of murder at Birmingham Crown Court on July 29, 1997. Sentenced to life in prison with the recommendation that she serve a minimum of 14 years, she immediately lodged an appeal claiming she was the victim of a miscarriage of justice because of the publicity about her case. It was thrown out in October 1998.

Two years later, Tracie finally admitted she had killed Lee Harvey, and in 2005 a television documentary was made about the case. A prison source said, "Andrews has… admitted to the murder, which has surprised a lot of people. Although she has accepted her guilt, nobody really believes that she feels much remorse. She sees this as her first step on the way to parole. Andrews is manipulative and devious. Officers believe she will say or do anything to get out of jail."

ABOVE: Tracie Andrews arriving at Birmingham Crown Court on July 29, 1997, to hear the verdict in her murder trial.

Either wracked with guilt or in fear of being found out, Tracie took a drug overdose the next day, but survived. She was arrested in hospital on December 7, while recovering. The police had been unable to find any witnesses to the road rage attack and not a

BELOW: The sleepy village of Alvechurch was shocked by the murder of Lee Harvey in 1996.

Herbert Armstrong

A keen gardener who often used his hobby to escape from the sharp tongue of his domineering wife, it was only natural that when Armstrong finally decided that he couldn't take anymore he turned to a remedy he'd found effective in his beloved garden: weed killer.

The marriage of solicitor Herbert Armstrong and his wife Katherine was never a particularly happy one. Although the couple had three children together, she was a tyrant. Armstrong was forbidden to drink or smoke, two pleasures that he much enjoyed, while Katherine often took her own pleasure in humiliating him in front of friends. Like many men who find they have married a domineering nag, he found refuge in the garden where he could avoid Katherine's sneering. He was never able to avoid her completely though and over the years his anger. At the age of 53, Armstrong finally decided that enough was enough: his wife had to die. First he made sure that a new will was drawn up for her under which he was the sole beneficiary and then he replenished his stock of weed-killer. After all it had rid his garden of unwanted pests, so why not other areas of his life, too.

In August 1920, Katherine Armstrong's physical and mental health collapsed to such an extent that she was admitted to the Barnwood Asylum in nearby Gloucester. By January 1921 she was well enough to be discharged and returned home to the care of her husband on the 22nd. And take care of her he did—again with doses of arsenic based weed-killer. A month later Katherine was dead. The local doctor, Thomas Hincks, certified that the cause of her death was heart disease. She was buried with due ceremony.

ABOVE: English solicitor Herbert Rowse Armstrong, in a photograph from the 1920s.

Armstrong was now free to get on with his life in peace, and presumably take up drinking and smoking once more, but having gotten away with murder so easily he was tempted to turn to the weed-killer again. This time it wasn't a wife who needed to be removed, but a business acquaintance with whom he had fallen out—Mr Oswald Martin. Armstrong bought a box of chocolates, made a small hole in the bottom of each and carefully inserted his poison. Then he had the box delivered anonymously to Martin's house. A delighted Mrs. Martin ate some, and the box was also produced at a dinner party. Martin escaped with his life, but one of the guests quickly became ill and suspicion fell on the chocolates. The small holes in the base of each were soon discovered, as was the arsenic they contained.

Armstrong wasn't going to give up easily though. On October 26, 1921, he invited Martin to visit his

BELOW: Witnesses Dr. Webster (left) and Dr. Thomas Hincks (center) outside the courtroom in Hereford, Gloucestershire, during the 1922 trial of solicitor Herbert Rowse Armstrong for the murder of his wife, Katherine.

ABOVE: Crowds gathering outside the courtroom in Hereford, Gloucestershire, during Herbert Rowse Armstrong's trial.

house for afternoon tea, during which he passed his guest a scone, apologizing for using his fingers. Later that evening Martin became ill. Dr. Thomas Hincks, who had also treated the unfortunate Katherine Armstrong, was called in and faced with many of the same symptoms from that case, he became suspicious. A urine sample was sent to the Clinical Research Association for analysis and revealed the presence of arsenic in Martin's system. The police were called in and after making discreet investigations they exhumed Katherine's body. It, too, contained arsenic. On January 19, 1922, Armstrong was arrested and charged with the murder of his wife.

His trial began on April 3, 1922. Armstrong represented himself skillfully, arguing that his wife had taken the poison herself either in an attempt to relieve her illness or in a suicide attempt, but it wasn't enough. The Martin poisoning was used as evidence, as was the fact that when Armstrong was arrested he was carrying a small bag of the poison. Herbert Armstrong was found guilty of the murder of his wife, and sentenced to hanging. After a failed appeal he was executed on May 31, 1922.

Arnold Axilrod

A man whose sexual appetites were matched only by his depravity, dentist Arnold Axilrod drugged his patients so that he could rape them while they were unconscious. He also kept a lover, and when she fell pregnant the evil man decided to terminate the fetus, and his mistress with it.

On the morning of April 23, 1955, John J. Cowles, Jnr., of the Cowles publishing empire was backing his Pontiac out of his garage, in Minneapolis, when he noticed what appeared to be a bundle of clothes in the alley. The "bundle" was the body of a young woman. Her face had been scratched and bruised, and her throat had a bluish mark. Police were called and when they searched the woman's coat pockets found a wallet containing a five-dollar bill, a doctor's prescription slip, and a driver's license. The woman was identified as Elizabeth Mary Moonen aged 21.

An autopsy revealed that she had been strangled, and that Elizabeth had been three months pregnant. It also found traces of semen in her vagina, which suggested that she had had intercourse just prior to her death. It seemed likely that her sexual partner would also be her killer. Here the mystery deepened, for police enquiries found that Elizabeth's husband was a serviceman stationed in Korea.

The starting point in the hunt for Elizabeth's lover was Dr. Glen Peterson who had issued the prescription found in Elizabeth's wallet, and he immediately pointed police in the right direction. He told them that she had named the baby's father as local dentist Arnold Axilrod, 49, who had a reputation as something of a ladies' man.

In fact, Axilrod was much more sleazy than a simple womanizer. His surgery was above a seedy nightclub called the Hoop De Do, and his patients were mainly nightclub performers and hat-check girls. Despite the fact that he had a spotless reputation, there were doubts about his activities. In late 1954, a phone call had been received by the police during which an anonymous woman told an officer that Axilrod had sedated her to operate on her teeth and then raped her while she was unconscious. But as she refused to give her name or file a complaint, the allegation was never investigated.

Axilrod buckled quickly under police questioning. He admitted that he'd given Elizabeth a ride on the evening of her death, and said that the two had quarreled after she accused him of being the father of her child. He claimed she had also threatened to expose him. The next thing he knew, Axilrod continued, was that he'd blacked out and when he came to, Elizabeth was no longer in the car. What he said next surprised the police. When they told him that she had been strangled, Axilrod replied, "If she was strangled, I must have done it. I was the only one there." He later withdrew that statement.

When the case hit the newspapers, 20 women came forward to say they had also been drugged by the dentist. One was Elizabeth's sister who said that Axilrod had talked suggestively to her. Axilrod went on trial for murder in Hennepin County District Court in late 1955. Despite public outrage, the evil dentist was not convicted of murder though. At the end of his trial, the jury found Axilrod guilty of manslaughter and given a prison sentence.

Arthur Bagg

When jealousy enters an already unbalanced mind, the results can be tragic. And few minds have been as fevered as Arthur Bagg's. His was a life lived in fantasy, worshipping the mythical Count Dracula, and the murder he committed was every bit as ghastly as any from a horror story.

When 17-year-old Marjorie Patricia Rosebrook's **stabbed and mutilated body was found** beneath a viaduct outside Johannesburg, South Africa, suspicion immediately settled on her boyfriend, artist Arthur Bagg. The detectives' certainty that they had found the killer hardened when he told them that he hadn't been with Marjorie on the day of the murder—November 23, 1937. In fact, they already had several witnesses who reported that they had seen the couple together.

Determined to get a confession, the police continued to interrogate the 23-year-old. Eventually he broke down and willingly took officers to the scene of the crime, even going so far as to re-enact the killing for them. In a jealous rage over her conduct with another man, he had had stabbed her twice. Nevertheless, that didn't explain the mutilation and there was also the question of Marjorie's missing clothes and the murder weapon. At this point Bagg's co-operation dried up, for the full extent of his lunacy was yet to be uncovered. He tried everything he could to stop a police search of his home, and once there it soon became apparent why.

Beneath the floor of his bedroom was a secret earthen chamber hidden by a trapdoor; a "ritual site" where Bagg worshipped Count Dracula. It was also where he had hidden the murder knife and Marjorie's blood-stained clothing. Along with the incriminating evidence detectives found a piece of leather on which Bagg had carved the words, "I hereby defile the living God and serve only the Dark One, Dracula; to serve him faithfully so I may become one of his faithful servants."

Ironically, it was the evidence that he had tried to conceal that would save Bagg from execution. At his trial, on February 28, 1938, he withdrew his confession to Marjorie Rosebrook's murder and claimed she had committed suicide. He said he had only told police he had killed her to save her from shame. But after two hours deliberation, the jury found Bagg guilty of murder and he was sentenced to death. However, after assessments of his mental state were made—which took into account his strange shrine to the vampire—the sentence was commuted to life imprisonment. Bagg was released in 1947 after serving nine years.

BELOW: Arthur Bagg's obsession with Count Dracula led him to commit the horrendous murder of Marjorie Rosebrook.

George Ball

While the murder of Christine Catherine Bradfield was not a classic crime of passion, it certainly occurred during a moment of terrifying and passionate fury.

George Ball was the 22-year-old clerk of a shop that sold tarpaulins in Liverpool, England. Unfortunately, it was not a job he enjoyed, for the simple reason that the store's manager was a bitter woman with a sharp tongue. Nothing Ball ever did for Christine Bradfield was right. She constantly barked orders at him and was swift to get angry.

Humiliated by the woman on a daily basis, Ball's anger also steadily grew, until on December 10, 1913, he snapped. In a turmoil of hatred, Ball gave in to a temptation of a different sort, the temptation to take revenge. He grabbed Christine while she was counting the day's takings, raped her, and battered her to death with a piece of wood.

As his rage subsided, Ball was faced with the consequences of his crime: a dead body for which he would hang if caught. Quickly he enlisted the help of another young man who worked in the shop, Samuel Angeles Elltoft, who was just 18 years old and a person of extremely low intelligence. Easily led, Elltoft agreed to help dispose of the body.

Catherine's body was wrapped in tarpaulins and loaded onto a handcart, in which Ball and Elltoft planned to push it to the local Leeds and Liverpool Canal where it could be dumped. Unfortunately for the

---

BELOW: A modern view of Walton Prison where George Ball was hanged on February 26, 1914.

pair, there was someone standing between them and the canal. Walter Eaves was waiting outside the shop for his girlfriend. The murderer and his accomplice could go nowhere without being spotted. The situation took a turn for the worse when one of the shop's shutters blew open, putting a dent in Eaves' bowler hat. Seeing Ball through the window, he immediately began complaining that the shop was responsible for ruining his best hat. Panic-stricken Ball was forced to offer Eaves two shillings in compensation.

As Eaves continued to wait for his girlfriend, Ball decided that he had to get rid of the incriminating evidence immediately. The bowler-hatted suitor was still there when Ball and Elltoft came past pushing a tarpaulin-covered handcart that to contain a heavy load. Although Eaves didn't see them throw Catherine's body into the canal, he would remember the odd bundle the next day when the corpse was found. For it did not sink as Ball had hoped, and nor was it washed into the River Mersey and out to sea. Instead the sack containing the body got caught in a lock gate where it was discovered the next day.

On reading newspaper reports of a woman's body being found in the canal Eaves went straight to the police. Elltoft was quickly arrested, but Ball went on the run, adopting a disguise that seems almost designed to attract attention to him. Shaving his eyebrows, the inept killer covered one of his eyes with a pirate's eye patch and then wore a pair of spectacles over the top. It must have looked ludicrous and certainly didn't help save him from the clutches of the law, particularly as the whole of Liverpool was soon searching for him. The detective leading the murder inquiry had a flash of inspiration. He organized for Ball's photograph to be flashed up on screens of all the city's movie theaters, accompanied by the message: "George Ball, Wanted for Murder, Reward." Ball was recognized and arrested on December 20, 1913, as he left a football match.

But Ball's bizarre attempts to free himself were not yet over. For his trial the following February, he concocted a story that could have come straight from a boy's comic. The court heard that two desperate men had sprung up from where they were hidden beneath tarpaulins and killed Catherine Bradfield. Having murdered her, Ball insisted that they had put a revolver to his and Elltoft's head and threatened that if they did not dispose of the body, they too would be killed. In response, the prosecution simply asked that if that had been the case why did Ball not ask for Eaves' help during the dealings over the dented bowler hat.

Unsurprisingly, Ball was found guilty of murder and sentenced to death. While awaiting his execution in jail, he finally realized there would be no reprieve and confessed to the murder to the Bishop of Liverpool. He was hanged at Walton Prison on February 26, 1914. Elltoft was given a four-year prison sentence.

Susan Barber & Richard Collins

If Susan Barber had ever been faithful to the man she married, it was a short-lived fidelity. Within weeks of her wedding, the 17-year-old bride was welcoming her 15-year-old neighbor into her bed every morning, shortly after her husband left for work.

Believing Susan's six-month old baby daughter to be his, Michael Barber accepted his responsibilities and married her. The couple set up home in a small house in Westcliffe-on-Sea, Sussex, England; three houses away from 15-year-old Richard Collins who soon caught Susan's eye. Within weeks the boy was eagerly awaiting Barber to leave for his 5am start at the local cigarette factory each morning so that Collins could slip into his still-warm spot in the marital bed and his wife's arms.

The pair enjoyed many dawn sex sessions together, and over time Susan had two more children.

Their affair might have gone on indefinitely, but for one morning when Barber left home at 4am for a fishing trip with friends. As usual Collins took his place soon after he had left the house and he and Susan became so involved in each other that they didn't notice the weather getting worse outside the window. Barber decided that he'd rather be inside in the warm and dry and returned home to find his wife and teenage neighbor in bed together. His rage was terrible and neither of the lovers escaped his fists, but after Collins

BELOW: Paraquat herbicide crystals, of the type used by Susan Barber to poison her husband.

had been sent packing Susan agreed that she would end the relationship.

She never had any intention of fulfiling her promise and continued to write to Collins and see him when she could. Meanwhile, she grew bitterly resentful of the husband who had put a stop to her daily fun.

Michael Barber started to feel unwell on June 4, 1981. His illness started with a severe headache, but was soon accompanied by sickness and stomach pains. Three days later he was having difficulty breathing and was rushed to the Intensive Care Unit at Southend General Hospital. Still, his condition deteriorated and he was transferred to London's specialist Hammersmith Hospital. Doctors were puzzled by his condition.

No specific infection could be found, but his symptoms matched those of paraquat poisoning. Instructions were given for blood and urine samples to be taken and sent to the National Poisons Reference Centre for analysis, but there was a mix up with paperwork. Although no samples were ever taken or sent it was believed that they had been and that a negative result had been sent back. Michael Barber died on June 27 and at a postmortem his major organs were removed and preserved.

On July 3, the rest of Barber's body was cremated and the same day Richard Collins took his belongings three doors down the street and moved in with Susan. Flush with cash after her husband's employers paid out a death benefit of £15,000 and with a further £3,300 a year promised for each of the three children, Susan did not waste any time grieving. Instead she threw wild drink and sex parties and bought herself a CB radio, giving herself the handle "Nympho."

In September, the hospital where Michael Barber died finally received a postmortem report that showed he had ingested a toxic substance, probably paraquat. A check on the relevant files showed that the supposed blood tests had never taken place, let alone been sent off for analysis. Realizing the mistake, the hospital took tissue samples from Barber's organs at the mortuary and sent them to ICI, manufacturers of paraquat, and to the National Poisons Unit. The results came back quickly, both confirming the presence of paraquat.

Susan Barber and Richard Collins were arrested nine months after Michael Barber's death. Susan was charged with murder, conspiracy to murder, and of administering poison with intent to injure. Collins was charged with conspiracy to murder. Both pleaded not guilty at their trial at Chelmsford Crown Court, which began on November 1, 1982. Susan admitted putting the poison on her husband's food but claimed she had just wanted to make him ill so that she could get away without him coming after her. Both defendants were found guilty: Barber was sentenced to life imprisonment and Richard Collins to two years.

Elvira Barney

The acquittal of Elvira Barncy was nothing short of jaw-dropping. The evidence stacked against her was damning, yet still the jury found her not guilty.

The marriage of 24-year-old, gin-swilling, wealthy socialite Elvira Barney and her husband Stephen was known to be a rocky one. Neighbors would later testify that on one occasion they had seen Elvira leaning

BELOW: Socialite Elvira Barney arriving at her parents' home in London shortly after being acquitted of the murder of her lover Michael Scott Stephen.

from a window firing shots at her husband with the very gun that later killed him. In fact, the couple had separated, but drunken, jealous Elvira was determined that no one else would have Stephen.

On May 31, 1932, Elvira and Stephen passed an evening together at the Café de Paris in an attempt to patch up their relationship. As was usual they drank a lot of alcohol, and as was equally usual a row broke out. It would be the couple's last. They returned to Elvira's London home in Knightsbridge and the argument escalated. At first, neighbors assumed it was just another raging quarrel, but then they heard the words, "I will shoot you!" followed by gunshots.

In a panic, Elvira telephoned her doctor and told him a "terrible accident" had happened. He arrived to find Stephen Barney laying dead at the foot of the stairs, shot in the chest at close range. The police were called and they quickly found a .22 Smith & Wesson revolver with two empty chambers. The gun, Elvira told them, had gone off accidentally during a struggle. She had picked it up to threaten suicide if her husband left her for good

and Stephen had attempted to wrestle it away from her. They didn't believe the story and Elvira was formally arrested and charged with murder on June 3.

During the trial at the Old Bailey, Elvira's lawyer Sir Patrick Hastings presented only the flimsiest of evidence in her defense. At one point he demonstrated that the revolver used in the alleged murder had no safety catch and could be fired by just the slightest pressure on the trigger. The ballistics expert Robert Churchill disagreed, telling the jury that the model was one of the safest guns ever made. The jury also heard that all the forensic evidence pointed to murder and listened to the neighbors' tale of hearing Elvira's threat shortly before the gunshots were heard. They were also told that she had been seen taking pot-shots at her husband from a window on an earlier occasion.

Incredibly, Elvira was found not guilty. The jury simply refused to believe that she had intended to kill her husband. The scandal took its toll on the heavy-drinking socialite. Elvira moved to France and was found dead in a Paris hotel bedroom four years later.

Adelaide Bartlett

That Theodore Edwin Bartlett was eccentric is undeniable. To marry a beautiful young woman only to encourage her in a sexual liaison with a man of the cloth seems more than a little perverse. Yet it still seems unlikely that Bartlett would knowingly swallow enough chloroform to kill himself in a bid to attract his own wife's attention.

Suffering from rotten teeth and halitosis and having spent many of his 30 years building up a chain of grocery shops, love had taken a back seat in Bartlett's life until his brother introduced him to the 18-year-old Adelaide Blanche de Tremoile. Vivacious and lovely, she was a young woman who might have found a much better match save for the fact that she had been born out of wedlock. There were few greater social stigmas in the Victorian age, so when Bartlett asked Adelaide's father for her hand he was accepted. Not many men as wealthy as Bartlett would have been eager to marry an illegitimate girl. Strangely though, Bartlett proposed

to both Adelaide and her father that their marriage be purely platonic. It is impossible to say with any certainty why he would have wanted to avoid sexual contact with his pretty new wife, but it seems obvious that Bartlett's sexuality was different to what would have been considered the acceptable norm in those days and it is possible that he did not want her to discover this. Time would make him less concerned though and he would later press his unwanted attentions on Adelaide.

As part of the bargain he made with Adelaide's father, she was sent first to finishing school and then spent some time in a convent, both at Bartlett's expense, before returning to become his wife. From the start, the marriage was stormy. Bartlett's father initially came to live with the couple and made life so unpleasant for Adelaide that she ran back to her former lodgings and, Bartlett was firmly convinced, into the arms of his brother Frederick who still lived there.

But while Bartlett may have been jealous of his wife's affection for his own brother, he had no such pangs when it came to the Methodist minister George Dyson. Indeed, Bartlett encouraged their relationship as much as he could. A man of dubious reputation, Dyson was invited to tutor Adelaide and to join the couple on trips. And he also soon began sharing Adelaide's bed, an arrangement her husband seems to have been delighted with.

It appears that his wife and her lover were less happy with the arrangement. Toward the end of 1885 Adelaide bought four small bottles of chloroform and on New Years Eve, Edwin Bartlett went to sleep at the couple's apartment in Pimlico, London. He never woke up.

Such a sudden death was suspicious and a postmortem was performed. It found that Bartlett's stomach was full of chloroform, and Adelaide and Dyson were quickly arrested on suspicion of murder. Dyson immediately rushed to protect himself by laying all the blame at the feet of the young woman whose sexual favors he had only recently been enjoying. He became a witness for the prosecution.

Adelaide's trial began in February 1886. Defending her was one of the finest legal minds of late Victorian England, Sir Edward Clarke, who set out to show that Bartlett was mentally unstable

BELOW: Adelaide Bartlett, accused and acquitted in the Pimlico Murder case of 1886.

and had committed accidental suicide. The jury heard that Adelaide had bought the chloroform to make her husband sleep and thus avoid his unwanted sexual advances. No one, it was argued, could be poisoned with such a large amount of such an evil tasting liquid without immediately knowing it. Bartlett, Clarke told the jury, had grabbed the bottle and swallowed its contents as a way of getting his wife's attention.

The sensational case soon became known as The Pimlico Murder, and as the lurid details of Bartlett's sexual oddities became known, Clarke was able to convince the jury that the suicide theory was possible if not likely. Adelaide was acquitted, with the head of the jury stating, "Although we think there is the gravest suspicion attaching to the prisoner, we do not think there is sufficient evidence to show how or by whom the chloroform was administered." Adelaide Bartlett left the court a free woman and with cheers resounding in her ears. Amazingly she took up again with the man who had been so quick to denounce her, then she and George Dyson vanished from the public eye.

Earl Leo Battice

An old sailors' tradition holds that women on board are always bad luck, and that certainly proved the case when ship's cook Earl Leo Battice insisted on taking his mistress onto the merchant ship Kingsway. First his wife discovered his attempt to have some extramarital fun on the high seas, and when she turned the tables on him the voyage of the Kingsway became a voyage into disaster.

In 1926, the four-masted schooner **Kingsway** set sail from Perth Amboy, New Jersey, headed for the Gold Coast of Africa with a cargo of timber. First though, the captain took her into port at Puerto Rico, where he went ashore to look for a cook. He found Earl Leo Battice, who seemed a good candidate for the job but who insisted that his wife join him on the trip. The captain refused, thinking that a woman among the all-male crew on such a long voyage could only mean trouble. Time was tight though and Battice adamant. With a schooner full of men needing to be fed, the captain reluctantly agreed. But it wasn't Battice's wife who came aboard, but his mistress Emilia Zamot—a poor Creole girl from the streets. The captain's first taste of trouble arrived when Battice's real wife Lucia heard about his departure, boarded the schooner, and sent Emilia packing. Then she took her place as the Kingsway set sail on December 15.

At first, the husband and wife arrangement on board appeared to work well much to the relief of the captain. But then Lucia became close to a muscular and aggressive German engineer, Waldemark Karl Badke,

RIGHT: A street scene from the Puerto Rican port where the captain of the Kingsway hired Earl Leo Battice.

a man who no one wanted to upset. The two didn't bother to conceal their affair, and fearing a mutiny—as well as Badke's anger—the captain made no move to intervene in the affair.

Battice, however, was driven to the point of jealous insanity and when, on February 4, 1927, he caught his wife and Badke together in a ship's storeroom he slashed at Lucia with a razor until Badke overpowered him. Lucia died from her injuries a week later and her body was dropped overboard into the sea. Battice was clapped in leg irons for the rest of the outward journey, but was released on the return as the captain desperately needed a decent cook to replace the new African employee, who was making half the crew ill.

The Kingsway re-entered American waters in August 1927. Battice was arrested and charged with second degree murder. He was found guilty of the murder of his wife Lucia Battice and sentenced to 10 years imprisonment in the Federal Penitentiary in Atlanta.

Ann Beddingfield & Richard Ringe

This tale of illicit love and deadly intentions dates to the mid-18th century and is particularly notable for the stupidity and clumsiness of the mistress and servant who plotted to kill the master of the house.

A **man of good and wealthy stock,** John Beddingfield was 24 when he married Ann. The couple received a large farm in Suffolk as a wedding present from his parents and settled down to a life of sleepy comfort in the English countryside. Ann, however, soon grew bored of talk about crops and rearing stock, and longed for something to break the boredom of life as a well-

to-do farmer's wife. She found it in one of the servants. Soon Richard Ringe was performing household duties by day and sexual duties in Ann's bed by night.

While she certainly wasn't the first lady of the house to tumble into bed with one of the staff, Ann made the mistake of falling in love with her servant beau. And while her husband had graciously turned a blind eye

ABOVE: Richard Ringe was hanged for his part in the murder of John Beddingfield.

to her nocturnal pleasures, a life of illicit sex was no longer enough for her. If John Beddingfield were to die though, she knew that she would become the sole owner of the extensive farm and free to marry again. Although it might cause a minor scandal, she could raise Ringe from his position of servitude to become master of the property.

Ringe was easily persuaded and together they plotted. Unfortunately, they were as inept at murder as they had been at hiding their affair, and may as well have advertised their intentions. First Ann told another servant that her husband would soon be dead and then she asked a kitchen maid to add the poison she had bought to the master's drink. When she refused, Ringe decided more drastic action was called for.

One night in March 1763, Richard Ringe crept into John Beddingfield's bedroom and strangled him as he slept. He then burst into Ann's room and announced,

"I have done for him!" If he had looked around the room before speaking he would have noticed that a young maid was also present. She was so alarmed she ran to see that her master was unharmed.

Unbelievably, at the Coroners Court none of the servants gave evidence and a verdict of "death by natural causes" was returned. The jury believed John Beddingfield had somehow strangled himself with his own bedding while having a nightmare. Still Ann Beddingfield and Richard Ringe were in fear for their lives since the servants knew everything. Their love now melted away.

They were right to be afraid, for the maid who had been in Ann's room the night of the murder had simply been waiting to collect her wages before going to the authorities. She told them her story, and the couple were charged and brought to trial in April, 1763. Ann pleaded her innocence while Ringe, after hearing testimony from the servants, confessed his part in the crime in the hope of being shown mercy. It never came. Richard Ringe and Ann Beddingfield were both found guilty of murder and sentenced to death. On April 8, 1753, they were drawn by sledge to Rushmore, near Ipswich, where Ringe was hanged and Ann burned alive at the stake.

RIGHT: Ann Beddingfield was burned alive at the stake after being found guilty of the murder of her husband John.

Cyril Belshaw

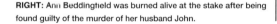

The mysterious disappearance of Betty Belshaw began a murder investigation that remains unsolved to this day. While her husband Cyril—who was having an affair at the time she vanished—was not convicted of her murder, since the day after the couple arrived in Paris she has never been seen again.

In 1978, Cyril Belshaw was a highly respected academic and head of the anthropology department at the University of British Columbia. Editor-in-chief of the journal of the Current Ethological Sciences and adviser to the United Nations Bureau of Social Affairs, he was well known on the lecture circuit and had written many papers about his work. He was also cheating on his wife, Betty.

Nevertheless, the couple decided to put their academic work (and Belshaw's secret lover) behind them for a year so they could indulge their passion for travel. They crossed the Atlantic and first went to

Montana Vermala in Switzerland before moving on to the romantic French capital of Paris. It was here that the mystery began. On January 14, 1979, the couple booked into the Novotel Bagnolet hotel and stayed in their room until breakfast the following morning. Then they decided to go their separate ways. Betty wanted to carry out some research at the Bibilotheque Nationale, and Cyril wished to explore the city. They left the hotel together and parted at Bourse Station. Betty failed to show up at the lunch date she and her husband had arranged for 1 pm and was never seen again.

It was not until the next day that Belshaw reported his wife missing to the police. He also notified the Canadian Embassy, and called the couple's two adult children to tell them what had happened. Once police investigations were under way, Belshaw made what might be thought of as an odd decision. He left Paris and returned to Switzerland on January 18.

A little over a month later, on March 28, workers repairing a mountain road near Le Sepey in Switzerland found the nude, mutilated body of a middle-age woman wrapped in rubbish bags and tied up with twine. The body lay in a ravine used as a rubbish disposal site and attacks by animals had made identification near-impossible.

Nevertheless, the local police immediately suspected the body was Betty Belshaw's and spoke with fellow police in Paris and Canada. During the investigations it came to light that Belshaw was involved with another woman. Thinking they had found a motive for murder, police moved in quickly and arrested Belshaw, charging him with the murder of his wife.

But there was more confusion to come. With Belshaw willingly helping them, Interpol located Betty's dental records and were amazed to find that they did not match the corpse. With only the body of a mystery woman as evidence, the legal battle was long and complicated, but in the end Cyril Belshaw was allowed to walk free from court—neither exonerated nor found guilty, but acquitted. Belshaw returned to Canada and carried on his academic work. The body of his wife was never found.

Karla Biddle

Technical consultant Ashley Watson was by no means the first man to think that he could enjoy relationships with two women at once and get away with it. Tragically for everyone involved in the love triangle though, one of his lovers decided to confront her rival rather than the man who had strung them both along. The fight that broke out between the two women ended in disaster.

Ashley Watson and Karla Biddle's was a long established relationship by the time he began an affair with Emma Bradshaw. The couple had met in 1993 and by 2002 owned a house together. While there had often been talk of marriage, the plans were later shelved when their relationship began having difficulties. Unbeknown to Karla, the couple's problems were probably largely due to the fact that Watson had been splitting his time between two women for four years. He had met Emma Bradshaw at a Mercedes Benz dealership where they both worked in 2003 and, soon after, began sleeping with her. With his original relationship disintegrating, Watson moved out of the home he shared with Karla and into Emma's West Midlands house in 2007.

Although it was a sad situation, it was not an unusual one—except that Watson was still sleeping with his ex-girlfriend. And so began a potentially disastrous balancing act during which he would sometimes send Karla affectionate SMS text messages while he was having dinner with Emma. Sure enough, catastrophe was soon to arrive.

On May 14, 2008, Karla decided that she had had

enough of her lover's two-timing and drove to Emma Bradshaw's home to inform her of her own continuing sexual relationship with Watson. Although Karla had no intention of harming her when she arrived at the house, less than an hour later Emma's life was bleeding from numerous stab wounds as she banged on neighbors' doors. Eventually, an ambulance was called and she was rushed to hospital where she died of her wounds. Karla, meanwhile, returned home, changed out of the nightclothes she had been wearing, and went to work. There, she sent "chatty" text messages to Watson in the hope that it would divert police attention away from

BELOW: Karla Biddle, in the back of a police van, being driven from Warwick Crown Court.

ABOVE: Karla Biddle being escorted from Warwick Crown Court where she was tried for the murder of Emma Bradshaw.

her.

Her efforts failed. Karla Biddle was arrested and appeared at Warwick Crown Court in April 2009, charged with murder. This was later changed to manslaughter after the court heard that she had not gone to Emma's house armed, but that Emma had grabbed the knife as the argument became more heated. There was a struggle and in a frenzy of rage at the woman who had stolen her partner of so many years, Karla took the knife from her and stabbed at Emma over and over again.

Despite the fact that this was a crime of passion committed in a moment of insane rage, Judge Griffiths Jones said he could not ignore the severity of the crime, or the number of times the knife had been used. Many of Emma's wounds were on her hands making it obvious that she had tried to defend herself from the frenzied attack. He also added that Karla's fleeing the scene was a "profoundly unattractive act." After the month-long trial she was found guilty of manslaughter on the grounds of provocation. The jury spent 17 hours deliberating on their verdict and, taking into account that the killing was not premeditated, Griffiths Jones gave Emma a sentence of seven years in prison.

In conclusion he gave a short address that might very well be applied to many other crimes of passion, saying, "This case is an absolute tragedy in which there can be no winners, only losers. You were a respectable, intelligent, and successful young woman. I accept that your relationship with the man concerned had ground you down emotionally. The uncertainty of his fidelity and commitment to you, and your love for him had caused you a great deal of pain and anxiety which was clearly reflected in perfectly reasonable and understandable inquiries to find out where the truth lay. It is also a tragedy because your rival in love was also a thoroughly decent and valuable woman."

Edward Black

Deeply in debt and bitterly regretting the decision he had made to marry a woman 14 years older than himself, Edward Black decided that he needed a fresh start and that only his wife's death could give it to him. Accordingly, he bought two ounces of rat poison, and told the shop assistant that he needed it to eradicate the vermin in his house.

In 1921, **Edward Black** felt himself relatively young at only 36, but his life hadn't turned out quite as he had hoped. His job as an insurance salesmen didn't pay enough to keep him in the lifestyle he aspired to, and his wife Annie, who owned a sweetshop, was now 50. Her looks were fast fading and Black's love for her had died completely. The future seemed to hold nothing but poverty and caring for an elderly, unattractive wife who frequently suffered from gastro-enteritis. But with the application of a little arsenic, he hoped that he could still find the happiness that had so far eluded him.

Black bought two ounces of rat poison from the Timothy White's store in St. Austell, Cornwall, England, and on October 31, sprinkled a killing dose onto his wife's breakfast. Then he fled. While his wife's condition spiraled downward toward death, he hid at Cashin's Temperance Hotel in Liverpool.

Annie Black succumbed to the poison in less than a fortnight. By November 11, she was dead. Of the two doctors who had treated her, one believed that gastro-enteritis was to blame, but the other was more puzzled. The symptoms didn't seem to match so, to be certain, he ordered a postmortem. Sure enough, traces of arsenic were found in Annie's body.

Suspicion immediately fell on her absent husband, and the police rapidly tracked him down to the hotel in Liverpool. When he knew the game was up Black made a botched attempt at cutting his own throat.

Having survived the half-hearted suicide attempt, he was arrested, and taken back to Cornwall to stand trial. Black denied the murder of his wife but had done nothing to cover his tracks. His signature was on the poison register at Timothy White's and, despite his protests that someone else had bought the poison and forged his name, Black was found guilty at Bodmin Court after a jury deliberated of just 40 minutes. He was hanged at Exeter Prison on March 24, 1922.

BELOW: Bodmin Assize Hall, Cornwall, where Edward Black was convicted of the murder of his wife.

Mary Blandy

An unlikely killer, it is thought that Mary Blandy's only crime was to put her trust in the man she loved; a man who had already proved himself capable of cheating and lying to obtain what he wanted.

Mary Blandy's was a happy home in the pleasant riverside town of Henley in southern England. Her father was a lawyer, Francis Blandy, and her future prospects were good. Nevertheless, on meeting the charismatic army officer Captain William Henry Cranstoun in 1746, her life would become more like the plot of a gloomy novel. Cranstoun was already married but became determined to win the £10,000 that he was told Mary would inherit on the death of her father. He courted her tirelessly, winning her love and her promise to marry him while also gaining the affections of her mother, for whom he paid a small debt of £40. A date for the wedding was set for 1751, but before it could take place Captain Cranstoun had a big problem. He had to get rid of his other wife who lived hundreds of miles to the north in Scotland.

Cranstoun's strategy was to write to his wife, telling her their marriage was preventing him from rising through the army ranks. He asked if she would, instead, say that she was his merely his mistress. Confused, but wishing to help with her husband's career, Mrs Cranstoun wrote back as suggested. The devious captain then passed the letter around to friends and family and began divorce proceedings against her, claiming that the marriage was not valid and using his wife's letter as proof. The hapless Mrs Cranstoun was forced to show lawyers that they were, indeed, legally married.

Inevitably, news of Cranstoun's predicament reached the ears of Mary's father. Francis Blandy immediately ordered his daughter to end their relationship until such a time as Cranstoun's domestic arrangements were resolved. In spite of a deathbed appeal from his wife, who begged Blandy to allow Mary to marry her lover, Mary's father remained firm. He was becoming increasingly suspicious that Cranstoun did not intend to leave his wife, but was simply after money.

The events leading up to Blandy's murder were always murky and have grown more so over two and a half centuries, but the following tale is widely

Miſs MARY BLANDY

LEFT: A portrait of English murderer Mary Blandy, along with a depiction of her execution at Oxford in 1752.

her father standing between them. What's more, while Blandy lived, Cranstoun knew he would not be able to get his hands on the lawyer's money. However, he devised a murder plot that would solve both problems and leave him free of blame should it be discovered. The keys to his plan were his young fiancée's unquestioning adoration and her innocence.

Appearing desperate to be married to Mary, he gave her a potion. It was magical, he claimed, and after drinking it her father would no longer object to their marriage. Eager to wed, Mary agreed to slip the potion into her father's drink. Cranstoun was right. After drinking the potion Francis Blandy no longer objected to the marriage—for the simple reason that he was dead. The potion had contained a deadly dose of arsenic.

The crime was discovered and according to plan, the practiced liar and cheat Cranstoun wheedled his way free of justice. Mary was tried on March 3, 1752, and found guilty. Six weeks later, on Easter Monday, she was hanged outside Oxford Prison. The debate over whether or not she was to blame for her crime

ABOVE: Murderess Mary Blandy talking to a visitor in Oxford castle where she was held. She can be seen wearing leg irons under her dress to prevent her escape.

accepted as being the most accurate. While Mary was still deeply in love with him, Cranstoun realized that their marriage was becoming less and less likely with continued for years after her death. Cranstoun was never charged, but in an odd twist discovered that he, too, had been deceived. The fortune he had hoped to take from Mary had never existed; Francis Blandy was nowhere near as rich as he pretended. Cranstoun died in battle in Flanders, six months after his lover.

Lorena Bobbitt

Although Lorena Bobbitt did not actually kill her husband, she inflicted on him a terrible—and now infamous—wound. In an odd twist of fate, she was not punished for her crime and instead became something of a heroine to feminists.

It was an incident that grabbed headlines around the world. John Wayne and Lorena Bobbitt returned to their home in Manassas, Virginia, on June 23, 1993, after an evening of partying and drinking, and Lorena would later allege that Bobbitt raped her. She told a court that it was just the latest abuse in a long list of others. Her husband was often violent toward her and made no secret of the fact that he was having sex elsewhere. On one occasion, she said that he had forced her to terminate a pregnancy against her wishes. This time, however, John Wayne would pay a terrible price for his behavior.

After the attack, as John lay sleeping, Lorena got out of bed to fetch a glass of water from the kitchen. As the tap was running, she spotted a carving knife and, as she stared at it, the years of abuse that she had suffered at the hands of her husband all came flooding back. Overwhelmed with anger and

ABOVE: Lorena Bobbitt waving to cheering demonstrators as she leaves the Prince William County Courthouse in Manassas, Virginia.

BELOW: The knife used by Lorena Bobbitt to cut off the penis of her husband.

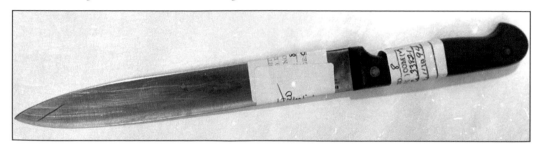

At this point Lorena came back to her senses, and realizing that she had committed a terrible crime she called the emergency services. Bobbitt was rushed to hospital while police combed the field for his penis. It was eventually found and the police packed it in ice and rushed it to the hospital. It took nine-and-a-half hours in surgery to successfully re-attach the severed body part.

Lorena defended her actions in court by maintaining that she had been the victim of constant abuse. Her lawyers told the jury that suffering from depression and post-traumatic stress disorder she had simply snapped. While John Wayne denied all of his wife's allegations, Lorena was able to supply witnesses to support her claims and she was eventually found not guilty of sexually wounding her husband.

In 1994, it was John's turn to face the judgement of the court. He stood trial for raping Lorena, but he, too, was acquitted.

By 1995 the couple were divorced. Although she had tried to avoid media attention,

ABOVE: Lorena Bobbitt (left), being escorted from the courtroom in the Prince William County Courthouse, Virginia, following the not guilty verdict.

hardly knowing what she was doing, Lorena Bobbitt picked up the knife, walked back to the bedroom, and sliced off more than half of Bobbitt's penis. Then she picked up the severed organ and drove a short distance before throwing it into a field.

Lorena Bobbitt had by now become a feminist icon, and in the years that followed she founded Lorena's Red Wagon, an organization devoted to bringing an end to domestic violence. She later obtained a degree and gave birth to a daughter by a new partner, though when she and John were both guests on the Oprah Winfrey Show in 2009 she insisted that she would never marry again. John Wayne Bobbitt, however, used his new notoriety in a different way. He formed a band called The Severed

Parts and appeared in adult movies. He also continued to abuse women and after two more court cases for domestic assault was convicted in 2004.

LEFT: John Wayne Bobbitt (center) arriving at the Prince William County Court House for the first day of his wife's trial on charges of malicious wounding.

BELOW: Supporters of Lorena Bobbitt hold signs and shout their support as she leaves the courthouse.

Mary Bolton

From almost the day that she was married, in 1922, Mary Bolton was a dreadful thorn in her husband's side. And as time went on she became more and more unbalanced, to the point where she was willing to kill rather than lose him.

A good-natured, hard working, and patient man Charles Bolton most certainly didn't deserve the woman he married. Almost immediately after the wedding, he realized that he had made a terrible mistake: Mary nagged him constantly and made wild accusations. Each day he went to his office and each night he returned home to face her jealousy. She was convinced that he was having affairs and became so frenzied in her rage that she would even beat him and, on one occasion, slashed his face with a razor. The hapless Bolton was forced to tell police who came to investigate when neighbors reported the violent row that he had cut himself shaving.

None of Mary's accusations was true. Bolton was a decent man and despite his wife's temper tried hard to make their marriage work. His protestations and attempts to calm Mary were futile though, and the strain was affecting his work. His employers even suggested that due to his personal problems he might be better off working for himself.

After enduring her emotional and physical torments for 14 years, Bolton finally came to the end of his tether, and filed for divorce on January 25, 1936. Mary, however, was not going to let him get away so easily and spent months harassing him to change his mind. And when she realized that Bolton was determined to be rid of her, she decided that she would get rid of him first.

Mary bought a revolver on June 11, and drove to her husband's office. All the way her rage grew and by the time she was riding the elevator to the 10th floor her fury was uncontrollable. Finding her husband in his office, Mary fired six shots. As Charles Bolton lay bleeding to death on the floor, she asked, "Why don't you get up and stop faking?"

Mary Bolton was originally sentenced to death in the electric chair but this was later commuted to a sentence of life imprisonment. However, Mary did not fancy spending the rest of her life—perhaps another 40 years—behind bars. She died on August 29, 1943, after slashing her wrists with a pair of scissors.

Lizzie Borden

Not all crimes of passion are triggered by lust or passion turned sour. For Lizzie Borden it was hatred of her stepmother and a domineering father, as well as good old-fashioned greed, which turned her into a brutal killer. Perhaps one of the most famous murderers in history, Borden was never convicted of her crime, but looking back it seems almost impossible that she got away with it. Never able to give a clear account of her whereabouts at the time of the double murder, she was lucky enough to have a judge who owed her defense counsel a favor and she also threw herself on the sympathy of the jury, and their misplaced belief that a mere woman could not have committed such a frenzied slaying.

B orn in Fall River, Massachusetts, in 1860, Lizzie's mother died when she was just two years old. Her father married again, a woman called Abby Gray who was 10 years his junior, and as Lizzie and her sister, Emma, grew up they came to despise their stepmother. To them she was a simple gold-digger who was frittering away their inheritance. Matters came to a head when their father, who was notoriously mean with money gave his wife's sister a large sum to save her from financial ruin. Lizzie wanted revenge.

The opportunity presented itself in the summer of 1892. Emma had gone to stay with friends at the nearby country town of Fairhaven while Lizzie remained at home with just a maid in the house along with Lizzie and her stepmother and father.

On August 4, Lizzie's father was away from the house for a short while. Around 9.30am, Mrs Borden was cleaning the steps to a spare bedroom when she was struck from behind with an axe. The blow to her head was enough to kill her instantly, but eight more rained

Father's dead. Someone came in and killed him!" The police were soon on the scene and under questioning, Lizzie's own story changed constantly from the outset. First she said she had been out in the yard when her father was killed, then she "remembered" that she had actually been in the barn. At the inquest that would change again, with Lizzie recalling that she had been in the kitchen when her father returned home. Although at one time she also said she had been on the stairs, she maintained that she had not noticed her stepmother's body there.

Nevertheless, the early investigation focused on John Morse, the brother of Mr Borden's first wife, who had recently stayed with the family for a few days. That avenue of investigation proved short-lived when Morse provided a solid alibi. The police were left with just two suspects—Lizzie and Bridget Sullivan. Quickly they narrowed it down to one as it was established that the maid had no motive for the crime while Lizzie had made no secret of the fact that she hated her stepmother. Her contradictory statements were also arousing suspicion.

By the time Lizzie Borden came to trial in June 1893, public opinion was already behind her. The folk of Massachusetts could not bring themselves to believe that one of their own, a God-fearing woman, could have committed such a crime. Lizzie had also cannily appointed one of the best criminal lawyers in the state to defend her. George Robinson was a former governor of Massachusetts and, crucially, had been responsible for appointing one of the three judges who now sat on the bench before him. The judge repaid the favor by agreeing with Robinson that damning transcripts of Lizzie's questioning at the inquest, during which her story had changed several times, were inadmissible. The prosecution case looked weaker and weaker, having finally to rest on the fact that Lizzie Borden was at the house at the time of the murders and that her evidence was conflicting.

Lizzie and her lawyer did their utmost to secure the jury's sympathy. Midway through the 10-day hearing she appeared to collapse in a faint, while Robinson later pointed to the soberly dressed, neat figure, saying: "To find her guilty, you must believe she is a fiend. Gentlemen, does she look it?" The tactic worked. The jury found Lizzie not guilty and she was set free. On

ABOVE: A colorized photograph of Lizzie Borden from the late 19th century.

down in quick succession. The same fate awaited her husband when he returned home an hour or so later; a killing blow was landed and again followed by a ferocious attack on his already dead body. Both heads were later removed for specialist forensic examination, which revealed "injuries consistent with a frenzied, almost psychopathic, attack, although both victims died with the first blow such was the force with which it was delivered."

The alarm was raised when the maid, Bridget Sullivan, heard Lizzie screaming, "Come down, come down.

ABOVE: The Borden house in Fall River, Massachusetts where the grisly murders were committed.

soon after with, it was often said, a large quantity of cash from the late Mr Borden's bank account given to her by Lizzie.

The jury may have been convinced of her innocence, but the public was not so satisfied. and as the years passed it became the widespread belief that Lizzie had gotten away with murder. She may have escaped the law, but for the remainder of her days would be taunted by a popular rhyme: "Lizzie Borden took an axe. And gave her mother forty whacks. When she saw what she had done. She gave her father forty-one!"

Lizzie Borden initially lived with her sister and then by herself until she died aged 67 in 1927. She was buried in the same family plot as those who died on that sweltering August day 35 years before.

being acquitted of murder, she inherited much of her father's money and used it to buy a house in a wealthy suburb. Suspiciously, Bridget Sullivan returned to Ireland

Cordelia Botkin

Cordelia was most definitely a "woman scorned." Having won her younger lover, he deserted her and returned to his wife. Love turned to seething fury and when Botkin's attempts to ruin his marriage failed, there was only one course of action left: revenge. Not on the man who had broken her heart, but on the woman who had taken him from her.

At 41 years old, Cordelia Botkin was a sophisticated woman of the world. Separated from her wealthy grain broker husband, he nonetheless supported her financially, leaving her free to indulge a busy social life and numerous flirtations. But when she met John Preston Jack Dunning in 1896, she felt a powerful attraction that appeared to be mutual. He was 32, nine years her junior, and a highly regarded reporter for the Associated Press in California. Soon the couple were

involved in a passionate affair. It was not Dunning's first, and when his wife found out that once again he was cheating on her, she decided that she had had enough. She left, taking their small daughter away to her father's home. Cordelia was overjoyed. With Mary Dunning out of the picture she could at last take a more public position in her lover's life.

The affair lasted three years. During that time, Dunning began to drink more and more heavily, and became addicted to gambling. Eventually, he was sacked by the Associated Press after embezzling $4,000 dollars to pay gambling debts, and though he found work on local San Francisco newspapers was quickly fired by them too; this time for habitual drunkeness. Homeless and penniless, Dunning was forced to move into the hotel where Cordelia lived. There, he surveyed the wreckage of his life and decided to clean up his act.

Well aware of Dunning's talent, in 1898 the Associated Press agreed to give him another chance and hired him as their lead reporter. It meant leaving San Francisco, but he seemed all too keen to return to the life he'd had before it had all gone so disastrously wrong. Although Cordelia pleaded with him desperately, her agonized pleas fell on deaf ears. Dunning left her, was reconciled with his wife, and left for news assignments in Cuba, where he became a hero at the battle of Santiago Bay when he helped save survivors of the Spanish battleships that were sunk.

BELOW: The California State Prison at San Quentin where Cordelia Botkin lived out her final days.

Already heartbroken, when Cordelia heard of her faithless lover's new success and the mended relationship with his wife, she became incensed with jealousy. Having supported and loved Dunning through all his troubles, it was the final humiliation. At first she tried to vent her rage by sending Mary Dunning anonymous letters that gave intimate details of all her husband's affairs, but it didn't have the effect she had hoped. More radical measures were called for.

One morning, Mary Dunning was delighted to receive a box of candies at her father's home in Delaware. An unsigned note attached said, "With love to yourself and baby," but the fact that the handwriting was the same as the poison-pen letters she had received obviously didn't register. Mary ate three and shared the rest. The candy contained a real poison this time: arsenic. Two days later, Mary was dead, alongside her sister Harriet. Miraculously, four others who had eaten the sweets survived.

It didn't take the police long to follow the trail back to Cordelia. Mary's father noticed that the note accompanying the candy was in the same hand as the poison pen letters his daughter had been receiving, and the box of candy was traced back to San Francisco. Cordelia Botkin denied the murder charges, but the case against her was open and shut. She was convicted in December 1898 and again at a retrial in 1904.

Sentenced to life, she eventually died in 1910 at San Quentin State Prison, her life destroyed by jealousy. And hers was not the only one. If vengeance on the man she loved was what she was after then Cordelia succeeded. The loss of his wife and the ensuing scandal tipped Dunning into a downward spiral. He died, virtually destitute, before she did.

Leone Bouvier

Leone Bouvier's life was one of abuse, and when the man whom she believed would save her from it betrayed her too, it proved too much for her to bear.

The daughter of a drunk father and unsympathetic mother, at 16 years old, Leone Bouvier had already lost her virginity during a fumbled encounter in a field and been taken advantage of by various local lads. Illiterate and unloved, she had little in life to look forward to when she met a 22-year-old garage mechanic named Emile Clenet. For the first time Leone believed that someone cared about her. Clenet would visit her on a Sunday, take a hotel room, and the couple would spend the day making love, taking rests to laugh together and talk about marriage.

But like many a naive young girl, she was deceived. While Clenet certainly enjoyed the promise of certain sex on a Sunday, he had little love for her. Leone had already suspected that he had a cruel streak, but in a haze of love she had made excuses for him. And when she fell pregnant in 1951 she continued to trust him. On hearing the news, Clenet refused to live up to his responsibilities and instead, callously told his teenage lover to get rid of the baby. Leone obediently had a termination. It left her ill; the headaches and depression she had previously suffered from grew so bad that she eventually lost her job at a shoe factory. Her drunk father beat her when he was told that she would no longer be bringing a wage home. In desperation Leone cycled 30 miles to Nantes in the hope of finding comfort in the arms of her lover, but Clenet briskly told her she had broken the "Sundays only" rule and refused to speak to her.

Jobless and abandoned by her lover and family, Leone lived on the streets and earned money for food the only way she could; by prostituting herself. Despite all that had happened she still loved Clenet and hoped against hope that they might marry, but as time passed their meetings became few and far between and, when he did show up, he showed no compassion for her plight. Much of her life was now spent at the docks where she sold her body. Sick, heartbroken, betrayed, and with her thoughts dwelling on revenge, Leone spent what little money she had on a pistol.

Still, disaster might have been averted if Clenet had returned just a little of the love that Leone had given him. But it was not to be. At a final meeting, during which the couple visited a carnival, Clenet announced he was to leave France to work in North Africa. Leone begged him to stay, but he simply shrugged and told her that he would never marry her. In response Leone pulled his reluctant face to hers for a parting kiss. Then she shot him at point-blank range in the neck.

Leone was arrested in a convent at Angers where she had sought shelter with her sister who had become a nun several years before. She was charged with murder and brought to trial in December 1953. Fate still had one final misfortune for her. Although she had killed a man, if anyone deserved to be treated leniently under the French traditions of the crime passionnel it was Leone Bouvier. Nevertheless, she was unlucky enough to be assigned an unsympathetic judge. When he heard that her sister was a nun, he chastised Leone for not making anything of her own life, and even the appearance of a drunk father and long-suffering mother in the dock did nothing to sway him. He told her that killing her lover as he bent to kiss her was an act of gross atrocity and took no notice of Leone's weeping or her whispered words, "But I loved him."

After deliberating for just 15 minutes, the jury saved Leone from a death sentence by finding her guilty of murder without premeditation. However, she received the full penalty of the law: a life sentence with a minimum of 20 years to be served.

Eliot Bower

It is rare indeed that someone who confesses to killing a love rival is set free, yet in Paris in the mid-1800s that is exactly what happened. The British defendant used the French plea of crime passionel rather than pre-meditated murder, and he was set at liberty, with many even agreeing that he had done the honorable thing by slaying his wife's lover.

Like many men of his time, Elliott Bower was a hypocrite whose double standards are easy to see in these more enlightened days. An English foreign correspondent working in Paris, he thought nothing of betraying his wife, Fanny, with a series of women. Such was his arrogance that he hardly bothered keeping his numerous mistresses a secret from her. For the unfortunate Fanny Bower, life became a series of heartbreaks as she discovered time and again that her husband had been cheating on her with yet another. Needless to say, while Bower pleasured himself with the ladies of Paris, his wife was expected to be completely faithful and uncomplaining.

Emotionally crushed after her husband's latest fling was revealed to her, Fanny finally turned in desperation to a close friend of her husband's who had always been kind to her. Saville Morton was also a foreign correspondent, working for a rival newspaper, and during happier times he had become almost part of the family, dining often with the Bowers and accompanying them for Parisian nights out. Now, Morton's relationship with the distressed Fanny deepened into something more and, as time passed, they became lovers. Soon, Fanny fell pregnant.

When the child was born (Fanny's fifth), she instantly declared it to be, "just like Morton!" At first, fearing scandal, Morton stayed away, but his lover's fragile emotional state had been further weakened by the birth of another man's child. She summoned Morton to her bedside and banned her husband from the room. He

must have been suspicious, and his fears were confirmed on the night of October 1, 1852. At last called to his wife's side, he heard her confess in a fevered outburst that he was not the father of her child.

In a frenzy of rage that he—the serial adulterer—should be deceived in his turn, he confronted his former friend. Morton admitted everything. Bower, in a fury, took up a long carving knife and ran him through with it.

To escape punishment Bower deserted his family and fled to England. But soon came the news that French police considered his act a crime passionnel, and not premeditated murder. Knowing that this would be treated much more leniently, Bower returned to France and gave himself up. At his trial, which started on December 28, 1852, Bower listened to the heated defense put up by his counsel; that he had been driven to kill because of Morton's seduction of his wife, his close friend's dishonorable and treacherous behavior, and the ultimate humiliation of the birth of a child which was not his. In fact, he was presented to the jury as the real victim of the affair, and the murder of his wife's lover not only understandable, but a deserved punishment and an act of honor.

He was lucky to be tried in a country that prides itself on having the legal defence of a crime passionnel. Perhaps he would not have been given such a sympathetic hearing anywhere else. Acquitted of the crime, and virtually hailed as a hero by the French press, Bower left the court a free man.

Martha Bowers

Taking another human life is a terrible crime and one that affects killers in different ways. Some suffer the torture of their own conscience as they realize what they have done, others remain defiant. A few seem to feel no remorse whatsoever. When Martha Bowers husband died she threw herself on his body, weeping hysterically. But less than two hours later she was spotted laughing and joking with her lover.

Martha Bowers married her third—and final—husband in San Francisco in 1902, but such happiness she may have had with Martin Bowers, a bridge builder,

did not last long. Martha was not the type to be satisfied with just one man and before her marriage was a year old she was enjoying the attentions of a lover, Patrick

Leary. It wasn't long before Bowers became aware of his wife's infidelity, and he insisted that the affair must come to an end.

Soon after, on June 5, 1903, a doctor was called to their home. Martha asked Dr. Carl Von Tiedmann if he could prescribe medicine for her husband saying that he had become ill as a result of ptomaine poisoning caused by eating too much ham. Over the following days, Martin's condition deteriorated until a second doctor was called in. This time, Bowers was taken to a convalescent home and finally he began to recover. After a month he was judged fit to return home. Not long after, he was critically sick again and was rushed to hospital where he died on August 25, with his wife pouring out her grief over his lifeless body.

Harry Bowers—Martin's brother—was perplexed. Something about the death didn't seem quite right. He requested a full postmortem be carried out, which found four grains of undissolved arsenic in Martin Bowers' stomach. By now the possible murder was making news reports and caught the eye of a pharmacist who recalled a woman coming to him on August 20, with a prescription for arsenic. He told police the prescription was memorable because though signed by a Dr. McLaughlin, it was written on a plain sheet of paper and not a normal prescription form. However, the description of the woman the pharmacist gave turned out not to match that of Martha, but it did lead police to her sister, Zylpha Sutton.

In Bowers' home, police found a school composition book with a page torn out. It matched that upon which the phoney prescription had been written and so, too, did the handwriting in the book. The police also heard from witnesses of how Martha had been seen playfully cavorting in public with Patrick Leary less than two hours after the death of her husband.

With further revelations about how Martin Bowers had attempted to put an end to the affair, it was more than enough to condemn her. Martha Bowers was found guilty on January 20, 1904, and sentenced to life imprisonment. Her sister Zylpha was released through lack of evidence.

Maria Boyne

Maria Boyne's murder of her husband was committed simply because she could not bear to lose anything she thought of as hers. While she wasn't prepared to part with her lover she had no intention of losing her London home in a divorce either. In her attempt to have it all though, as so many killers had found out before her, she made sure that she lost everything.

Maria's eight-year marriage was over in all but name when she took a knife to her husband. She was already pregnant by her 24-year-old lover, Gary McGinley, and divorce was imminent. The only thing Maria was afraid of was that she might lose her house in the legal battle with her husband. In the weeks before the killing, she told her friends that she just wanted Boyne dead so that she could bring McGinley into her home.

Finally, her murderous intentions were fired up by a particularly vicious argument with her husband. Maria grabbed a knife and brutally stabbed him 31 times, then calmly took a gold chain from around his neck. She would use the money raised from pawning it to celebrate her husband's death with a passionate night in a hotel with McGinley. Boyne's body was found by his elderly father, Michael, who would die soon after giving evidence in the trial. The shock he received on finding his son's bloody corpse meant he too became a victim of Maria's crime.

Maria couldn't evade justice for long, though she was prepared to go to any lengths to do so. In fact, when it became clear that she would face trial for her crime she threw her lover to the wolves, telling the police that it was he who had killed Boyne. No one was fooled.

The jury cleared the apparently naive McGinley, but Maria faced the full penalty of the law, damned almost as much by her own lack of remorse and her attempts to shift the blame as by the crime itself. As Judge Paul Worsley, told Maria, "You were motivated by sex and selfishness. You were scheming and devious."

In February 2009, the 30-year-old Maria was found guilty at the Old Bailey, London's central court, murdering Boyne in his bed in April 2008. She was sentenced to life on March 4 and told she would serve a minimum of 24 years in prison. In seeking to serve only her own needs she had killed an innocent man and left two young children, as well as her baby daughter, motherless. In an emotional and touching statement shortly before he died, Boyne's father told the press, "My son thought the world of her despite her numerous affairs. He loved her."

Betty Broderick

After putting so much time, emotional energy, and effort into helping her husband achieve his dreams, to be betrayed at a time when she should have been enjoying the fruits of her labors was a brutal injury for Betty Broderick to suffer. Her life, which had once promised so much, was torn to shreds. The only thing that could satisfy her was the deaths of those who had caused her so much grief.

Betty and Dan Broderick married in April 1969 after meeting at a football game and both shared the same dream: They wanted to be wealthy, secure, and happy—a family that had it all. During the first years of hardship, the couple put everything into their hopes for the future. Dan enrolled in law school, while Betty took jobs to support him. When their four children came along she took sole charge of them, allowing her husband to concentrate on finishing his studies and starting a career. He was offered a job at an established law firm in San Diego, California, and Betty—still determined to do her bit—took a job as a cashier at a restaurant in the evenings.

As the years passed, the Brodericks' dreams of financial security came true. They bought a beautiful house in the affluent Coral Reef suburb of La Jolla in San Diego, became members of exclusive clubs, and took foreign vacations. But along the road to success the shared goals and the loving closeness that had bound them together was lost. Dan became ever more distant from the family. He rarely saw the children and when he and his wife did spend time together it was usually at one of the legal functions or parties that Betty came to detest.

It was at one of these events that Betty overheard a stray comment from her husband that would mark the beginning of her breakdown into emotional chaos. Dan, who was talking to a friend, asked, "Isn't she beautiful?" After a brief moment of delight, Betty soon realized that Dan hadn't been talking about her but Linda Kolkena, a receptionist at the law firm.

Dan now became even more detached from his family than he had been before, and made no secret of his distaste for the woman who had worked so hard to help him climb the ladder of success. On one occasion he told Betty that he was tired of his life and that she was "old, fat, ugly, and boring." Meanwhile, he had taken Linda Kolkena on as his personal assistant.

Betty found out just how calculating her husband could be at the beginning of 1985. Having announced that he was moving the family to a new, bigger, rented house; soon after their belongings were unpacked Dan deserted them and returned to their old home. In a fit of anger and hoping that Dan might realize just how much she had done for him, Betty took all their children and dumped them on him. Her plan, however, backfired badly. Dan hired a housekeeper and finally began to spend more time with his children. Not only did he cope admirably, but his relationship with the children flourished. Betty, meanwhile, was sidelined. His relationship with Linda now openly acknowledged, Dan filed for divorce, and as a top lawyer he was not an easy opponent in a legal battle.

Having lost everything and faced with a long and painful fight, Betty's state of mind began disintegrating. She ignored legal advice, failed to turn up at court hearings, and left a series of telephone messages littered with obscenities and abuse. They would soon come back to haunt her during the divorce proceedings in court. But when she lost custody of the children and Dan took out an injunction preventing her from visiting her old home, something in Betty snapped.

She bought a gun and on November 5, 1988, drove to Dan's home, let herself in with a key she had stolen from her eldest daughter, and made her way to the bedroom. Seeing two shapes beneath the covers of the bed she used to share she shot them both. Dan and Linda were killed instantly.

In court, Betty's defense lawyers claimed that she had been driven to the edge of sanity by the latest developments in the long and bitter divorce battle and had gone to the house to reason with her husband one last time and to commit suicide if she failed to win his sympathy. But while the jury accepted that Betty suffered from psychological disorders they could not help but see the crime as being calculated and premeditated. The prosecution made full use of the hysterical messages Betty had left on her husband's answer phone and, again, they helped paint a picture of a bitter, vindictive woman.

Betty's first trial ended in a hung jury with two jurors preferring a manslaughter verdict rather than murder. At her second hearing, the jury returned a verdict of two counts of second-degree murder, and Betty Broderick was sentenced to two consecutive terms of 15 years to life and two years for the illegal use of a firearm. She was ordered to serve a minimum of 21 years before becoming eligible for parole.

Elizabeth Brown

The tale of the last woman ever to be hanged in Dorset, England, is a sorry one, for Elizabeth Brown's was a true crime of passion, committed in a moment of heartbroken anger. It is also a tale that has left a lasting mark. Her death was watched by a 16-year-old reporter named Thomas Hardy, who would go on to be one of Britain's greatest novelists. Elizabeth's tragic story made such an impression on him that it formed the basis of his greatest novel, Tess of the D'Urbervilles.

An attractive redhead, Elizabeth Brown married her husband John later in life than was usual in the mid-19th century. He was 20 years her junior, and it was rumored that he wed only for his wife's money, though the gossip doesn't have the ring of truth to it. Elizabeth was certainly not wealthy; both she and her husband were employed as servants. The couple settled down to married life in the village of Birdsmoorgate, near Beaminster in Dorset, and it soon became obvious that the relationship was not a happy one. Elizabeth became convinced that her youthful husband was unfaithful, and one fateful day in 1856 she was proved right. Returning home unexpectedly one night, Elizabeth caught her husband beneath the blankets of their marriage bed with another woman. Broken-hearted and humiliated she flew into a rage and a violent quarrel followed. Elizabeth hit out at John who in turn lashed her with a whip. She seized an axe and in the heat of the moment caught him a fatal blow.

Elizabeth then made a mistake that would eventually lead to her own death. Had she told the truth then it is very likely that the circumstances of her husband's death would have been taken into account, and she would have been treated leniently. Instead, the frightened woman told police that her husband's fractured skull had been caused by the kick of a horse. Her story was not believed, she was charged with murder, and went on trial at Dorchester Assizes where she continued to protest her innocence. It did not take a jury long to return a guilty verdict and she was sentenced to death by hanging. Only then did she tell what had really happened.

Although there was a swell of public support for Elizabeth, the Home Secretary refused to grant a reprieve because Elizabeth had lied for so long. She was taken to the scaffold at Dorchester prison on August 9, 1856, and—in a further cruel injustice—delivered into the hands of the infamous hangman William Calcraft, Britain's principal executioner from 1829 to 1874. He was noted for his "short drops," which meant a slow and agonizing death by strangulation rather than a cleanly broken neck.

A crowd of nearly 4,000 people gathered to watch Elizabeth accept her fate with calm and dignity. She had chosen a tight-fitting black silk dress for her execution. The noose was ill-fitting and Elizabeth's death was far from instant. A later report noted what a "fine figure she showed against the sky as she hung in the misty rain," and how "the tight black silk gown set off her shape as she wheeled half round and back" in her death throes. This grisly and salacious report was written by the young Thomas Hardy.

RIGHT: The acclaimed English novelist, poet and dramatist, Thomas Hardy who attended the execution of Elizabeth Brown at Dorchester Prison as a young reporter.

BELOW: An illustration from Thomas Hardy's Tess of the D'Urbervilles: Elizabeth Brown's tragic story made such an impression on Hardy that it formed the basis of his classic novel.

Ernest Brown

Dorothy Morton's first mistake was to cheat on her husband with Ernest Brown. Her second was to try and end the affair. For her lover had killed before and was determined to keep her by doing so again.

Having begun an affair with one of her husband's employees, a worker on his successful Yorkshire cattle farm, Dorothy Morton soon realized that she had made a terrible misjudgment. Her lover, Ernest Brown, was bad tempered and aggressive. Try as she might, he wouldn't let Dorothy finish the relationship. Instead, he continued to badger her for sex and treat her as if he owned her. On September 5, 1933, Brown found out that Dorothy had been swimming with another man and flew into a terrible rage during which he punched her to the ground. In fear for her life, Dorothy ran from her lover to the main house and stayed there, waiting for her husband, Frederick, to return. Instead, she heard the sound of a shot outside. Soon after, Brown appeared saying he had killed a rat in the barn. Dorothy waited in vain for her husband. In the early hours of the next morning, she heard an explosion and looked out to see the farm garage on fire. She grabbed her baby and with companion Ann Houseman, ran from the house to report the fire to the police.

When the flames were finally put out, the badly burned body of Frederick Morton was discovered among the cinders. He had been shot in the stomach then he and his two cars were doused with petrol and torched in an attempt to destroy evidence.

Ernest Brown was arrested and charged with murder. He was tried at Leeds Assizes and was soon found guilty. However, as the case had proceeded, it came to light that Brown had also murdered a woman called Evelyn Foster nearly two years earlier. She had offered a lift to a "smartly dressed man" with a bowler hat on January 6, 1931, and he had leaned over to touch her intimately as she drove. When she stopped the car to throw him out, he knocked her unconscious before setting fire to the car with her in it. Burned almost beyond recognition, Evelyn Foster had managed to whisper the man's description to police from her hospital bed before she died, and after Brown's arrest, police realized he was a match. Already sentenced to death it made no sense to try Brown for an earlier crime, but on the day of his execution—February 6, 1934—a chaplain told him, "You should use these last few moments to confess your sins and make your peace with God." As the hangman placed the noose around his neck, Brown murmured "Otterburn," the name of the village where Evelyn had lived.

Albert Burrows

A violent thief who had previously been arrested for horse stealing, cruelty to animals, and assault, when Albert Burrows met Hannah Calladine he added bigamy to the long list of crimes on his charge sheet. It was not, however, the last one he would commit.

Born in Cheadle Hulme, Derbyshire, England, in 1871, by the time World War I broke out, Albert Burrows had amassed an extensive police record. Although he sometimes worked as a laborer on building sites, he was not above raising extra income to take home to his wife and daughter through stealing and his temper had also landed him in trouble on more than one occasion. He was a man who felt that laws and morals just didn't apply to him. So when he began working in an ammunition factory and met a younger woman to whom he was attracted the fact that he already had a wife and child did not stop him starting an affair with her. As far as Hannah was concerned Burrows was a widower whose daughter was being looked after by a housekeeper friend in Glossop and when she fell pregnant in May and Burrows proposed, she accepted. The couple were married in October.

For a short while Burrows was able to secretly support both families, but when the war ended he found himself unemployed and unable to keep up payments. Added to which, Hannah had begun to have suspicions about her husband and wrote a letter to his daughter in Glossop. Burrows first wife was shocked to discover that there was another Mrs Burrows, and her husband was prosecuted, serving six months for bigamy.

Burrows returned to his original wife when he was released, but found that Hannah had obtained a legal order that he financially support her and her infant son, as well. When he couldn't pay up, she had him arrested and he was imprisoned for another three weeks. The situation was no better when he came out the second time. With no job and two families to maintain, Burrows was soon behind on payments again.

The situation grew even worse when Hannah arrived on his doorstep in a cold night just before Christmas in 1919 with his son and Elsie (her daughter from a previous relationship) and demanded to be taken in. With his outraged wife protesting, Burrows allowed Hannah to stay, saying that she couldn't be turned away on such a night—his wife walked out the following day. Hannah ended up staying the final three weeks of her life with her former husband.

On January 12, 1920, Burrows again appeared in court, but this time he had solved his problems.

He told the justices that Hannah had found a good job and left taking the children with her. Mrs Burrows returned to the family home soon after. Finally, it seemed that Albert Burrows had put the stresses and strains of supporting two families behind him. The true extent of his crimes, however, would later come to light in the most appalling way.

On March 4, 1923, a four-year-old boy named Thomas Wood went missing after having been seen with Burrows. He was quickly taken into custody and under police questioning broke down. The truth that was to be unravelled made his previous crimes look like minor misdemeanors. Burrows admitted that he had sexually assaulted the small boy, then dropped him down a mine shaft. When it was searched, little Thomas's body was indeed found, and alongside were the remains of Hannah Calladine and her two children, Albert, and Elsie.

The trial of Albert Edward Burrows for the murder of Hannah Calladine, 32, and her fifteen-month-old son was held at the Derbyshire Assizes and began on July 8, 1923. The horrified jury took less than a quarter of an hour to bring in a verdict of guilty. With the death sentence already passed, the authorities didn't waste any time bringing the cases for Elsie or Thomas Wood to court and Burrows paid for his crimes at Bagthorpe Gaol in Nottingham on the August 8, 1923 with a noose around his neck.

William Burton

A cheat and a liar, William Burton, made sweeping promises in order to seduce the young woman who had caught his eye. He had no intention of keeping them though, and when he found out that she was pregnant the cold-hearted Burton decided she had become a problem.

As a 29-year-old rabbit catcher at Manor Farm in the Dorset village of Gussage Saint Michael, William Burton was no great catch himself, though he possessed a certain amount of charm. It had won him a respectable wife, who worked as a schoolteacher, and the couple had recently welcomed a baby to their flat above the village post office. Burton was dissatisfied though. His wife was somewhat older than him and now a mother. His passion for her was waning, just as it was growing for another woman.

At Manor Farm there was a beautiful young cook named Winifred Mary Mitchell. Burton became determined to have her. He gave her the full benefit of his rough charm, but she was not the type of woman to give her love easily. For two months he tried to seduce her, and still she resisted, knowing that he was married man with a young child.

Winifred was finally won over when Burton promised to take her to Canada where they could begin a new life together. Convinced that Burton loved her enough to leave his family behind, Winifred's reluctance was cast aside. Burton's promises were empty. What had started for him as a challenge and then an enjoyable sexual liaison abruptly became a liability when Winifred fell pregnant. He could see only one solution that didn't involve the inconvenience of either making good on his promises or having his cheating brought to light with the birth of an illegitimate child.

On March 29, 1913, Burton again promised Winifred that they would soon run away together and arranged to meet her in a secluded spot. He then borrowed a gun, saying he needed it to kill a cat. When his lover arrived for their illicit tryst, he shot her and buried her body in a shallow grave.

Unfortunately for him, on May 2, the corpse was discovered, and when police discovered scraps of passionate letters Burton had written to Winifred, he was arrested. William Burton was found guilty of murder and became the last man ever to be hanged at Dorchester Prison on June 21, 1913.

ABOVE: An aerial view of Dorchester prison, William Burton was the last man to be hanged there.

Kitty Byron

The law is supposed to stand apart from public opinion, but in Kitty Byron's case her conviction for murder was followed by such an outcry that the Home Secretary himself stepped in, saving her first from the gallows and later allowing Kitty's release from prison after she served just six years of a life sentence.

Kitty Byron's was a woeful tale. She had the misfortune to fall in love with Arthur Reginald Baker. In public, Baker seemed to be respectable married man and was a member of the London Stock Exchange. However, in private Baker was a heavy drinker and prone to outbursts of violent temper, during which he often attacked his mistress. On one occasion he almost strangled her.

Baker lived a double life, with his wife in one home while Kitty was set up in lodgings on Duke Street in the West End of London. As far as the landlady was concerned the couple were Mr and Mrs Baker and unremarkable except for their furious arguments, which often ended in violence. On the evening of November 7, 1902, there was a particularly vicious quarrel that ended with Kitty appearing on the landing in her nightdress to avoid her lover's fists. The next morning, tired of the fighting, the landlady gave them two months' notice to leave.

The relationship calm down for a while after the incident, but it seems that Baker was growing bored of his mistress. After taking Kitty a cup of tea before leaving for work one morning, he took the landlady to one side and confessed she was not his wife, but a girl of "no class." He assured her that he would make sure Kitty left the premises the very next day.

Unfortunately for Baker, a housemaid overheard the conversation. The news, which she quickly passed on to Kitty, would cost him his life. On hearing how her abusive lover now planned to coldly abandon her and have her thrown out of her home, Kitty uttered the words that would come back to haunt her at her trial. Baker would die, she said, "before the day is out."

The landlady was mystified. Why, she asked, did Kitty stay with a violent, drunken bully if they were not married? Kitty's reply was short and simple: "Because I love him," she said, before going out to buy a sharp knife. She then sent a note via a post office messenger boy to Baker at his office. It read, "Want you importantly. Kitty."

Baker came at once, following the boy back to the post office where Kitty was waiting. As he approached the woman he had beaten so often she pulled the knife from where it was hidden in her muff and stabbed Baker twice.

Her trial began in December 1902 and Kitty's was a pathetic figure as she stood weeping in the dock. While admitting that she had killed Baker, she said that she did not know what she was doing and pleaded not guilty to murder. Public sympathy was with her, but the judge's less so. While the defense pleaded manslaughter, he did not agree and summed up in favor of a murder verdict though with a strong recommendation that the court should be merciful. But clemency was not forthcoming: Kitty was found guilty of murder and sentenced to death.

However, her fortunes were about to take a dramatic turn for the better. The trial had been widely reported in the press, and the public mood was that the sentence was far too harsh considering how Kitty had suffered at Baker's hands. While she awaited the gallows, a petition was circulated and 15,000 signatures collected before it was handed to the Home Secretary. It included the names of clerks who had worked with Baker in the City and knew exactly the type of man he was. A reprieve was duly granted, and Kitty's sentence reduced to life imprisonment. In 1907 it was reduced again and she was released from prison in 1908.

Frederick Bywaters

Percy Thompson was the victim of a classic crime of passion. In refusing to divorce his wife, Edith, so that she and the man she adored could be together, he brought the anger of both down upon his head. But while the lovers both eventually hanged for his murder, it is likely that only one of them was guilty.

In 1916, Percy Thompson married Edith Graydon. He was 21 and she was just 18, and the couple settled down to their life together in Ilford, Essex, England. Percy was a clerk at the Pacific and Orient shipping line, and Edith was a bookkeeper at a millinery firm. For almost six years, they enjoyed a life of quiet domesticity, but that was before Edith was swept away by a passion that she had never imagined possible.

In the summer of 1921, the Thompsons joined a group for a holiday visit to the Isle of Wight. Among the party was 19-year-old Frederick Bywaters, a shipping line employee and a confident young man with a

Bywaters could not be satisfied with the role of lover. Although the affair was made easy by the fact that he lived under the same roof as his mistress, he could not bear to watch her pretending to still be a dutiful wife. Before long, he confessed to Thompson that he and Edith were deeply in love and asked him to divorce her so that she would be free to marry again. Thompson was understandably furious. A huge argument erupted and Bywaters was thrown out of the house. Edith was told that her affair was at and end.

Nevertheless, the lovers continued to see each other whenever it could be contrived and, when they couldn't meet, sent each other long, passionate letters. In September 1922, Bywaters' ship docked in England. On the afternoon of October 3, he and Edith had a secret rendezvous in a London teashop. Later that night she and her husband went to the theater and returned late to Ilford. As they walked home an assailant leaped from the darkness. It was Bywaters.

As the young man repeatedly plunged a knife into Percy, Edith screamed and cried for help, pleading with her lover, "Oh don't, oh don't!" Her reaction was, said witnesses at her trial, one of genuine horror. She also pleaded with a doctor who rushed to the scene to save her husband's life. However, she did not tell the police that she knew the attacker though the thin protection this brought Bywaters soon failed. After talking to neighbors and discovering the stack of letters Edith had received from her lover, a motive for murder was established. Edith and Bywaters were arrested.

At their trial, the prosecution alleged that the murder had been planned that afternoon at the teashop rendezvous. Bywaters denied it and told the jury that he had tried to reason with Thompson again and ask him to divorce Edith, and in the ensuing an argument Thompson had threatened to shoot him. He insisted that he had acted in self-defense and even so had only meant to injure, not kill.

ABOVE: Frederick Bywaters, seated, at the inquest into the death of Percy Thompson.

strong personality. The mutual attraction between him and Edith Thompson was explosive. Before the short vacation was over, Edith confided to her sister that she no longer loved her husband.

Overwhelmed by her feelings for Bywaters, Edith set out to persuade her husband to allow him to become a lodger at their home, telling him that the extra money would be useful. Reluctantly, Thompson agreed, and Bywaters moved in. But such was his love for Edith that

However, the couple were betrayed by their own letters. When the prosecution produced 62 of them, sent from Edith to Bywaters, they painted a damning picture of adulterous lovers plotting to kill the man who stood between them. In each, Edith referred to her lover by his pet name "Darlint" and many told how she was trying to kill her husband by putting glass into his food, "Big pieces too, not powdered." She also wrote of trying to poison Thompson: "He puts great stress on the tea tasting bitter." And more: "I am going to try the glass again when it is safe." In one particularly passionate letter Edith wrote, "This thing that I am going to do for both of us—will it ever, at all, make any difference darlint? Do you understand what I mean? Will you ever think any the less of me?"

In response, Bywaters told the court there never had been a real plot to murder Thompson. The letters were just the fantasies of two people who adored each other but were forced apart. The letters also contained references to an abortion that Edith had had when she found she was carrying Bywaters' baby and it is interesting to note that such was the morality of the time that the ignorant jurors interpreted many of the phrases in the letter referring to the terminated pregnancy as being further death threats. Edith's defense counsel, however, made no attempt to clear up the jurors' misunderstandings. He feared that the knowledge that she had not only cheated on her husband but aborted her lover's child would lose the jury's sympathy completely.

The case against the lovers was strong, yet there was one thing in Edith's favor. A single hard fact that the defense case finally rested upon. The pathologist's report stated that no glass or traces of poison had been found in the body of Percy Thompson.

There was to be no mercy, however. The judge—Mr Justice Shearman—took pleasure in detailing Edith's "wicked affection" for her lover in his summing up, saying, "This is a squalid and rather indecent case of lust and adultery." The jury took two hours to consider their verdicts. Edith Thompson and Frederick Bywaters were pronounced guilty and the judge sentenced them to hang. They died on the gallows on the morning of January 9, 1923.

To the end, Bywaters remained both dignified and determined to protect the reputation of his beloved Edith. From his condemned cell, he wrote in her defence, saying "For her to be hanged as a criminal is too awful. She didn't commit the murder. I did. She never planned it, she never knew about it. She is innocent, absolutely innocent."

BELOW: Crowds lining up outside the Old Bailey, London, during the trial of Edith Thompson and her lover, Frederick Bywaters, for the murder of her husband.

Henriette Caillaux

Henriette Caillaux was discovered by shocked staff at the busy office of Le Figaro newspaper in Paris standing over the dead body of her victim. The corpse of the paper's editor, Gaston Calmette, was riddled with bullets and in her hand Madame Caillaux held a smoking gun. Even so, Caillaux eventually walked free, having befuddled a jury with a mixture of psychology and pure theater.

While crimes of passion may occur in all societies around the world, the French seem to have a certain flair for them, and have even made laws governing how a *crime passionel* should be judged. Even so, the case of Henriette Caillaux was a complicated one. Although the victim of her murderous fury was an old lover, their affair had been over for years and would have remained forever buried if Henriette had not gone on to marry Joseph Caillaux, who would become the French Finance Minister. Her former beau, Calmette, meanwhile became editor of Le Figaro, one of France's leading newspapers.

Henriette's rage was sparked when Le Figaro began lampooning her husband in a series of article and cartoons published in the newspaper and reached boiling point when she and the Finance Minister were further humiliated. Calmette had kept some letters from his days as Henriette's swain and they included a love letter from Caillaux written to Henriette 13 years previously when she was also his mistress.

Wearing a fur coat over a gown and with her hands tucked in a muff Madame Caillaux arrived at Le Figaro's offices during the early evening of March 16, 1914. As the wife of the Finance Minister and a woman of some standing, she was immediately ushered in to see the Calmette. Standing before the editor, Henriette asked a single question: "You know why I have come?" Caillaux barely had time to answer "Not at all Madame", before his old flame pulled a gun from her muff and shot him six times. Newspaper staff immediately poured into the office and attempted to seize the murderer. With French haughtiness, Henriette Caillaux shouted "Do not touch me. I am a lady!"

RIGHT: Gaston Calmette, the editor of Le Figaro, who was shot and killed by Henriette Caillaux.

Today, the result of the trial would certainly be a forgone conclusion, and even then the future looked bleak for Henriette. But, as Calmette had already discovered, she was a woman of considerable mettle who it was unwise to underestimate. French courts were notoriously sympathetic toward crimes of passion and she was determined to use that in her favor, even though she and Calmette had not been lovers for years. Appointing Fernand Labori, one of France's most

BELOW: Henriette Caillaux, in a photograph taken during the same year as her trial for the murder of Gaston Calmette.

LEFT: Fernand Labori, the counsel for the defence in the murder trial of Henriette Caillaux.

celebrated lawyers, to defend her, Henriette Caillaux went into court with every possible argument prepared. The jury heard Labori criticize the 1804 Napoleonic Code that discriminated against women then argue that a woman must be expected to vent her passionate feelings.

Henriette herself performed amazingly on the witness stand, managing to present herself as a highly romantic woman at the mercy of her emotions while offering scientific research that showed how the nervous system and unconscious mind could make people capable of terrible actions under extreme pressure. Henriette's entire defense was intended to make her appear a heroine of uncontrollable passion to the jury, and a victim of psychological laws to the experts. In popular opinion women of ungovernable passions were to be viewed sympathetically—such strength of feeling was even desirable—while temporary insanity placed her beyond the law.

It worked like a charm. After a seven-day trial in the Cour d'Assises in Paris, Henriette Caillaux walked free. After less than an hour of deliberations, the all-male jury decided the homicide was committed without premeditation or criminal intent. The jurors accepted her testimony that when she pulled the trigger, she was a temporary victim of (as Labori put it) "unbridled female passions."

Yvonne Chevalier

The term crime passionnel could have been invented for Yvonne Chevallier. Hers was a rags-to-riches story that had all the ingredients for a fairy-tale ending, for it wasn't the money or respect that mattered to Yvonne; it was the dashing hero she had married. So when her adored husband became involved with another woman her life was shattered.

At 24 years old, Yvonne was working as a midwife at a hospital in Orleans, France. The daughter of a peasant family, she had little money and was uneducated, unworldly, and very shy—quite the opposite to the intelligent and ambitious doctor Pierre Chevallier, who was from an excellent family. Nevertheless, he was only

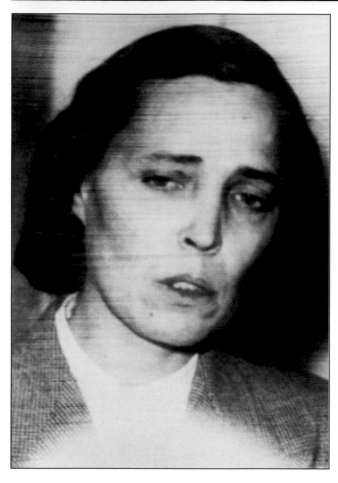

ABOVE: Yvonne Chevallier, pictured during her trial for the murder of her husband Pierre.

of their free time was spent between the sheets. Chevalier's family strongly disapproved of the relationship with a mere peasant girl, but he ignored their protests. When war broke out in 1939 he became an even greater hero in Yvonne's eyes, and those of many others. He served as a medical officer with the French Army, saving lives at the front line. While on leave—and with none of Chevallier's family present—the passionate couple married in 1939.

When France was overrun by Germany a few months later, Chevallier became the head of the local Resistance movement. As the Germans retreated in 1944, Chevallier became an even greater hero. He led Resistance forces against the Germans and drove them from Orleans. On a wave of public acclaim Chevallier was elected mayor of the city the same year.

That was the first step on what would become a high-profile political career. As mayor, Chevallier organized the reconstruction of the city—a challenge that won him further praise when it was officially declared the best rebuilt city in France. He became parliamentary representative for Orleans in 1951, and from now on affairs of state would mean he spent much of his time in Paris.

Meanwhile, the sweet and shy Yvonne remained in the background. She bore Pierre two sons who became good friends with the children of wealthy neighbor Leon Perreau and his wife Jeanne. And while the children played, Yvonne became close to the couple, recognizing in them a pair who were as mismatched, but happy, as she and Chevallier. What Perreau lacked in physical attributes—he was short, fat and bald—he made up with his personal charm, and his success as owner of Orleans' most prestigious department stores, Jeanne was 15 years younger than her husband and a red-headed, spirited beauty who easily held her own in

two years older than her and the attraction between them was instant and intense.

Just a few weeks after they met, in 1937, she had moved into his apartment, where Chevalier's unquenchable desire for Yvonne meant that much the political and social circles that made Yvonne feel so ill at ease.

Unfortunately, the state's affairs weren't the only ones that Pierre Chevallier was attending to. Ironically, unlike their both married couples, he and Jeanne were a perfect match and they were soon deeply infatuated with each other.

Even before she found out, Yvonne was displaying symptoms of a breakdown. Anxious over a husband who was so frequently far away, she smoked incessantly, drank endless cups of strong, black coffee, and was becoming increasingly reliant on the amphetamine and barbiturate drugs her doctor prescribed. It wasn't long before her intuition told her that her marriage had started to fall apart, and it was confirmed when one of her sons fell sick. She brought him into bed with her so that she could comfort him during the night, and Chevallier moved to a couch in his office. But when the boy recovered, her husband refused to move back into the marital bed. Where once he had been insatiable in his lust for Yvonne, now he would not touch her. She visited beauty salons and *haute couture* shops and even began trying to understand his political world in an attempt to win back his affections, but nothing worked. She was rejected and alone; her hero had now become her tormentor.

Her devastation became complete when she received an anonymous letter that explained her husband's new coldness. It told her that Chevallier was having an affair. This was confirmed when an increasingly distressed Yvonne discovered a letter

BELOW: Pierre Chevallier, in a photograph taken just a year before he was killed.

ABOVE: Yvonne Chevallier appearing in the dock at the Reims Court of Assizes charged with the murder of her husband Pierre.

was at first met with furious denials, then confession, and then a demand for a divorce so he could be free to marry Jeanne. Chevallier told his wife, "As far as I am concerned you are a free woman. Take a lover because I will never make love to you again."

In desperation, Yvonne turned to Leon Perreau, hoping with his help to break the lovers up. If the affair continued, she explained to him, she might kill herself from grief. Perreau's response was a shrug. He already knew about the affair and had accepted the humiliation of being a mari complaisant— compliant husband. Next, Yvonne visited the National Assembly to find her husband and beg him again to give Jeanne up. She was turned away, and Chevallier left to take a vacation with his lover, but not before telling his wife she was a "cow."

At first, Yvonne attempted suicide with poison, but it only made her ill. Then she obtained a firearms license and bought a Mab 7.65mm, a French-made semi-automatic with a nine-round magazine. It was the perfect weapon she later said, "to kill without any doubts."

On August 11, 1951, Pierre Chevallier returned to the family home to collect the last of his clothes and belongings. Imploring him to stay, Yvonne followed him to their sons' bedroom and watched as he kissed them both goodbye. The heartbreak of watching him say farewell to his children was overwhelming. Yvonne fell to her knees clutching at her husband's legs while he snarled at her to keep her hands off the Under Secretary of State. Then Yvonne ran to grab the gun she had bought earlier screaming that would shoot herself.

in one of her husband's jackets. It was addressed to "Dear Pierre" and went on to say, "Without you, life would have no beauty or meaning for me." The note was signed "Jeanne." A confrontation with her husband

Chevallier made an obscene gesture and sneered, "Do it then. But only when I have left." They were the last words he ever spoke. Yvonne fired randomly at her husband, shooting him in the forehead, leg, chest, and face. He fell dead to the floor with Yvonne crouched over him. Only thoughts of her children prevented her from turning the gun on herself. As she stood up, the gun accidentally went off again sending a final bullet into Chevallier's back.

When the news of his murder at the hands of his wife became public the response was outrage. Although Yvonne knew what a vile man her husband had become, to the rest of France he was a revered politician and a national hero. So intense were emotions in Orleans that it was decided Yvonne's court hearing should take place some distance away, where passions were running slightly cooler.

However, by the time the trial began on November 5, 1952, the public's sympathy had started to come round to Yvonne. Tales of her husband's infidelity were well publicized and the frail and lost woman with her white face and gaunt appearance was a sight to melt the hardest of hearts. As one journalist would later write, "The French press went crazy, throwing caution to the wind with police reporters, court reporters, sob sisters, psychiatrists, novelists, the works. The French felt they invented the crime passionnel. They were determined to leave nothing unsaid and they left nothing unsaid. The whole country was outraged, or outraged that anyone would be outraged."

As each new detail of the case came to light support for Yvonne grew. By the time Jeanne Perreau came to give evidence she was hissed in court while confessing that her affair with Pierre Chevallier had gone on for five years. Her arrogant declaration that, "Love does not make one ashamed. I believe that for love one is never punished," caused such a stir that she was asked to leave. Leon Perreau, meanwhile, became a figure of contempt for his acceptance of his wife's infidelity. He even spoke calmly of how Pierre Chevallier was the favorite of all his wife's lovers and shared her bed on average three times a week.

When Yvonne herself took the stand public sympathy became total. After hearing of how deeply she had loved her husband and how she had fallen at his feet to try and prevent him leaving, only to receive a rude gesture in return, even the prosecuting counsel said that the death penalty in this case was not appropriate, calling instead for just a two-year prison sentence.

The jury took less than an hour to reach its verdict. Yvonne was acquitted. The Catholic Church later granted her absolution for the killing, but gentle, sensitive Yvonne could not absolve herself so easily. She took her sons to live in one of France's notorious mosquito-infested colonies in French Guiana, West Africa—a place that had once been a penal colony and was now described as a tropical hell. A desolate community of people still lived there and Yvonne returned to her work as a midwife among them.

Vincent Ciucci

Although 36-year-old Vincent Ciucci dreamed of a happy life with the woman he intended to marry, his existing wife and children stood in the way. However, he wasn't about to let his existing responsibilities scotch his dreams so he came up with a vile plan that would free him to begin afresh and also allow him to collect insurance money on his wife's death.

On December 5, 1953, Vincent Ciucci chloroformed his wife Anne and their three children and then shot each one in the head. He then set fire to his Chicago apartment behind the grocery store he owned to make it look like they had died in the flames. Thinking it would put him beyond suspicion, the grocer stayed in the house and when the fire department team arrived, Ciucci made a great show of stumbling out of the smoke-filled apartment, choking and begging for his family to be rescued. He had wrongly assumed that if their bodies were burned, the bullet wounds would be impossible to see.

It was a bungled attempt to disguise a murder. After they had retrieved the bodies, the police quickly realized that this was no ordinary house fire and took Ciucci in for questioning. He denied everything, saying '"I admit that I am a gambler and I like to fool around with women. But I wouldn't do anything like that. How could a man kill his own children? He would have to kill himself instead." Becoming more desperate he then concocted a story that mysterious intruders had entered his apartment and shot his family before putting a torch to the building. Incredibly, he claimed that he would not have heard the four shots because he was a heavy sleeper.

Ciucci was charged with the four murders and stood trial three times before he was finally brought to justice. At the first two, he was found guilty of first degree murder of his wife and two of their children. At the third he was also found guilty of the first degree murder of the third child. His defense counsel's pleas for clemency fell upon deaf ears, and Ciucci became the last man to die in the electric chair in Chicago on March 23, 1962. The execution took place at one minute past midnight and was witnessed by nearly 30 people including journalists.

William Corder

William Corder was more than happy to indulge in a sexual dalliance with Maria Marten, as others had done before him, but he hated the idea of marrying her. Instead, he arranged to elope with her, and when she met him on the night they planned to run away, he shot her.

The gruesome story of William Corder and Maria Marten would later become known as "The Red Barn Murder" and began in the little village of Polstead in Suffolk, England, in the early 19th century when she was 24 and he was just 22.

Maria already had two illegitimate children by former lovers by the time she and Corder, the son of a farmer, became involved and quickly became pregnant with another. With his attempts to keep their relationship secret now rendered useless by her swelling belly, Corder said he would marry her, but kept putting it off. When the baby died (amid rumors that it had been murdered), he decided that he no longer owed Maria the wedding she craved. Nevertheless, she continued to badger him.

In the late spring of 1827, after several more postponements on Corder's part, the couple arranged to meet at the Red Barn, close to Maria's house, so they

RIGHT: An early-19th century illustration of William Corder, the perpetrator of the notorious "Red Barn Murder."

could elope. Although there was no real reason for them to run away together, Corder claimed he had heard that the parish officers were going to prosecute Maria for having bastard children. Maria Marten was never seen alive again.

Corder disappeared from the village for a time, but later returned to say he and Maria were now happily living in Ipswich. He also said he could not yet bring her back as his wife for fear of the anger of his friends and relatives. Already though, the village folk were suspicious, and the pressure on Corder to produce his wife eventually forced him to leave the area again. Now he wrote letters to her family claiming they were living on the Isle of Wight, and gave various excuses for the fact that she had not contacted them.

Suspicion continued to grow, and on April 19, 1828, Maria's stepmother persuaded her husband to go to the Red Barn and dig in one of the grain storage bins. He quickly uncovered the remains of his daughter buried in a sack. Maria's body was badly decomposed but was identified, by her sister Ann, from her hair, clothing, and a missing tooth. Corder's green handkerchief was discovered around her neck. Although it was obvious that there had been foul play, it was difficult to establish the exact cause of Maria's death. It was initially thought that a sharp instrument—possibly Corder's short sword—had been plunged into her eye, but this wound could also have been caused by her father's spade when he was exhuming the body. The handkerchief at her throat suggested strangulation while other wounds suggested she had been shot.

Corder was tracked down to Brentford, Middlesex, where he was running a boarding house with a woman he had married. The police charged him with "murdering Maria Marten, by feloniously and willfully

BELOW: William Corder being executed at the gallows in Bury St. Edmunds, Suffolk, on August 11, 1828.

BELOW: A contemporary pamphlet containing details of the "horrid murder" of Maria Marten by her lover William Corder.

THE MURDER OF
MARIA MARTEN
IN THE RED BARN AT POLSTED.
Containing the whole Account of the horrid Murder,
COMMITTED BY HER LOVER AND SEDUCER WILLIAM CORDER.
Which was revealed in a Dream by her Mother, and also a graphic
ACCOUNT OF HIS CONFESSION AND EXECUTION

shooting her with a pistol through the body, and likewise stabbing her with a dagger." And in order to be sure of a conviction eight other charges were brought against Corder, including one of forgery.

Corder's trial started on August 7, 1828, at Shire Hall, Bury St. Edmunds. The court was so swamped with hopeful spectators that admittance was by ticket only. Finally standing before a judge, Corder pleaded not guilty to the murder of Maria Marten. He admitted being in the barn with Maria but said he had left after they argued. He claimed that while he was walking away he heard a shot, ran back to the barn, and found Maria dead with one of his pistols beside her.

It took the jury just 35 minutes to return with a guilty verdict. He was sentenced to hang and afterward be dissected. Corder spent the next three days in prison agonising over whether to confess to the crime and make a clean breast of his sins before God and after several meetings with the prison chaplain, entreaties from his wife, and pleas from both his warder and the governor of the prison, he finally gave a different story. While he still hotly denied stabbing Maria, he now said he had accidentally shot her in the eye as she changed into her traveling clothes.

Corder was hanged in Bury St. Edmunds on August 11, 1828, in front of a large crowd. One newspaper claimed there were 7,000 spectators, another as many as 20,000. His body was later used to demonstrate the workings of the nervous system to medical students.

Cheryl Crane

Over the years Hollywood has been the scene of many murders, some every bit as dramatic as those on-screen. But there have been few stranger cases than the slaying of gangster Johnny Stompanato by the 14-year-old daughter of movie star Lana Turner.

As has often been the case with Hollywood folk, while Lana Turner enjoyed a thriving career in the movies her private life was much less successful. It was while she was coming to terms with the collapse of her most recent marriage that she received a telephone call that would end in death, and a murder trial for Lana's young daughter, Cheryl Crane. At the end of the line was a man, a complete stranger, who told the star that they had mutual friends and asked her out on a blind date. Showing an incredible lack of judgement, Lana agreed and so began a torrid relationship with local criminal Johnny Stompanato.

BELOW: American actor Lana Turner (center), wearing dark sunglasses, sitting next to her ex-husband, Stephen Crane, in a courtroom during the murder trial of their daughter, Cheryl Crane.

ABOVE: High-angle view of American actor Lana Turner (right) seated in a courtroom, surrounded by reporters during the trial of her daughter, Cheryl Crane.

An ex-U.S. Marine, con-man, and associate of known gangsters, Stompanato was a smooth talker who soon insinuated himself into Lana's bed, her Los Angeles mansion, and her bank account. And once he was firmly installed in her life things quickly turned sour. Stompanato bullied and abused his famous lover and gambled her money away. Lana's daughter Cheryl regularly begged her mother to end the relationship, but Lana replied, "I'm too afraid." As a court would later hear, Stompanato was an associate of big-time gangsters Bugsy Siegel and Mickey Cohen, and had already told

LEFT: Cheryl Crane, daughter of actor Lana Turner, sits in a chair at the time of her trial for the murder of gangster Johnny Stompanato.

Lana what would happen if she tried to leave him, threatening, "I'll mutilate you. I will hurt you so you'll be so repulsive that you'll have to hide forever." On another occasion he told her, "When I say hop, you hop. When I say jump, you jump."

Such threats became ever more frequent and on the night of April 4, 1958, Stompanato and Lana had a violet argument during which he again threatened to scar her, shouting, "I'll get you if it takes a day, a week, a month or a year. If I can't do it myself, I'll get someone who will. That's my business."

Outside the door Cheryl was listening. In fear for her mother's life and driven to a frenzy of hatred by the gangster's threats, she fetched a long-bladed kitchen knife, ran into the room, thrust it into Stompanato's stomach, and killed him.

As might be expected for a case involving such a high-profile celebrity, the ensuing inquest was a sensational. On live television, audiences greater than any she had received before watched Lana Turner give an account of the events leading up to Stompanato's death and a passionate defense of her daughter. As a minor, Cheryl did not appear in court, but gave evidence in writing. Her statement read: "They had an argument and he was threatening Mother. He said he would kill her and hurt Daddy, Grandma, and me. He said he had ways of doing it. My mother was very frightened. I went down to the kitchen and got the knife. I took the knife up to the room in case he hurt mother. I rushed into the room and stuck him with the knife. He screamed."

The jury returned a verdict of justifiable homicide, effectively clearing Cheryl of blame for the killing. On hearing it, a friend of Stompanato leaped up in the public gallery and shouted, "It's lies, all lies. The girl was in love with him as well. He was killed because of jealousy between mother and daughter." Cheryl was released from a juvenile prison to resume normal life with her movie star mother. The scandal had no ill-effects on Lana's career. In fact, she earned an $2 million from her next film, *Imitation of Life*—an incredible fee at the time. She needed the money: Stompanato's family sued her and received an undisclosed settlement.

Dr. Hawley Harvey Crippen

The case of Dr Crippen is one of the most famous in the history of crime. Involving a nagging, unfaithful wife, a sexually charged affair, a desperate escape, and grisly remains found in a basement, Crippen's tale contains all the ingredients of a thriller novel.

Crippen was an American doctor, who worked as a consultant ear specialist in England despite not being qualified to practice medicine outside of the United States. Flamboyant and dressy, he was charming in public but hid his private turmoil. All was not happy in the Crippen household.

Following the death of his first wife, Crippen had married again in 1892 at the age of 31, to a young woman of 19 named Cora. They had a complicated courtship. At the time, Cora was already the mistress of a stove manufacturer who paid for the singing lessons that would eventually propel her onto the London music hall stage under the name Belle Elmore. While she eventually agreed to be Crippen's wife, marriage did nothing to settle Cora. She liked to be center stage; to be adored and admired. Like many others of the same temperament, she tried to satisfy her need for attention in the arms of numerous men. Her string of lovers included an ex-boxer and several of the lodgers who took rooms with the Crippens. Meanwhile, she grew contemptuous of her husband and her bad temper often spilled over into nagging and arguments.

So, when Crippen met a 17-year-old Polish typist named Ethel Le Neve and was attracted to her, he felt no guilt. After all, he knew that Cora had affairs and made his life a misery. He hired Ethel as his bookkeeper and—surprisingly—the pair remained on professional, terms for seven years before becoming lovers.

It was Cora's vicious tongue that sealed her fate. When Ethel fell pregnant and had a miscarriage, Cora was quick to humiliate her husband, claiming to her music hall friends that the baby could have been fathered by any one of a number of men that Ethel had been sleeping with. Such accusations were rich, coming from a woman who delighted in her many affairs, and drove Crippen into a rage. Cora, he decided, had to die.

Crippen's chose poison as the cleanest murder method and accordingly gave his wife a strong dose in a nightcap on January 31, 1910. But when that didn't have the required effect he simply shot Cora in the back of the head, then dismembered her body and buried it in the cellar, covering the parts in quicklime to help them decompose more quickly. To cover his tracks he then told her friends that she had rushed to the bedside of a sick relative in the United States. As time passed and she didn't return, he said that she had become seriously ill, and then that she had died. Nevertheless, Cora's friends were suspicious. They alerted the police who questioned Crippen and searched the house. Although on that occasion they found nothing, Crippen was spooked, and decided to flee.

Together with Ethel, who was disguised as a boy, Crippen boarded the SS *Montrose*, which was bound for his homeland. But back in London the police returned and, finding the house deserted, this time searched more thoroughly. Before the ship left harbor, the tale of the grisly remains found in the coal cellar were splashed all over the newspapers along with Crippen's photo. And as the boat steamed out toward America, a copy caught the eye of the captain of the SS Montrose. Recognizing one of his passengers, he famously sent a message to shore, which read: "Have strong suspicion

BELOW: A photograph of Dr. Crippen from 1910, the year he is alleged to have poisoned his wife and dismembered he body before fleeing across the Atlantic Ocean.

that Crippen London cellar murder and accomplice are among saloon passengers." Crippen became the first murderer to be caught by wireless telegraph.

At the trial, Crippen gallantly played down Ethel's involvement in his wife's death, and she was acquitted of murder. Crippen also pleaded innocent, saying the remains found at the house on Hilldrop Crescent were not those of his wife, but the jury did not believe him. he was found guilty of murder and hanged on November 23, 1910.

However, it appears Crippen did not kill his wife after all. In 2007, DNA analysis of the body in Crippen's cellar suggested that the body was not Cora's. Instead the murder victim was an unknown man!

RIGHT: 39 Hilltop Crescent, London: The house where Dr Crippen was alleged to have murdered his second wife Belle Elmore.

BELOW: A detective leads Doctor Hawley Harvey Crippen from the SS Megantic, upon arrival in England, in August 1910.

Dr. Philip Cross

For some men entering the twilight of their lives, a new passion with a much younger woman is a chance to turn the clock back to a time when they were young and vigorous. Such infatuations can be so all-consuming that they become deadly.

Dr. Philip Cross had long preferred women who had a fresh glow of youth about them. When he married at the age of 44, his wife Laura was just 22. For 18 years, the couple lived comfortably and happily at Shandy Hall in the village of Dripsey, County Cork, Ireland. Dr Cross's practice was successful, and over the years the couple were blessed with six children. However, the contentment of the Cross family home came to an abrupt end when Laura took on a new governess for the children.

Effie Skinner was just 20, by then more than 40 years younger than Cross, and not strikingly pretty. Nevertheless, she had a youthful charm that immediately attracted Cross. Soon he had become totally besotted. Although the strength of his lust threatened to overwhelm him, Cross tried to suppress the emotion, but one day as Effie stood before him reporting on the children's' progress he could contain himself no longer. He leaned over and kissed her.

Cross regretted it immediately, fearing that the

shocked and unresponsive Effie might tell his wife or—even worse—that she might leave. Effie had no wish to give up a comfortable job though, and stayed quiet. But the longer she was in the house, the more intense became Cross's lust until it became so obvious that Mrs Cross could not help but notice. She immediately sacked Effie even though she protested that any sexual inclination was all on the doctor's side.

The governess left for Dublin and was pursued there by Cross. Now, at last, away from his wife's watchful eyes he allowed his passion free reign. Effie succumbed to his advances. It seems that finally having the object of his lust robbed Dr Cross of what remained of his senses, for he was now determined that she must become his wife, and mistress of Shandy Hall, whatever the cost. And the price that must be paid to satisfy his passion was Laura Cross's life.

It was easy for the doctor to arrange his wife's death. Having procured a good supply of arsenic, which he said was to be used for sheep dip, he began to poison her. As she grew unwell, the doctor reassured her that it was not a serious illness and gave her a remedy that contained yet more arsenic. Within a month she was dead. And within two weeks of that, Philip Cross was married to Effie Skinner.

Had he not been so quick to wed his mistress, Cross may never have been discovered, but Laura's friends and family were already suspicious about her death. She had always been a healthy, robust woman and never displayed any of the symptoms of the heart problems that Cross had said killed her. Although he tried to keep his new marriage secret, when he brought Effie back to Shandy Hall it couldn't be hidden for long. Suspicions became accusations, and the police exhumed Laura's body. A postmortem found no sign of heart disease, but plenty of arsenic and strychnine. Dr Philip Cross went on trial for murder at the Munster Assizes in Cork and was found guilty on December 18, 1887.

George Crossman

George Crossman's were not really crimes of passion in the true sense, yet the murders he committed are worth mentioning here because they were all in the name of love. A serial womanizer and bigamist, he married seven women—that we know of—and one by one he killed them.

At the age of 32, George Crossman was married to his fifth wife. His first three marriages had all been legitimate, but this was his second wedding conducted under a false name. Wife number five was a widowed nurse called Ellen Sampson. After her joyous wedding day in January 1903, she returned with her husband to her new home in Ladysmith Road, Kensal Rise, north London, without the slightest suspicion that it was already the home of wife number four, Edith. As soon as their wedding night was over Ellen became surplus to requirements. Crossman smashed her over the head and hid her body in a trunk in the attic. By the time Edith returned home from visiting friends everything in the house was normal. She would never know that her husband had found time for a bigamous marriage and a murder while she was away.

Incredibly Crossman and Edith lived a fairly happy married life for the next two years, though that certainly would not have been the case if she had known the truth: she was not legally married (there was yet another wife in the background), there was a body rotting in a trunk at the top of the house; and during that time Crossman married wives six and seven during trips away from home.

It was only when the couple's lodger William Dell started to complain about the awful smell coming from one of the upstairs room that Crossman's murdering secret was revealed. In March 1904, Crossman hastily tried to get the trunk out of the house, but it was too late. By then William Dell had already alerted police about what he strongly suspected was the smell of a rotting body, and Crossman was caught in the act or trying to remove the trunk on March 23. He managed to dash past the police, who gave chase. The certain knowledge that he was going to die a painful death on the gallows was too much for Crossman. After running almost a mile, he stopped to cut his own throat from ear to ear with a razor.

Sir John Henry Delves Broughton

The murder of a known womanizer in Kenya will probably never now be solved, but the prime suspect remains Sir Henry Delves Broughton. However, though he stood trial for the killing, with the help of his young wife—whose lover was the victim—Sir Henry was found not guilty of killing his rival.

Kenya's White Highlands were once nicknamed "Happy Valley" due to the excessive drink, drugs, and sex parties enjoyed by its wealthy inhabitants in the days when Kenya was still a colony of the British Empire. Foremost among the hedonists was Josslyn Victor Hay, 22nd Earl of Erroll and Baron Kilmarnock. Locally, he was known as "The Passionate Peer," for the 39-year-old aristocrat was a sophisticated, handsome, sexual predator; an accomplished seducer, whose favorite line was, "To hell with husbands."

On November 30, 1940, Hay was drinking at the Muthaiga Club, a watering hole favored by the wealthy British, when two recently arrived strangers entered. Sir John Henry "Jock" Delves Broughton was a property magnate and racing fanatic in his late 50s and on his arm was an ash-blonde beauty—26-year-old Diana Caldwell whom Sir Henry had married only weeks before the pair had emigrated to Kenya. Hay later told friends, "Never can I remember a woman having such an immediate impact on me. I saw her eyes boring into me and I knew then that I must have her. I walked over to her while Jock was at the bar and said to her, Well, who is going to tell Jock—you or I?'"

It did not take long for Hay to seduce the beautiful young bride. On January 18, 1941, Diana confessed to her husband that she had fallen madly in love, and reminded him of an extraordinary pact that Sir Henry had made with her before they were married. Aware of the great differences in their ages, Sir Henry had promised that if Diana ever fell in love with a younger man he would provide her with a quick divorce and several thousand pounds a year afterward. He had never expected the marriage to come to an end so quickly though. Instead of immediately honoring his promise, he asked his wife to take a three-month trip with him to Ceylon and told her that if she would just promise to reconsider then she could even bring Hay along.

Diana considered the generous offer for a couple of days and then rejected it. She walked out on Sir Henry, telling him that she was going to live with Hay.

Three days later, Sir Henry called the police to report a break in. Two revolvers, some money, and a cigarette case had been stolen. The same day he saw his lawyers about a divorce and later wrote the following words to a friend: "They say they are in love with each other and mean to get married. It is a hopeless position and I'm going to cut my losses. I think I'll go to Ceylon. There's nothing for me to live in Kenya for."

At 3am on January 24, 1941, a truck driver discovered Hay's body slumped under the dashboard of his car, which had left the road and plunged into a ditch only three miles from Sir Henry's home. He had been shot through the head at point-blank range with a .32 caliber revolver.

Strangely, the police didn't announce that they were treating it as a murder case until January 25, by which time the body had already been buried. But once they did, Diana quickly came forward and accused her husband of cold-bloodedly killing her lover out of jealousy. Sir Henry was taken into custody. In another

odd turn of events, however, Diana relented almost immediately. By the time police formally charged Sir Henry with the murder, she had flown to Johannesburg to hire top criminal lawyer Harry Morris to defend her husband. It was to be a worthwhile investment.

Morris called experts to prove that the three bullets fired at Hay could not have come from any gun owned by Sir Henry. The accused also performed masterfully in the dock, at one point saying, "She could ask who she liked. I should not have tried to stop her in any event. I see no point in it. We met every day at the club and I cannot see it makes any difference if a man comes to stay the night. In my experience of life, if you try to stop a woman doing anything, she wants to do it all the more. With a young wife the only thing to do is keep her amused." What motive, it was asked, could a man so coolly accepting of his wife's infidelity have in murdering her lover?

On July 1, 1941, Sir Henry Delves Broughton was found not guilty of murdering Josslyn Hay. The file on the crime has never been closed, and the murderer has never been caught. Sir Henry committed suicide in Liverpool on December 5, 1942, leaving a note that said he had found the strain of the trial and publicity too much to bear. Diana returned to Kenya where she remained until her death in 1987, a rich, enigmatic, extravagant lady to the last.

Geza de Kaplany

Most men who marry a beautiful and glamorous young wife celebrate their good luck in winning a woman that so many other men desire. But for Geza de Kaplany, his wife's good looks were a reason for jealousy and suspicion. When he was struck by impotence and could no longer make love to her, he found a solution to his problems: if he couldn't have her, then he would make sure that no one else wanted her.

Born in Hungary in 1926, Geza de Kaplany was working in a hospital in San Jose, California, when he met 25-year-old Hanja. She was 10 years his junior, a glamor model and ex-showgirl who had her choice of men, but the doctor's own good looks attracted her and she fell in love. He, in turn, was smitten by the lovely young creature and soon the couple were joined in marriage. Less than a month later, Hanja was brutally and fatally mutilated by her husband.

It began with an obsession that other men in their apartment building were pursuing the eager Hanja, but de Kaplany's unravelling mental state also meant that he could no longer sustain an erection. Sunk in black thoughts and comparing his own inadequacy to his gorgeous young wife's obvious sexual allure, he came to an insane conclusion: Hanja must be made ugly.

On the evening of August 28, 1962, loud classical music flooded the Ranchero Palms Apartments in San Jose, accompanied by equally loud blood-chilling screams. Neighbors quickly called the police, but by the time they arrived it was already too late. Hanja was found tied to her bed. De Kaplany had poured sulfuric and nitric acids over his wife, and mutilated her with a knife. She suffered third degree corrosive burns over 60 per cent of her body with most of the brutality focussed on her genitals. So bad was the damage that one of the ambulance crew had to be treated for burns sustained simply by touching her skin. Maimed beyond comprehension, still Hajna de Kaplany fought for her life. It proved to be a losing battle. After 33 days in hospital, she succumbed to her injuries.

De Kaplany told police that Hajna had been unfaithful to him, and that he had just wanted to destroy her beauty rather than kill her. Somewhere in his twisted mind he

ABOVE: Dr. Geza de Kaplany, who tortured his wife with acid on her face and knife wounds to much of her body.

protest and accusations that gruesome postmortem photographs of Hajna de Kaplany had been removed from his file prior to review by the California State Parole Board. After working in Taiwan as a medical missionary he broke parole conditions and got a job at a hospital in Munich in 1980. However, when his past became known he was swiftly fired. Incredibly, he found another woman willing to be his wife and became a naturalized German citizen in order to avoid extradition back to America.

BELOW: Hajna de Kaplany, pictured in her showgirl days. Her beauty, combined with her husbands insane jealousy, led to her horrific death.

was aware of the horror of his crime: When he saw police photographs of his wife wounds he broke down. At his trial in 1963, de Kaplany pleaded not guilty to his wife's murder on the grounds of insanity. He claimed to suffer from multiple-personality disorder and said that the sadistic crime was not committed by him but by his alter ego, Pierre de la Roche. Nevertheless, de Kaplany was convicted of first degree murder, though due to his irrational behavior before and during the trial he was sentenced to life imprisonment rather than death.

De Kaplany actually served less than 12 years for his insane and deadly attack. He was released in 1975 amid

Marie de Morell

Although the aristocratic French lieutenant Emile de La Ronciere was the one who served time for this crime of passion, with hindsight it is outrageous that he was ever convicted. It is far more likely that he was the victim of a crime of passion himself—a cruel plot levelled at him by a highly-strung girl determined to punish him for being attracted to her mother rather than herself.

The son of the **Count de La Ronciere**, Emile was a typical aristocrat of his time. It was true that he kept a mistress and had mounting gambling debts, certainly, but that made him no different from the majority of young noblemen at the beginning of the 19th century. In fact, his life may have passed in complete obscurity, of interest only to a handful of French family historians, save for the fact that in 1834 he joined the cavalry school at Saumur in the Loire Valley of France, and soon found himself at the center of a scandal.

La Ronciere's commanding officer at the school was the Baron de Morell, an intimidating fellow aristocrat

BELOW: The Royal School of Cavalry at Saumur, in the Loire Valley of France, where Emile de La Ronciere was stationed when he met the de Morell family.

who was known for being even more wayward in his habits than most Frenchmen of high birth. Nevertheless, La Ronciere's progress was unremarkable at first and like the other well-born officers he would often dine and socialize at the baron's home where he met the baroness and her daughter Marie.

Although La Ronciere was obviously attracted to the baron's wife and the pair indulged in flirtation, that was not so unusual in French society at that time, and there is no suggestion that the two were involved in an affair. One evening though La Ronciere was surprised and humiliated when the baron turned on him and ordered him out of the house in front of the assembled guests. It was a terrible insult and one followed by a puzzling revelation when the next day de Morell produced letters he had received threatening his family. He accused La Ronciere of sending them.

The lieutenant assured him that he could not possibly have sent them, and pointed out that they contained details that would have been known only to the family. But this was just the beginning of his problems. On the night of September 24, 1834, Marie de Morell burst into the room of her English governess in hysterics. La Ronciere, she explained through her tears, had forced his way through her window and made obscene threats to her. Having bolted the door so that she could not escape he had grabbed her breasts, bitten her, and forced her to pull up her nightshirt, then cut her naked thigh. She had been frightened for her life, she managed to choke out, but eventually La Ronciere had left by the window he came in at.

The next day brought more trouble in the shape of another poison-pen letter, this time addressed to a lieutenant whom Marie de Morell was known to be close to. His honor insulted, the young man accused La Ronciere of sending it and challenged him to a duel. The challenger lost, but even though wounded refused to withdraw his accusation.

With all these charges stacked against him, La Ronciere was given an ultimatum: If he confessed then matters would be quietly dropped, but if he persisted in protesting his innocence then his father would be told and the full scandal revealed.

He was given a night to make a decision. In the morning La Ronciere foolishly signed a confession of guilt in an attempt to save his name from being blackened, then rode for Paris hoping to let matters settle. His hope was in vain. Letters continued to arrive at the de Morell household. Some said that Marie was pregnant, others said that the baron and his wife would soon be murdered. All were full of the most vile insults. With his patience at an end Baron de Morell had La Ronciere arrested.

The evidence at his trial was shockingly flimsy, and La Ronciere's defense pulled it to shreds. The court heard that he could not have burst into Marie's room in the night. It was on the top floor and the house was surrounded by guards. To get in he would have needed a long ladder which would have been seen immediately, and even if he had managed it, why was it that the governess who slept next door had heard nothing of the violence until Marie had come into her room? The glazier who had mended the broken window was also brought to the witness stand to testify and said that he had been surprised to see that all the broken glass had fallen outside, suggesting that the window had been broken from the inside and that it would have been impossible for anyone to reach the latch from the hole that had been made.

The defense also asked why the supposedly violated Marie had immediately gone back to sleep that night and how had she recovered from her terrifying ordeal so easily as to have been seen enjoying herself thoroughly at a ball two nights later. There was also the matter of the wound on her thigh. It had not been examined immediately after the attack and when someone did look at it, it appeared to be no more than a light scratch.

And there was yet more evidence that shouted La Ronciere's innocence. The poison-pen letters he was accused of sending were still arriving when he had been away from the country and after he had been arrested and jailed. And though it would be a stupid criminal indeed who signed his letters, these bore La Ronciere's initials and signature, twice with the name spelled wrongly.

Although Marie de Morell took the stand to give evidence against La Ronciere, the defense was not allowed to ask her any questions at all. She calmly denounced him and then was allowed to leave the court. If the defense had cross-examined her, it is possible that they may have succeeded in getting her to admit that she had an unrequited passion for La Ronciere herself and, jealous of the attentions he gave to her mother, she had set out to destroy his reputation and prospects. As it was, the court preferred her word over all the evidence that suggested she was a liar. La Ronciere was found guilty of sending threatening letters and the attempted rape of Marie. He was imprisoned for a decade.

Julio Diaz & Nicole Garcia

It was a case that shocked America: Nicole Garcia didn't just help her lover to murder her husband, but arrived at her husband's funeral with the young man on her arm! Before her husband had been dead a week, his murderer was living in his house, driving his car, and looking after his children.

Although Nicole Garcia later claimed that the decision to kill her husband had been sparked by his drunken abuse of her, friends of the couple testified that Jason Garcia had been a good and decent husband who had never laid a finger on his wife. Many people have suggested that, in fact, when she and her lover, Julio Diaz, entered the Garcia family home in New York City on May 10, 2008, their only motive was to remove an obstacle to their relationship.

What happened next is also unclear, for the stories offered by Nicole and Diaz never matched. Nicole told police that Diaz had confronted her husband and a fight broke out, at which point she ran from the room. She said that when she returned Garcia had been wrapped in a blanket. Diaz, however, claimed that Nicole had awoken her husband when they got to the house, argued with him, and that Garcia had then attacked. Having pushed his opponent over a table, which had knocked him unconscious, Diaz said that he had checked Garcia's vital signs and told Nicole to call for help. It was she who had fetched the blanket and told her lover to wrap Garcia in it.

Both stories agree that at the end of the fight Jason Garcia had been swaddled in a blanket, and an autopsy later revealed that he had still been alive at this point. That would not be the case for long though. Diaz now choked his lover's husband with his bare hands and then strangled him with a rope. For good measure, he then wrapped Garcia's head in a plastic bag and tape.

Finally sure that their victim was dead Nicole and Diaz carried the wrapped body to a car and drove it around New York—from Brooklyn to Queens and back to Brooklyn again—before choosing the aptly named Great Kills Park over in Staten Island as a suitable dumping ground.

When the body was discovered the murder was initially thought to have been a random killing committed by a stranger, but suspicion and rumor spread like wildfire, especially after Diaz escorted Nicole to her husband's funeral. He had also moved into the family home.

On September 15, 2008, Nicole Garcia was pulled in by police on a drink-driving charge after she crashed her large Chevrolet Suburban vehicle just a block away from her house. She had drunk more than twice over the legal limit of alcohol. The next day Julio Diaz was arrested for murder. Friends and family of Jason Garcia had not been the only people suspicious of events surrounding Garcia's violent death and now, under further questioning, investigators had finally begun to find out the truth.

While Nicole Garcia was charged with hindering prosecution and tampering with physical evidence, Diaz first faced a charge of second-degree murder and a 25 year to life prison sentence. But under a plea deal, he admitted the lesser charge of first-degree manslaughter. At his final court appearance Diaz was sentenced to 17 years behind bars.

Nannie Hazle Doss

What drove Nannie to kill was not love and passion, but the lack of it. As hard as she tried to find a husband who would match up to the dashing men in the bodice-ripping books and true romance magazines she had become addicted to, none of them ever did. And to make way for the next unlucky husband, one by one they had to die.

N annie Hazle Doss—who also became known as "Arsenic Annie," the "Jolly Black Widow," and the "Giggling Grandma"—was a cuddly creature with twinkling eyes and a wide smile by the time she finally stood trial for her crimes. Beneath the sweet exterior was a woman who killed without a second thought. She had been born Nancy Hazle, in 1905 in Blue Moun-

RIGHT: Nannie Doss pictured with her grandchildren, in a courthouse corridor during a hearing to decide her fate for the death of her husband, Samuel Doss.

BELOW: Nannie Doss looks happy and relaxed as she talks with homicide detective Captain Harry Stege before her arraignment on a charge of murder.

tain, Alabama, and, in a similar tale to many women who turned murderer, led a miserable childhood. Beaten cruelly and forced to work on the family farm by a father who may also have sexually abused her, Nancy—now known to all as Nannie—escaped her hellish home at the age of 15 by marrying a man named Charlie Braggs who she had met only four months previously.

The marriage was doomed from the start. Braggs insisted that his mother come live with the newlyweds in Tulsa, Oklahoma, and before long started staying away from home for nights at a time while he played around with other women. Meanwhile Nannie was swamped with children—the couple had four daughters in four years—and having failed to find the love for which she had always yearned, turned to drink and lost herself in romance magazines.

Nevertheless, as it turned out Braggs was the most fortunate of her five husbands, though the same can't be said for two of the children. He returned home one day in the spring of 1927 to find them dying on the floor (they were later alleged to have been Nannie's first victims) and he walked out, taking the surviving oldest child and leaving his wife with the youngest. He later said that he had left, "because I was frightened of what she would do." His instinct probably saved his life. Braggs filed for divorce and it was finalized the next year, by which time Nannie had already lined up husband number two.

This one didn't last long. He failed to satisfy and within a year of the marriage Frank Harelson died of stomach trouble. Husband number three must have come closer to fulfiling Nannie's fantasies because he survived until 1952 before the same death took him, too. Number four, Richard Morton, left a healthy insurance policy, and by now Nannie had hit her stride and felt that she no longer needed to confine herself to husbands. In short order, Nannie's mother, her two sisters, and the nephew of one of her deceased husbands were added to the list of mysterious deaths.

It was only upon the death in 1954 of Nannie's fifth husband, Samuel Doss, that an autopsy was ordered. It was discovered that there was enough arsenic in him to kill 20 men. Arrested, she chuckled and giggled through police interrogation, not appearing to understand the gravity of her crimes. She was still smiling when, at her trial, the court was told that her estimated tally of victims was 11. Nannie Doss showed neither regret nor remorse and calmly explained that she had poisoned the last four of her five husbands because they were, "dullards." None of them had lived up to the glamorous fictional men in her paperbacks and magazines. She was sentenced to life imprisonment and died in prison of leukaemia in 1965.

BELOW: Nannie Doss, pictured in a mug-shot taken in Tulsa, Oklahoma in October 1954.

Pauline Dubuisson

As little as she valued the faithful young man who adored her while they were together, Pauline Dubuisson was determined that he wouldn't find happiness. If she couldn't have him, then no-one could.

A young woman who was used to having everything she wanted, Pauline Dubuisson clearly didn't have much time for morality. During World War II, the young Frenchwoman had become the mistress of an enemy German Army officer when she was just 17 years old, and when she enrolled as a medical student at the French University of Lille after the war, she soon showed just as little regard for right and wrong.

At university in 1946, she met a charming and gentle-natured fellow student, Felix Bailly, and the two began a relationship. But during the stormy three years they were together, Pauline was anything but faithful. Smitten by his wild lover, Bailly proposed to her again and again and—just as frequently—Pauline turned him down and cheated on him.

Emotionally drained and heartsick, Bailly eventually came to the end of his tether. Leaving the wanton Pauline and Lille behind, he went to continue his studies in Paris where he soon met the beautiful Monique Lombard, a woman deserving of Bailly's love and who returned it fully. Finally happy, Bailly became engaged to Monique at the end of 1950.

Back in Lille, Pauline was furious when she heard the news. Although she had cared little for Bailly when she had the chance, she was the kind of woman who believed that she could treat men as her playthings and wasn't used to losing a lover to another woman. Her pride demanded that she win him back. But the tables were turned. The man who would have once done anything to win her love now rejected Pauline's advances, telling her that he was blissfully happy. His fiancée was the love of his life.

With venom in her heart, Pauline returned to Lille where she spent some money she had been given as a birthday gift on a .25 caliber automatic pistol. She then wrote a letter saying she intended to kill Bailly after which she would commit suicide. The note was soon found by Pauline's landlady who quickly sent a warning to Bailly. When Pauline arrived in Paris, Bailly refused to let her into his apartment, insisting that anything she wished to say to him could be said in public at a café. Having arranged a meeting, he duly arrived with a friend to protect him.

Pauline never turned up. But she was watching as he returned home. Soon after, Bailly answered a knock at his door, believing it to be another friend who was arriving to watch over him. Pauline raised the gun and fired three times. She then turned it upon herself and pulled the trigger. But the gun jammed. An attempt to gas herself also failed when a neighbor arrived to investigate the gun shots. Pauline was arrested and sent to jail to await trial. While there she would hear that the shame brought upon him by her actions had caused her father to write in sympathy to Bailly's family and then poison himself.

After attempting to slash her wrists the day before her trial began, Pauline Dubuisson was finally brought before a court in November 1952. Her lawyer attempted to soften the jury by using the old French defense that hers had been a crime passionnel. The jury found it unconvincing: her relationship with Bailly had ended 18 months before she murdered him. The suicide attempts were also seen as dramatic grabs at sympathy, and the court heard exactly how wayward Pauline's lifestyle was. She had kept a journal of all her lovers' performances, including Bailly's, and they were read out. When Monique Lombard took the stand, her good-nature and calm serenity left the jury with no doubt that the vicious and manipulative Pauline had been seething with rage at losing a lover to a woman so obviously superior to her.

Fortunately for her—and many said that it was more than she deserved—Pauline Dubuisson was found guilty of murder, but without premeditation. As a result, she escaped execution, but received a sentence of life imprisonment.

Ruth Ellis

Since immortalized in literature and film, the tale of the last woman in Britain to be hanged is one of tangled relationships and immorality set in the murky world of sleazy London nightclubs. It is also a warning. When someone allows their life to slide into depravity, the results can be disastrous.

Ruth Ellis began life as Ruth Hornby in the Welsh seaside town of Rhyl. Born on October 9, 1926, as she grew up her one ambition was to get out of the stifling town and away from her unhappy childhood home. By the age of 17, she was working in a factory in London during the war years and had met a Canadian

RIGHT: Ruth Ellis, in a photograph probably taken in the flat above her club on the Brompton Road in Knightsbridge, London.

BELOW: Ruth Ellis posing in stockings and suspenders, in a picture was taken by a Captain Ritchie in 1954.

serviceman. He took the opportunity of being on the opposite side of the Atlantic from his wife and children to have an affair with the pretty young teenager and showered Ruth with gifts while escorting her around London's nightspots. Sadly, his passion waned when he found out that his young lover was pregnant. Like many girls of her day, Ruth was literally left holding the baby when the war ended and her boyfriend returned to his family.

Devastated, Ruth declared that she would never trust or love a man again and persuaded her mother to take care of her infant son. Then she returned to London to seek work. One particular advert caught her eye, it read, "Wanted. Model for Camera Club. Nude but artistic poses. No experience necessary." Ruth attended an interview, stripped off her clothes, and was awarded a job posing for photographers who rarely bothered to fill their cameras with film. She also happily escorted the men who paid to look at her naked out to dine and dance in London's West End.

It wasn't long before Ruth forgot her pledge not to become involved with men and she took up with another who saw her as an easy target. Morris Conley owned the sleazy Court Club, had served time for fraud and illegal gambling, and employed women who would satisfy all needs of his customers. Ruth soon became an employee and quickly mastered the art of flirting with the men who came to the club and tricking them into buying fake Champagne and overpriced food. For her troubles, Ruth received a ten percent commission on top of her five pounds a week wage. However, there was even more money to be made by allowing customers to purchase her body as well, and Ruth proved herself a willing and able prostitute. As one client later reported, "She was an artist. She gave you the full treatment and by the time she had finished you felt on top of the world." At the same time she was also sleeping with Conley who felt he had the right to sex with his hostess employees. They were rewarded for complying with gifts of beautiful gowns, and should they refuse the dresses were slashed, and the girls fired.

At the age of 23, Ruth fell pregnant again, but this time opted for a dangerous backstreet abortion. Within a year, she was married to 41-year-old divorced dentist George Ellis and pregnant again, though there was no guarantee that the child was her new husband's. Nevertheless, Ruth decided to keep the baby and her daughter was duly placed in the care of her mother while Ruth and George continued to live a decadent lifestyle in London's seedier hangouts. The marriage wasn't destined to last though. Ruth's husband was an alcoholic with a violent temper, and the couple were constantly separating and reuniting as passion and possessiveness alternated between contempt and hatred between them. Eventually, George used doubts over their daughter's paternity as an excuse to desert his wife. By 1951 they were divorced.

With George's financial support withdrawn, Ruth returned to her job at the Court Club, which by now had become the Carroll Club, though the activities within its walls hadn't changed in the slightest. Ruth's enthusiasm for her work was rewarded with a rent-free, two-bedroom Mayfair apartment supplied by Conley while her expertise as a prostitute brought numerous gifts from clients. One admirer bought her a race horse, Ruth's wardrobe was filled with expensive designer clothes, and her purse with bundles of banknotes given to her by rich, international businessmen. She now counted celebrities among her friends including the World Champion racing driver Mike Hawthorn, who introduced Ruth to the man that would end her life.

David Blakely was engaged to another girl when he took up with Ruth. Three years younger than her, he followed a by now well-established pattern in Ruth's lovers, turning violent and abusive when drunk. But unlike previous boyfriends he had had a decent education at a public school, and when sober had excellent manners and treated her with more respect than most other Carroll Club customers. For once Ruth was sleeping with a man because she wanted to, rather than because he was just part of the job. When she became pregnant again in 1953, Blakely seemed ready to take responsibility. As Ruth would later recall, "David was very concerned about my welfare. Although he was engaged to another girl, he offered to marry me and he said it seemed unnecessary for me to get rid of the child, but I did not want to take advantage of him. I was not really in love with him at the time and it was quite unnecessary to marry me. I thought I could get out of the mess quite easily. In fact, I did so with the abortion."

After the latest pregnancy was terminated, Ruth's affections for Blakely waned and she began seeing other men without his knowledge. Among them was company director Desmond Cussen whose help she began to rely on. Due to Blakely's jealousy and suspicions about her activities, Ruth had not been able to entertain clients at the Carroll Club and had subsequently lost her job. Cussen set her up in a flat and became a frequent visitor. Nevertheless, she was still sleeping with Blakely and their relationship had become increasingly stormy, swinging from warm embraces to violent arguments. And despite her own infidelities and the fact that he was still engaged to Mary Dawson, when she found out

that he was having another affair—with an au pair—Ruth was furious. On one occasion she drove to the house where the girl worked and, seeing her Blakely's car outside, proceeded to smash every window at the front of the house.

Then, surprisingly, for a short while, Ruth's life looked as though it might finally settle down. Blakely broke off his engagement to Mary Dawson and proposed to Ruth. She was delighted and told friends that it was a turning point in her life. The relative peace and happiness was just the eye of the storm though. Blakely was still visiting his au pair lover and quickly became tired of Ruth's possessiveness. One night in January 1955, while drunk, he punched Ruth so hard in the stomach that she miscarried his child. The years

BELOW: The gun that Ruth Ellis used to shoot David Blakely.

ABOVE: Crowds gathering outside Holloway Prison before the execution of Ruth Ellis.

of brutal, drunken rows, dalliances with other partners, and terrible behavior finally came to a head on Easter Sunday that year.

The lover she had so much hope for had turned out no better than any of the other men in her life, so Ruth made her way to the Magdala public house in Hampstead, north London. In her bag was a .38 Smith and Weston revolver given to her by Desmond Cussen who not only showed her how to use it, but also drove her to the pub that night. On seeing Blakely in the Magdala, Ruth was overwhelmed with an icy, calm fury. As she later explained to a court, "I had a peculiar idea to kill David."

When Blakely left the pub with his friend Clive Gunnell, headed towards a night of pleasure with his au pair girlfriend, he heard Ruth scream "Get out of the way Clive!" Then a bullet ripped into him and he fell. Ruth fired three more shots as Blakely lay in the gutter. His life of womanizing and drinking was over.

Ruth went on trial at the Old Bailey on June 20, 1955. The jury took just 14 minutes to find her guilty of murder, and the sentence was death by hanging. Many suggested that she had brought it upon herself, having shown no remorse in court and making it perfectly clear her one intention on the night in question was to kill her lover. Nevertheless, there was an immediate public outcry. While no-one disputed that Ruth was a murderer, the campaign against capital punishment in Britain had lately been gathering pace, and to hang a woman who had been so taken advantage of and abused by so many men was deemed too harsh. On July 13, 1955, more than 1,000 people gathered outside Holloway Prison crying for Ruth to be reprieved. They added their voices to the many petitions sent to the Home Secretary. One petition alone bore 50,000 signatures.

The protests fell on deaf ears. Ruth's head was put through a noose and moments later the trapdoor beneath fell away. Writing in the Daily Mirror newspaper that day, the popular columnist Cassandra moved the nation with the words, "If you read this after nine o'clock in the morning, the murderess Ruth Ellis will have gone. The one thing that brings stature and dignity to mankind and raises us above the beasts of the field will have been denied her—pity and the hope of ultimate redemption."

Ruth Ellis was buried in an unmarked grave within the walls of Holloway Prison. In the early 1970s the prison underwent a program of rebuilding, during which the bodies of all executed women were exhumed for reburial elsewhere. Ellis's was reburied at St. Mary's Church in Amersham, Buckinghamshire. The headstone in the churchyard was originally inscribed "Ruth Hornby 1926–1955," but in 1982 it was destroyed by her son Andy shortly before he committed suicide.

Sergeant Frederick Emmett-Dunne

Often, the victims of crimes of passion are the innocent people who happen to be close to those caught up in powerful emotions. The murder of Sergeant Reginald Watters, for example, shows how love can set an otherwise decent man to kill his best friend.

Tall, handsome Sergeant Frederick Emmett-Dunne and his five-foot, one-inch friend Sergeant Reginald Watters were stationed in Duisburg, Germany, as part of the British post-war occupation force. While in Germany, Watters met and married a beautiful ex-nightclub singer called Mia. At first, Emmett-Dunne tried to repress his feelings for his mate's wife, but the more time he spent in their company the more his passion for her grew and the more he came to resent the fact that his unremarkable, short friend had married her when she should have been his. Slowly the bonds of friendship were overwhelmed by jealousy, to the point where Emmett-Dunne was prepared to kill the man he had once shared so much with.

On November 30, 1953, the body of Reginald Watters was found hanging from the banister at his barracks on the British Army base. It was Emmett-Dunne who broke the news to Mia, telling the widow that he would be constantly at her side to help her through her ordeal. He also gave a statement to the police saying that he had driven Watters back to his quarters at 7pm the night before, bid him good night, and left. The doctor who conducted the postmortem concluded that death was caused by shock, brought on by strangulation. Watters, he wrote on his report, had committed suicide by hanging.

There was something amiss though. Despite the verdict, gossip began to circulate. It was whispered that

Watters had committed suicide because his wife was having a secret fling with his best friend. The marriage of Mia and Emmett-Dunne in England just seven months later did nothing to still the wagging tongues.

But it wasn't just gossips who were suspicious of the events. The marriage was also viewed with suspicion by one of the official army criminal investigators named Sergeant Frank Walters. He had previously been bothered by the suicide verdict, too, and did not believe that Watters was type to take his own life, no matter how serious his personal problems were. When he heard about the wedding, Walters contacted Scotland Yard to report his concerns.

In February 1955 an order arrived at British headquarters in Duisburg to exhume Watters' body. Examination by a more experienced pathologist revealed that he had died not by hanging, but by a "severe blow across the front of the throat"—just the kind of blow that might have been inflicted by someone trained in unarmed combat. At the same time Emmett-

Dunne's half-brother Ronald, who had been a private at Duisburg, confessed to his own involvement in Watters' death. He told investigators that he had helped Emmett-Dunne hang Watters up on the bannister after his panicked half-brother told him he had killed him by accident.

Emmett-Dunne was arrested at the home in Taunton, Somerset, he shared with Mia. Despite his claim that he had acted in self-defense when Watters threatened to shoot him and had only meant to stun, he was charged with murder. The case, held before a seven-man army court, was covered extensively in the British and German press. On July 1955, Emmett-Dunne was found guilty of murder and sentenced to death. However, he escaped a fate that many thought he richly deserved. West Germany had abolished capital punishment, and foreign army bases had to conform with the law of the country. Instead Emmett-Dunne was given a life sentence. He served 10 years in Britain before being released.

Dr. Yves Evenou & Simone Deschamps

Twice divorced Yves Evenou had the good fortune to find his third wife in the strikingly beautiful and young Marie-Claire. But though she was undoubtedly stunning, she could not satisfy his cravings for perverted sex games: for that he turned to an older, plain woman. And when his desire for both waned he formed a plan to get rid of them in one disgusting act.

What Simone Deschamps lacked in looks she more than made up for with her zealous participation in sexual masochism. Almost as soon as she came into his surgery one day in the mid-1950s Dr Yves Evenou realized that she was a woman with whom he could explore his secret dark lusts. Before long he had moved his sex partner into the flat below the one he shared with his wife, Marie-Claire. It was a perfect arrangement for Evenou; a loving, respectable and beautiful wife in one flat, and a subservient mistress willing to satisfy all his perverted desires, in the flat below. Evenou even told a friend, "She may not be beautiful, but she knows how to love."

A willing conspirator in the duping of Marie-Claire, Simone even made herself useful to her lover's wife, helping her with chores around the house that were too heavy for the sickly doctor's wife. But as Simone and Evenou pushed their sexual boundaries to the limit, so the doctor grew ever more tired of his wife and his lover, too, and began plotting to get rid of them both in one foul swoop. To a twisted and sadist mind such as his, the plan he hatched must have had an elegant simplicity: he would incite Simone to kill Marie-Claire and then inform on her to the police. The plan also had the merit of providing one last, horribly depraved, sexual thrill.

Evenou warmed his lover up to the idea slowly. One night he told her, "My first two wives left me of their own accord but this one sticks like mustard plaster." After a day or two, he announced, "I feel that I should kill her, or maybe that you should do it for me." By the following day, after six glasses of port, the doctor appeared to make his mind up. "We must kill her," he told Simone. Without a word, she rose from her chair, went to the local hardware store, and bought a knife.

That evening Marie-Claire complained of a toothache, and her husband suggested a sleeping pill to ease the pain. As soon as she was asleep, Evenou rang the apartment below and Simone arrived within moments, naked except for a coat and shoes, which she slipped off. Then Evenou gently uncovered his wife's breast and said, "Strike here!" Simone obeyed. Marie-Claire woke in a shock as the knife plunged into her body and cried out, "Simone!" and then, "No! No!" But Evenou held her in his arms and whispered, 'There, there, everything's all right'. Befuddled with drugs and not yet feeling any pain, Marie-Claire relaxed, and Simone struck her again and again: 11 times in all. Then the lovers kissed. When it was over, Simone went to the bathroom to wash her hands, and Yves Evenou slipped out of the door. A few minutes later he arrived at the police station and told them that Simone Deschamps had murdered his wife.

What may have been an elegant plot in Evenou's mind didn't stand up to police investigations and questions. He was arrested alongside his sado-masochistic lover, but escaped trial by dying before the case could be heard. For her part in the murder, however, Simone Deschamps received a life sentence.

Dr. Renzo Ferrari

When Tranquillo Allevi drank from a bottle of liqueur that contained enough strychnine to kill 500 men, the Italian police were baffled at first, but one by one they exonerated his wife's lovers until they found the man who poisoned him.

At 38, Renata Allevi was a sophisticated woman of the world. She loved her wealthy dairy farmer husband who kept her in all the luxuries she could want, but also delighted in the intrigue and passions of her illicit liaisons and kept a stable of men to admire her. Nevertheless, the charmed life she had been leading shuddered to a halt on August 26, 1973.

Two days earlier a bottle of liqueur had arrived from Milan with a note explaining that the established Italian drinks manufacturer who made it was planning a sales campaign in the local area and asking Tranquillo Allevi if he would consider becoming the company's local representative. Allevi was an influential and highly popular man, and often received this kind of offer, so when the bottle arrived Renata thought nothing of it. She signed for it and left it on her husband's desk. When he returned he put it in the refrigerator to cool and then forgot about it.

On the 26th, after taking his wife out to dinner at a local restaurant, Tranquillo Allevi went to his office to entertain two friends. He remembered the bottle and took it from the fridge, poured three glasses, and—while his friends politely sipped their drinks—knocked his back in one. Death came quickly. Allevi was screaming by the time the liquid hit his stomach and his body quickly went into uncontrollable spasms. He was rushed to hospital but died soon after he was admitted. The diagnosis was obvious, for his friends too showed signs of poisoning, though mercifully their small sips saved them from death.

The police immediately suspected Renata, but it was apparent that her grief was genuine, and she made no

ABOVE: Renzo Ferrari gesturing in front of microphones as he answers questions by the president of a Court of Assizes in Imperia on the Italian Riviera, during his 1964 trial.

secret of the fact that she had signed for the bottle and even suggested to her husband that he put it in the fridge. Perplexed they looked elsewhere, but Allevi was a popular man and had no enemies that anyone knew of. Then, reluctantly, Renata admitted that she had three lovers with whom she regularly met: her husband's book-keeper, an army officer, and the veterinary surgeon who looked after Allevi's herds.

Another clue was the bottle itself, which had been sent from Milan on August 23. Checks with the drinks company confirmed that though over 100 complimentary bottles had been sent out, Allevi's name was not on the mailing list and the accompanying letter was not on the company's headed paper. Tests showed that a massive dose of strychnine had been injected into the bottle through the cork.

The police began to question Renata's lovers. The first two had alibis to prove that they had been nowhere near Milan the day the parcel was posted. The book-keeper had been with a client in San Remo, while the army officer had been in Tuscany on maneuvers. Detectives were left with the veterinary surgeon, Dr. Renzo Ferrari, who had been in Milan on that very day to renew his professional license. He had also purchased strychnine. And a check on the town hall offices Ferrari used in his post as a local government officer, revealed the typewriter upon which the accompanying letter had been written.

On September 1, 1973, Ferrari was charged with the murder of Tranquillo Allevi. At his trial the truth finally emerged. He pleaded not guilty, and his defense counsel told the court that he had no motive. Ferrari, they argued, had recently become engaged to the daughter of a wealthy family and had broken off his purely sexual relationship with Renata. He was looking forward to a good future and there was no reason to jeopardize it. Renata, however, painted a very different picture for the jury and one that fit the facts. On the witness stand she said that her husband had found out about the affair and that while she saw other men for pleasure it was him she loved, so she had agreed to finish with Ferrari. On being notified that their affair was over, Ferrari refused to accept it and when she told him, "I will never return to you", he had replied, "We will see about that."

A representative of the drinks company supplied the final, damning, piece of evidence. He stated under oath that no sample had been sent to Mr Allevi. However, one bottle had been dispatched, with an invitation on company notepaper, to one Dr. Renzo Ferrari.

The jury did not need any further evidence. Ferrari was found guilty of murder with premeditation on May 15, 1974. His combined sentence amounted to 30 years, including consecutive terms for the attempted murder of Allevi's two drinking companions. Although he has never admitted to it, it is very possible that the murderer had hoped that Allevi and his wife would open the bottle together and that he would thus have killed both of them. Once the bottle was delivered, Ferrari had no way of controlling who drank the poisoned liqueur, which suggests that he did not care which of the Allevis he murdered.

Sheila Garvie and Brian Tevendale

In retrospect it is hardly surprising that Max Garvie was eventually murdered, for the sex games he delighted in grew so astonishingly depraved that it was almost inevitable that sooner or later there would be an emotional backlash.

In 1955, **Sheila Watson** considered herself lucky to have landed Max Garvie for a husband. He was handsome, rich, and the owner of a large farm in Fordoun, Kincardineshire, Scotland. Over the following years the couple had two daughters and a son and had Max not been so bored of his tranquil existence the family might have enjoyed a happy family life. At first Garvie tried to liven up his life with the expensive toys of the rich. He filled his driveway with fast cars and bought a private plane, but nothing seemed to bring the satisfaction he craved and he eventually began looking for excitement elsewhere.

It started innocently. Garvie created his own so-called "nudist colony," and groups of his wealthy, thrill-seeking friends were invited to weekend parties where they would frolic naked within a triangle of trees and thick bushes Garvie had planted for just that reason.

It was not long, however, before the guests' inhibitions were set aside completely and Garvie's nude parties turned into sex orgies.

Sheila Garvie wasn't interested, and tried to ignore the naked flesh and debauched scenes in her garden. Instead, she tried to shield the children from what was happening outside the house and shrugged off her husband's continual demands that she join in the fun. Eventually, however, she was worn down by his pestering. Sheila gave in and went on to become a willing, and even enthusiastic, member of the group.

By this time West Cairnbeg Farm had become known locally as "Kinky Cottage," and guests at the house were playing a dangerous game of jealousy and broken rules. Garvie took his sexual adventures further with homosexual couplings and then brought 20-year-old Brian Tevendale into his home—not for

his own pleasure but for Sheila's. His wife was appalled at the idea. She saw sex sessions in the company of her husband as acceptable, but not the intimacy of one-to-one lovemaking.

Nevertheless, she gave in again. One night in 1967, when Tevendale was staying over, his bedroom door was suddenly opened and a naked, shivering Sheila shoved into the room by her husband. Garvie had at last broken his wife's will. Now the games took a new turn with Garvie and Tevendale tossing a coin to see who would sleep with Sheila. When Garvie lost he insisted the three go to bed together. Then Garvie started an affair with Tevendale's sister, Trudi Birse, wife of a policeman. Trudi joined in four-in-a-bed romps with the Garvies and her own brother. Trudi's husband even joined in,

ABOVE: Sheila Garvie on her way to the High Court at Stonehaven, Scotland, in 1968.

though Max thoughtfully arranged another female partner for him.

Still Garvie craved new sensual pleasures and further erotic adventures. Growing bored with Trudi, he suggested to Sheila that they both move on to new bedmates. Sheila refused. The one thing her husband had not considered was that amid all the debauched coupling real affection might blossom, but now his wife was passionately in love with Brian Tevendale. Used to getting his own way, Garvie tried to come between them. The man who had forced them together now tried to prize them apart.

On the morning of May 15, 1968, Sheila Garvie reported her husband missing to the police. She said when she had woken up that morning, Garvie was not in bed or anywhere to be found. Whether to cover her tracks or because she was genuinely innocent, Sheila confided in her mother, Edith Watson, that she thought Tevendale had killed her husband, and an appalled Mrs Watson went straight to the police.

Max Garvie's putrefying remains were eventually found in the drains of Laurieston Castle, St. Cyrus—Tevendale's home village—on August 17, 1968. The police's investigations led them straight to the depraved goings-on at the farm and Sheila Garvie, Brian Tevendale, and one of his friends, Alan Peters, were arrested and charged with Garvie's murder.

The sensational trial began at Aberdeen High Court on November 19, 1968. While details of the sordid events became public, Sheila and Tevendale accused each other of the murder. Sheila claimed she woke in the middle of the night to discover Tevendale and Peters had murdered her husband; Tevendale said the killing was Sheila's idea and he had gone along with it because of his infatuation with her. The prosecution, however, maintained that Sheila and Tevendale had plotted the murder together in order to stop Garvie from splitting them up. They suggested that on the night Garvie died, Sheila had slipped out of the marital bed to let Tevendale and Peters into the house and given them a gun. She then watched as Tevendale used it to smash Max's skull before putting a pillow over his face and shooting him in the head. The men then wrapped the body in a blanket, put it in the boot of Peters's car, and dumped it in the drains of Laurieston Castle. Throughout the proceedings, both the jury and the nation were horrified by the perverse events and the crime itself. One juror fainted when the yellowed skull of Max Garvie was produced as part of the prosecution evidence.

In the end, the prosecution prevailed—barely. The jury unanimously found Tevendale guilty of murder and Sheila was also found guilty by a majority verdict—enough under Scottish law to sentence her. The case against Peters was not proven.

Tevendale and Sheila were both released from prison in 1978, but never saw each other again choosing to lead anonymous lives. Tevendale married and became the landlord of a public house in Perthshire. He died in 2003. Sheila married twice—she was divorced once and then widowed—and led a quiet life running a bed and breakfast.

William Gardiner

The so-called Peasenhall Mystery of 1902, is one of the most notable of murder cases in British criminal history with a cast of characters reads like an Agatha Christie novel. William Gardiner was a Sunday school teacher, devout church minister, and married father of six; the victim—Gardiner's pregnant lover—a choir girl at the village church. Officially "unsolved" it is likely that Gardiner would have been convicted had it not been for the alibi provided by the very wife he had been cheating on.

The affair between 23-year-old Rose Harsent and Gardiner was much gossiped about in the small Suffolk village of Peasenhall. She was a domestic servant who sang in the choir and he taught Sunday school and delivered sermons from the pulpit. While it was rumored that Gardiner was only one of several men that Rose was involved with, the pair appear to have been irresistibly attracted to one another. Some said that the vicar had been called upon to intervene after they were caught in a compromising situation, but even his warnings had failed to cool their passion and the secret trysts continued.

On June 1, 1902, Rose was found dead by her father at Providence House where she worked. Her half-naked body was at the foot of the stairs with the throat cut from ear to ear. There were wounds on her shoulders and her nightdress was burned. It seemed that whoever had killed Rose had tried to set fire to her to destroy the evidence. Further examinations of her body revealed that she had been pregnant.

It did not take long for Gardiner to become the prime suspect. A police search of Rose's room soon turned up a note in his handwriting addressed to her and arranging a secret midnight meeting. He was arrested two days later.

Gardiner's trial began on November 7, and the case against him was strong: A bloodied knife had been found at his home (though Gardiner said he had used it to kill rabbits) and neighbors spoke of a late-night bonfire in the Gardiner's garden on May 31. The police suggested that Gardiner and his wife had been burning his blood-stained clothes. Nevertheless, Mrs Gardiner insisted that they had passed an unremarkable evening together before retiring to bed where they had both stayed until morning.

Of the 12 jurors, 11 thought Gardiner guilty, but without a unanimous verdict a retrial was ordered to begin on January 21, 1903. Again, the jury failed to reach a unanimous decision, this time with 10 of their number finding him innocent. Arrangements were quickly made for yet another trial, but before it began the Home Office decided that there was no prospect of securing a conviction and lodged a verdict of nolle prosequi—not proven. The case against Gardiner was dismissed and he was released from custody, having neither been convicted or acquitted.

Lilian Getkate

Every so often, someone slips through loopholes in the law, and so it proved in the case of Lilian Getkate. A former Brownie leader and church-goer, Lilian fully expected to serve a prison sentence for the crime of shooting her husband with his own rifle, but despite failing to convince many that she had good cause to kill, the jury found her guilty of the lesser charge of manslaughter and sentenced her to just 200 hours of community service. In a second stroke of luck, Lilian's conviction preceded a change in the law by just three weeks. Under the new ruling anyone convicted of manslaughter using a firearm was to be sentenced to at least four years jail time.

L ilian's was a problematic case. Her defense lawyer told the jury that she had been subjected to years of constant abuse by her husband, Maury. During their 16 years of marriage she had been dragged by her hair, made a virtual prisoner in her own home, raped, and threatened with death. Lilian also claimed that what finally provoked her to kill was her husband threatening to sexually abuse their daughter. According to a report in the Canadian newspaper, the Ottawa Citizen, Maury Getkate had been a tall, well-built man; a "paramilitary buff and aspiring ninja" who had a collection of "exotic weaponry." Two psychiatrists who examined and interviewed Lilian testified that she fitted the criteria for "battered woman syndrome."

The evidence was not so clear-cut though. Relatives and friends of the couple gave a different story, saying that to all outward appearances the Gatkates had been a happy, ordinary couple, devoted to their children and Lilian more than satisfied to be a stay-at-home mother. Maury Getkate, they said, was a hard-working, successful professional admired by his colleagues.

In fact, as crown prosecutor Julianne Parfett pointed out to the court, the only evidence they had for Lilian's plight came from Lilian herself. "No one could corroborate it," Parfett stated. "Not a bruise, not a hospital record, not a police report. Nothing... that's what is most troubling about this one. We simply say, 'Yes, you were abused. Fine. You walk.' That's what this sentence was all about. I think it's an appalling message to send to the public." With no third-person testimony or physical evidence to corroborate Lilian's tales, Parfett suggested that, at most, she may have suffered "moderate abuse."

Nevertheless, a jury made up of 10 women and two men found Lilian guilty only of the lesser charge of manslaughter, and she was ordered to do community service and attend meetings of Co-Dependents Anonymous, a support group for emotionally dependent people. It was not a verdict that pleased Ms Parfett. After hearing the sentence, she said, "The decision to spare her jail sends a message that women can kill, claim they have been abused, fail to prove it, and remain free."

Lilian's defense lawyer, Patrick McCann, was quick to respond, saying, "There's a long tradition in Canada that women who have been abused by their husbands or partners and have reacted to that and killed the man, have been convicted of manslaughter and not received custodial sentences. This is nothing new."

In the middle of the legal fuss was Lilian Getkate. She was as surprised as anyone to be walking free. And her surprise must have turned to relief when it was announced that from January 1996 there would be mandatory prison sentences of at least four years for manslaughter offences in which firearms are used. Lilian shot her husband in December 1995.

Chester Gillette

Born to a deeply religious family, Chester Gillette traveled around the United States during his formative years. By the time he reached age 22 in 1905, Gillette had settled in New York City where he worked as a foreman at his wealthy uncle's shirt factory. It was here that he met the pretty young secretary Grace Brown, who was just 18 years old.

Grace fell for the dashing nephew of the boss, and in a whirl of passion she was soon sleeping with him. The result was a pregnancy. Expecting Gillette to make an honest woman of her, Grace returned to her family home to come to terms with approaching motherhood and to await a marriage proposal. It never came. Instead, Grace discovered that Gillette had never been faithful and was now openly seeing other women. The final blow came when she discovered that the man she loved had met an attractive and wealthy socialite at a dance, and that he had become engaged to her. Her heartbroken letters to her lover became increasingly desperate, but still Gillette would not acknowledge her or the coming baby. Eventually, with nowhere left to turn, Grace threatened to tell Gillette's uncle the whole story and expose his dreadful conduct.

The threat seemed to work. In July 1906, Gillette told Grace to pack for a weekend trip away. Excited, and possibly believing that the trip would involve a

wedding ceremony, she packed her entire wardrobe. Gillette, meanwhile, packed almost nothing.

At first the couple checked into a rented cottage on Tupper Lake in Herkimer County, but the resort was too busy for what Gillette had in mind. At his insistence, they moved onto Big Moose Lake, taking separate rooms in a hotel there. Gillette then hired a rowing boat under the name of Carl Graham (careful to matching the initials on his suitcase) and rowed his pregnant teenage lover out onto the water. When they were some distance way from the shore, Gillette battered Grace with a tennis racket, then tipped her over the side, and rowed back alone. The unconscious Grace was left to drown. Gillette's social climbing ambitions were safe.

Back on shore, Gillette tried to cover his tracks by moving on to the Arrowhead Hotel on Eagle Bay. However, he made a fatal error in asking the check-in clerk if there had been any reported drownings. When Grace Brown's body surfaced the next day, the clerk

ABOVE: Chester Gillette's heartless murder of his one-time lover led to his eventual execution.

ABOVE: Grace Brown's only crime was to fall in love with the wrong man—who turned out to be a killer.

remembered Gillette's strange question, and the killer came under immediate suspicion. The tennis racket used to bludgeon Grace was found on the shore of Big Moose Lake, and under police questioning Gillette was nervous and shifty.

In court, the jury heard the extent of Gillette's callousness as Grace's heart-rending letters to her lover were read out, one by one, by the lawyers acting for the prosecution. He was found guilty of murder on December 4, 1906, and sentenced to death in the electric chair.

Gary Grinhaff

While some killers' fury vents itself in an uncontrollable outburst of deadly rage, others channel it into a cold, calm plan for revenge. Convinced that the affair that his wife had confessed to was still continuing, Gary Grinhaff approached murder—and his own suicide—in a highly methodical manner.

rinhaff discovered the affair his wife, Tracey, had been having in February 2008. A few weeks later he confronted her, and in order to try and resolve the situation peacefully her lover and his wife were called over to discuss it. It was an unusual step, but seemed to work; the unfaithful pair agreed that they would end their illicit relationship.

Over the following weeks though, Grinhaff became convinced that Tracey had not kept her promise so, ignoring his wife's protests of innocence, he set about to prove that she was still arranging secret love trysts. First he bugged her car so that he could listen to conversations and fitted it with a tracking device. Then he secretly bought another car in which he could follow her undetected. By May 1, he had the proof he needed. Tracey was a cheat, and with the same efficient calm Grinhaff made plans for retribution.

At 6am on the morning of May 3, 2008, the Grinhaff's three-year-old daughter Niamh woke her older sister Chloe. She was standing on the landing outside her parents' bedroom crying because she couldn't find her mother. Thirteen-year-old Chloe went to investigate and found her mother and father's bed empty and the duvet laying on the floor. Downstairs she found the note in the kitchen pinned to the cooker

hood. It was in her father's handwriting and gave her certain instructions. The teenager phoned a neighbor who told the girls not to go to school and contacted the police.

When the police arrived they found signs of an attack in the Grinhaff's bedroom, though an effort had obviously been made to make it tidy and to hide bloodstains from the two girls. Later, the bodies were discovered. Tracey Grinhaff's was found in the shed at the back of her garden. She had been strangled and bludgeoned to death with a heavy object. Shortly after, police found Gary Grinhaff's corpse in woodland nearby. He had killed himself by cutting into his own leg and arm with the saw attachment to his cordless electric drill. They later also found the car that Grinhaff had used to follow his wife, with notes inside so that his daughters wouldn't discover them. One was addressed to the wife of Tracey's lover and read, "This cannot go on; this is my only way out."

At the inquest assistant deputy coroner Donald Coutts-Wood said that Grinhaff had gone to considerable lengths to confirm his wife had resumed her affair and once satisfied had set out to kill her. He recorded verdicts that Mrs Grinhaff was unlawfully killed and that her husband committed suicide.

Albert Guay

There are no words to describe the sheer depravity of Albert Guay's crime. Even if we cannot understand the minds of many of the murderers who have been pressed to kill by their passion we can, at least, begin to imagine how a person may have come to feel so violently angry that they wished to punish the person who caused their pain or stood in the way of their future happiness. But Guay's crime goes far beyond that, for in planning to murder the wife who stood between him and his teenage mistress he saw no obstacle in causing the deaths of 22 other people, four of them children.

oseph-Albert Guay was born on January 12, 1919. The youngest of five children he was spoiled as a youngster and the temper tantrums that followed his not getting exactly what he wanted were something that he would take into adulthood with him. As a young man Guay sold watches and jewelry on commission and

when World War II broke out, he got a job at Canadian Arsenals Limited at St. Malo. There he met the woman who was to become his wife, Rita Morel. When the arsenal closed in 1945, Guay left with a little money, which he spent on buying a jewelry and watch repair shop. Life should have been sweet for the shop owner and his new wife, but from the start the couple argued frequently, and the fights grew worse after the birth of their child. The shop was not doing well and the financial strain was added to by a new tension in the house. Like many immature men, Guay felt slighted that he was no longer the center of attention in his own household. His natural inclination toward jealousy and possessiveness grew more pronounced as he realized his needs now came second to that of his son. Eventually, after eight years of marriage, he decided that the only way he would feel important again was to find someone who doted on him as his wife once did.

The girl he chose was 17-year-old nightclub waitress Marie-Ange Robitaille, who liked to be called Mary Angel. To help prevent his wife finding out about his pursuit of a teenager, Guay gave a false name when he first met her and it became the name he used throughout their relationship, which—despite his own family's financial worries—was conducted at an apartment Guay paid for. He also promised to marry her. Duped by his lies, Marie-Ange had no reason to doubt that she was not being seriously courted by a gentleman called Roger Angers who dearly wished to walk down the aisle with her.

But despite his careful tactics to avoid discovery Rita found out everything, and chose the place to confront her husband to cause the maximum damage to his affair. When Guay visited Mary-Ange at her parents' home one day, he found his wife waiting for him and the secret life he had built completely destroyed. Mary-

RIGHT: Albert Guay, pictured with his wife Rita, who was one of the victims of the plane crash that he callously engineered.

Ange was ordered out of the house by her appalled mother and father and the Guays soon followed, arguing viciously. When they returned home Rita packed some clothes and took the couple's five-year-old daughter to live at her mother's house.

If Rita had meant to finish his relationship, she failed. None of this seemed to bother Guay. He continued to see his young lover, and in most respects his life was little changed. The confrontation had, however, altered the relationship with Mary-Ange forever. Now she insisted that Guay make an honest woman of her and told him that if he didn't then she would end the affair. With divorce in the largely Catholic province of Quebec rare in the 1940s, Guay realized that the only way could marry his pretty young lover was to bring about 28-year-old Rita's death.

Initially, Guay considered killing his wife with poison, but he was afraid of discovery. After all, there were numerous people who knew he had a good motive for killing his wife. Instead, he concocted a twisted plan that he thought no-one would ever suspect. He traveled frequently by plane in his business as a jeweler to deliver or pick up items for his shop and came to the conclusion that if he could get his wife to take his place while he planted a bomb that would bring the plane down then there was every chance of the crime remaining undiscovered. And if he could time the bomb so the wreckage landed in the St. Lawrence River, any evidence would be washed away.

The more he examined his idea, the more he liked it, but there was a drawback. For a murder on this scale he would need the help of others. Unfortunately, he knew just where to find them.

The rewards that Guay must have promised those willing to join his evil scheme must have been huge, but he soon had his co-conspirators. The first was one of his employees, wheelchair-bound watchmaker Genereux Ruest, who would help him build and package a time bomb. Although Ruest had worked in the munitions factory alongside Guay, he did not have the detailed knowledge required for bomb-making or, indeed, how to go about blowing up a plane so he and Guay decided that a trial run would be needed. In preparation, the pair consulted local explosives experts, using the bizarre cover story that they needed to dynamite a pond. With all the information he needed and with help from Guay, Ruest worked on the bomb-making project from his wheelchair. He eventually created a simple, but effective, timed device from 20 sticks of dynamite, an alarm clock, and a battery. The second person that Guay enlisted was 41-year-old Margeuritte Pitre. She was Ruest's married sister and another former mistress. It would be her job to deliver the bomb to its destination.

All Guay had to do now was persuade Rita to make the plane journey. Guay insisted to his estranged wife that though their marriage was all but over, there was no reason why she shouldn't continue to help him with the business. It was imperative, he told her, that she should go to Baie Corneau to collect some jewels he had ordered from the mining community. Rita refused, but her estranged husband insisted that he was too busy to go himself and pointed out that her income depended on him doing well. When she protested again he told her that he had already bought the ticket. He failed to mention that he had also taken out a $10,000 insurance policy on her life, on top of another for $5,000 that he had purchased back in 1942. Finally, Rita agreed, though the couple argued fiercely as Guay drove her to Quebec City airport on the morning of September 9, 1949. They continued their row inside.

Meanwhile, Pitre was also on her way to the airport in a taxi. She had with her a very heavy parcel, which she told airport authorities was a religious statuette that had to be delivered to a Mr Larouche at an address in Baie Comeau. The 26 pound parcel was duly checked in as freight.

Shortly afterward, Rita boarded the Canadian Pacific Airlines DC-3 together with 22 other passengers. The plane was five minutes late leaving Quebec City and took off at 10.25am, a delay that upset Quay's carefully laid plan. It climbed into the sky and headed northeast toward the St. Lawrence River. And exploded 20 minutes later, scattering debris over the shore of the river rather than into the water. A fisherman near Sault-au-Cochon, 50 miles north of Quebec City, later told how he saw the smoking plane crash toward Cap Tormente on the wooded north shore of the river. Other witnesses said the plane's engines were still running as it hit the ground, which meant that investigators could immediately rule out engine failure as the cause of the crash.

Five workers at a nearby railway line witnessed the terrifying sight, too, and rushed to the scene. But there was nothing they could do. As flames flashed through the aircraft it was clear there would be no survivors. One of the rail workers gave a report to Montreal's La Patrie newspaper, saying: "Arms, legs, and severed heads were lying on the ground. The forward part of the plane looked intact. The bodies were piled up in there as if they had been thrown forward when the plane crashed… There was nothing we could do so we rushed to alert the railway authorities."

News of the disaster was soon being broadcast on radio stations throughout the province and police and Mounties descended on the crash site. The dead included the four crew, four children, and three American executives from the Kennecott Copper Corporation. Guay and his co-conspirators had succeeded in the murder of Rita Guay, but, in total, the lives of 22 other people were also lost. And all so that Albert Guay could marry his teenage sweetheart.

However, Guay would never make his trip down the aisle. Forensic analysis of the plane's debris soon revealed traces of dynamite and investigators concluded the plane had crashed following the explosion of a time bomb in the forward baggage compartment. Within days, Pitre, Guay, and Ruest were arrested. The investigation into the explosion had thrown up many clues, but the one that led straight to Guay was found in a simple tally of the freight list. All but one of the items on board were from regular shippers, and were easily checked. There was, however, no record of the sender of the "religious statuette." Nevertheless, a conversation with the taxi driver who took Pitre to the airport revealed her address and he also remembered that the lady dressed in black had specifically warned him not to drive over any bumps in the road. The driver recalled the woman had added, "These aren't eggs I'm carrying."

When police called at the home of Margueritte Pitre she wasn't there. In fact, she was in hospital recovering from a failed suicide she had attempted after realizing the enormity of the crime she had helped commit. Believing that the police were already watching her, Margueritte had taken an overdose of sleeping tablets.

She lived, but only to face death by less gentle means. Under interrogation she maintained that she had not known what the package she had delivered contained, but no-one believed her. Neither did anyone believe her story that Guay had threatened to bankrupt her if she didn't help him, though the tale that he had encouraged her to commit suicide after the crash seemed slightly more plausible.

Before his arrest Guay had presented himself to the world as a man deeply in mourning for his beloved wife. He urged investigators to "get to the bottom of this" and carried a large cross of flowers to Rita's funeral and placed it on her coffin, telling a priest, "If God wanted it, I accept." He was, however, swiftly forced to drop the pretence after he was arrested on September 23, 1949. and charged with murder.

Reust's arrest followed soon after. The three killers appeared at separate trials at the Supreme Court of Canada throughout 1950 and early 1951. Guay was charged with the killing of 22 people along with the assassination of his wife and found guilty. Imposing the death sentence, the judge told him, "Your crime is infamous. It has no name."

Albert Guay was hanged on January 19, 1951, in the Bordeaux Jail near Montreal. As was the ritual there, a chime sounded seven times to announce the execution of a man. (It sounded ten times to announce a woman's death.) Newspapers reported that his last words were, "Well, at least I die famous."

Reust fruitlessly claimed that he had not known his homemade bomb would be used to kill people. There were witnesses, however, who had seen him on the terrace of a hotel on the day of the crash; a vantage point he had chosen because it offered a fine view of the aircraft's course and, therefore, of the crash itself. Ruest was taken to the gallows in his wheelchair and hanged on July 25, 1952.

Pitre's trial began in March 1951, too late for Guay to testify against her as he had done against Reust in an effort to avoid the death penalty. Although she protested her innocence throughout, she was also found guilty and became the last women to be executed in Canada on January 9, 1953.

Frances Hall, Henry Carpender, & Willie Stevens

It is most likely that this bloody and shocking double murder was instigated by a scorned wife who was all too aware that the infidelity of her minister husband was common knowledge. However, while some murderers successfully appeal to the sympathy of the court and others are set free through lack of evidence, Mrs Hall and her partners in crime appear to have spread enough confusion for the case against them to be completely botched.

The bodies of the Reverend Edward Wheeler Hall and his mistress, Mrs Eleanor Mills, were found laying side by side on September 16, 1922. She wore a red-spotted blue dress and black stockings as well as a blood soaked silk scarf around her neck. Her left hand rested on the knee of the Reverend Hall while his right arm was under her shoulder. Propped up against one of his shoes was a business card and all around were shreds of torn up letters. When pieced together one read: "Oh, honey. I am fiery today. Burning flaming love." Hall been shot once over the right ear. Eleanor had been shot three times in the right temple, under the right eye, and also over the right ear. In what could only have been a furious personal revenge, the choir singer's tongue had been cut out after she was shot and her larynx removed. It looked like a classic crime of passion.

Reverend Hall had been the pastor of the Episcopal Church of St. John the Evangelist in New Jersey; Eleanor Mills a singer in the church choir. Both were married. Hall's wife was Frances Noel Stevens, heiress to a sum from the Johnson & Johnson Company while Eleanor's husband James was sexton at St. John's. There were few people in the parish who didn't know about the affair. Hall and Eleanor had been involved for four years and a neighbor later told how the couple met every afternoon at Mills' house.

It was nothing out of the ordinary then, when Eleanor telephoned the Hall house on the evening of September 14. Both the maid and Mrs Hall herself would later testify that Eleanor had called the reverend about a medical bill, and that he had left the house on the pretext of discussing it with her shortly after.

However, it was no ordinary evening. After years of illicit meetings and secret passion Eleanor and Mills had finally decided to elope.

At the Mills' house, Eleanor told her husband that she was going to call Reverend Hall soon after dinner. When she returned she said that she was going to the church and there was a slight scene, during which she scornfully told Mills to follow her if he dared. It was the last time that Eleanor would be seen alive. The worried Mills waited until 11pm then went to look for her at the church. Finding nothing, he returned at 2am. Again, there was no sign of the lovers.

When he went to work at the church the next morning, he asked Mrs Hall if she thought their spouses had eloped. She told him that she thought they were dead. At around the same time, Mrs Hall's brother, Willie Stevens, told the maid, Louise Geist, that "something terrible" had happened during the night. Strangely, the bodies had yet to be discovered.

That changed the next day, and the police quickly took four suspects in for questioning: Frances Hall, Stevens, another of Frances' brothers named Henry (who was known to be an excellent marksman), and her cousin, Henry Carpender. Not long afterward, Hall, Carpender, and Willie Stevens were all charged with the murder of Reverend Hall and Eleanor.

The court hearing that followed was confused and mismanaged from the start and was eventually dropped for lack of evidence. But a few years later evidence that the defendants had perverted the course of justice began to emerge. In 1926, Geist's estranged husband claimed that his wife had received $5,000 from the Hall

family. He said that the maid had learned that Reverend Hall planned to elope and had forewarned his wife. The money was a payment to ensure her silence. Later, a state trooper who had been on the investigative team also claimed that Carpender had paid him to leave the state.

ABOVE: Two New Jersey State policemen (center), with two traffic policemen, waiting to escort a witness to The Hall-Mills Murder Trial, 1926.

A new court case also brought forward a compelling witness. Mrs Jane Gibson (also known as "The Pig

ABOVE. Willie Stevens on the witness stand during the trial in which he was jointly accused of the murder of Reverend Edward Hall and Eleanor Mills.

Woman," because she owned a pig farm) testified that she had witnessed the killings. She identified Carpender as the shooter, and told that he had been at the scene with Frances Hall and Willie Stevens. Gibson claimed to have returned to the bodies after the murder and had then seen Mrs Hall crying over her husband's dead body. Nevertheless, her testimony was ignored because she had given quite a different account in 1922. Despite a fingerprint on the business card left at the murder scene belonging to Willie Stevens, all three defendants were finally found not guilty on December 3, 1926. Some observers said the jury's verdict was a gesture of defiance to a Jersey City prosecution counsel who had called them "country bumpkins."

Gavin Hall

When hospital radiographer Gavin Hall found messages on his wife's computer that detailed a sordid affair it sent him into a catastrophic mental breakdown that ended in tragedy. But while his unfaithful wife escaped his murderous intentions, their three-year-old daughter did not.

One evening in October 2005, Gavin Hall's 31-year-old wife Joanne thoughtlessly forgot to switch off the computer. And when her husband came to look at it, the double life she had been leading was revealed before his disbelieving eyes.

Joanne had joined a sex contact web site for married people. A distraught Hall discovered that his wife saw herself as "an incredibly bored married woman" and "an easy lay." There were messages, too, from her lover; a 45-year-old married district judge called James Muir-Little. His profile said that he was a "38-year-old non-smoker" who had "a very active imagination and I think about sex all the time."

As Hall read the messages they had swapped, it became obvious that the pair were already involved in a highly sexual relationship. They had swapped naked photographs of themselves and described in graphic detail the sexual acts they would like to indulge in. The judge had also suggested setting up a sexual threesome.

When confronted, Joanne admitted the fling, but told Hall that it was over. She was lying. As her husband's mental state deteriorated she continued her liaison with Muir-Little all the while reassuring Hall that he had nothing to worry about.

Eventually, Hall's mental state had reached a point where he could no longer work, and he took sick leave due to personal problems. Now, he broke down completely. Suicide, he thought, was the only answer to his mental anguish and he also decided that his and Joanne's daughter Amelia—or Millie as the family called her—should die too. As he later explained to the court, the little girl had told him repeatedly that she wanted to "come with Daddy."

On November 29, 2005, Gavin Hall fed Amelia anti-depressant pills to make her drowsy. Father and daughter said farewell—"like Romeo and Juliet" as he later described it—before he smothered her with a rag soaked in chloroform.

Although Hall later told a court he had no memory of the night, he then sent lengthy text messages to his wife and her lover. One, sent to Joanne at 2.57am, said, "I loved you. Millie asked to stay with me. I've dealt with your deceit for two months, now you have the rest of your life to deal with the consequences." Shortly before 4am he again texted his wife. This time the message read, "Goodbye, Millie sends her love. She died at 3.32am. Love till death us do part I said and this is what I meant."

He then dosed himself with the chloroform and slashed his wrists. Millie died just two days before her fourth birthday. Her mother Joanne found her under a duvet on the living room floor that morning.

Hall's attempt at suicide was unsuccessful though. He was convicted of murder in November 2006 after a six-day trial and told by the judge he would serve a minimum of 15 years in prison.

Muhammed & Ahmed Hanif

The 14-year affair of Arshad Mahmood and Zahida Hanif might have gone on undetected for much longer had Arshad not decided to use his lover's passion for him to extort money from her. When her family found out, their revenge was terrible.

Doorman Arshad Mahmood's secret relationship with the married Zahida Hanif had begun in the early 1990s when he was in his late 20s. Although he was a cousin of her husband, Muhammed, for years the couple met for sex sessions without arousing suspicion until an argument over money started between Muhammed and his wife's lover. Arshad had recently helped Muhammed's younger brother Ahmed come to the United States from Pakistan, and thought he was owed $20,000 for his trouble. Muhammed disagreed. Arshad also disliked the fact that Ahmed was now living with the Hanifs, making meetings with his mistress more difficult. Blackmail, he decided, was the perfect answer to his problems.

During a particularly steamy session with Zahida, Arshad had filmed himself and his mistress making love. Now he threatened to show it to her husband if Zahida didn't give him the $20,000 he deserved and make sure that Ahmed was evicted. For months the petrified, unfaithful Zahida struggled to meet his demands, but eventually the strain became too much for her to bear. She broke down and confessed all to her husband.

Muhammed decided that rather than go to the police, the matter was best kept within the family and enlisted his young brother to help punish the blackmailing doorman.

The two men grabbed Arshad when he arrived at his cousin's home after work, smashed him in the face with a metal pipe and strangled him with their hands and scarves. They then put the body in Muhammed's car, tearing his clothes, and removing all his possessions to make it look like a robbery, before dumping him on 54th Avenue near his Elmhurst home. Unfortunately for the killers, police found the explicit video in Arshad's work locker on June 9, 2005, and the whole case began to unravel. Muhammed and Ahmed were quickly arrested and charged with murder, though they appeared to have no remorse for their crime. A police spokesman later said, "They were kind of proud of it. They were joking around."

By the end of the month both men had been convicted and had begun their long sentences. Muhammed was found guilty of manslaughter and sentenced to 18 years in prison, while Ahmed got 21 years. At the trial, Robana Mahmood—Arshad's daughter—made it clear who she thought was to blame. Pointing to Zahida Hanif, she said "You all did it because she said so."

Jean Harris

When respected school principal Jean Harris met a man she liked and admired, murder was the last thing on her intelligent mind. But over years of betrayal and disappointment, love can turn even the most sensible of people into vengeful killers.

At 42, Jean Harris was a divorced and rather shy woman who was well-respected by her friends and colleagues at school. She was also not unusual in hoping that she might again find love in middle age, and at a dinner party in 1966 Jean thought she might have finally met a man who could make her happy. Dr. Herman Tarnower was a brilliant researcher at the Scarsdale Medical Center and would later earn himself a certain amount of fame on the publication of the successful book, The Scarsdale Diet. There was an instant chemistry between the pair and they began dating. Soon, Jean was deeply in love with Tarnower.

But he was not the type of man to be satisfied with a single lover, especially after he became something of a celebrity. Over the course of the 14-year relationship, he cheated again and again. Jean, who had never been very confident, turned a blind eye while her self-esteem sank with every new revelation.

The situation came to a head in 1980 when Tarnower began a sexual liaison with Lynne Tryforos, who worked as a receptionist at the medical center. Jean feared that there was something between her long-term partner and the receptionist that went beyond his usual flings and became certain that she was about to lose Tarnower for good. On March 10, she wrote a ten-page letter to her lover, revealing all her insecurities and expressing her own self-loathing for having become so desperately needy. With the attention to detail that might be expected of a highly organized school principal she also finalized her will. Then she drove to Tarnower's home and would later claim that the gun she took with her was intended for her own suicide.

Jean said that she had fully expected her final pleas for love to be fruitless and wanted only to take her own life. But when she reached her lover's apartment the sight of Lynne Tryforos's lingerie in Tarnower's bedroom sent her into a rage and she shot her lover four times at point blank range.

Jean was arrested and charged with second degree murder. Released on $40,000 bail she then admitted herself to a psychiatric hospital. When her case came to court, on November 21, 1980, she pleaded not guilty to murder, insisting that the gun had gone off accidentally as Tarnower tried to wrestle it away from her. It was an obvious deception and courtroom observers at the time asked why her defense attorney had not pleaded that the murder was committed while Jean was in a state

ABOVE: Jean Harris, photographed just hours before being found guilty of murdering her lover, Dr. Herman Tarnower.

of extreme emotional disturbance with a view to her being convicted of the lesser charge of manslaughter. That, however, is exactly what her defense counsel had wanted. She refused.

After a 14-week trial, Jean was found guilty of murder and sent to the Bedford Hills Correctional Facility in Westchester County, New York, for the minimum of 15 years to life. Numerous appeals followed the conviction, but the higher courts all agreed that she had received a fair trial. She served 12 years of her sentence and was finally pardoned in December 1992.

Catherine Hayes

The death of the last woman ever to be executed at Tyburn, London's infamous killing ground, was as gory as the one she inflicted on her husband. Catherine Hayes had an appetite for the wild side of life. She enjoyed nothing more than heavy drinking and romping with her two teenage lovers. However, her fun was spoiled by the presence of a husband. For Catherine the answer was simple: John Hayes must die.

The method Hayes chose for murder was direct and extreme, as might be expected of a woman who delighted in her own wildness. And it didn't take much to convince her two strong and virile young lovers to help. Catherine Hayes, Thomas Billings, and Thomas Wood prepared for their evening's work by drinking at the Brawn's Head tavern in London's New Bond Street. They then returned to the Hayes' home and, pretending to be friendly, plied John Hayes with enormous amounts of drink.

After drinking six pints of wine, Hayes staggered to his bed and collapsed. Even had he been conscious Hayes would have been in no state to defend himself from what happened next. Billings smashed him on the back of the head with a coal hatchet, fracturing his skull, and as Hayes gurgled in his death throes, Wood entered the room and hit him twice more. Then Catherine joined her young bedmates, and all three of them decapitated the body.

Hayes' head was taken in a blood filled bucket to be thrown in the River Thames, while the rest of his body was dismembered and stuffed in a trunk that was hidden in the local woods. However, in their haste and drunkenness, Wood and Billings made a mistake. Hayes' head was not washed away on the tide, but came to rest on the river's shore. Night watchmen soon discovered it, and the next day it was paraded on a pole around the streets of London in a ghastly identity parade.

It did not take the law long to catch up the murderous trio, and all three were found guilty at the Old Bailey, London's central criminal court, on April 30, 1726. Catherine Hayes and her lovers each received a death sentence.

RIGHT: Catherine Hayes hacking off the head of her husband John Hayes with the aid of her young lovers, Thomas Billings and Thomas Wood.

While in Newgate Prison awaiting her execution, Catherine sent letters to Wood and Billings showing remorse for involving them in the horrendous act. In a perverse twist, it was later whispered that she had also confessed that Billings was actually her son from a previous affair. Wood caught a fever in prison and died before he could be executed.

On May 14, Catherine Hayes was driven on a cart to be burned at the stake. Reports of the time tell us that, "She was fasten'd to the stake by an iron collar round her neck, and an iron chain round her body, having an halter also about her neck, which the Executioner pulled when she began to shriek. In about an hour's time she was reduced to ashes."

Frances Howard & Robert Carr

For the young Frances Howard, daughter of the Earl of Suffolk, the temptations of sexual adventures at the court of King James I proved too great to resist. Caught up in a web of passion that may have involved the king himself, she conspired to poison her lover's other sexual partner.

Young, beautiful, and from an old noble family, Frances Howard was an excellent marriage prospect. She was duly married off to the teenage Earl of Essex in 1610. However, either his sexual interests lay elsewhere or he was simply too young to appreciate the pleasures of the bed chamber. The marriage was not consummated, and soon after Frances' new husband left court bound for a long stay in France.

The passionate young woman, left alone in a court simmering with sexual intrigue, soon found herself tempted to join in and before long was sharing her bed with a young, handsome page called Robert Carr. While Carr was also involved in a homosexual relationship with Thomas Overbury, who was 11 years Carr's senior, he seems to have been more than happy to satisfy Frances' appetites. In addition to this pair of sexual partners, it was also whispered that Carr was the king's bedmate too! He was certainly much favored by the monarch, and while Carr and Frances pleasured each other on nights that Carr didn't spend in someone else's bed, he rose quickly in the king's service. Having been given a position in the Royal court, Carr, in turn, employed Overbury as his secretary.

Trouble began to brew with the return the Earl of Essex, Frances' husband. The earl was now eager to prove himself a man and whisked his wife off to the country in order to finally consummate their marriage. Sadly for him, his clumsy approaches were rejected by a woman who was, by now, more used to the expert touch of her youbg bisexual lover. Frances refused to have sex with him, and the frustrated earl instead sought a divorce. The marriage was dissolved by the Archbishop of Canterbury.

The divorce came as a shock to Thomas Overbury. Convinced that a now single Frances would steal Carr away from him , he became hysterical and made such a public scene that King James had him thrown into the cells at the Tower of London. In fact, both Frances and Carr were eager to be rid of Overbury, whose revelations were an embarrassment to both of them. With the help of Sir Gervase Elwes, Governor of the Tower, and a chemist's assistant, they conspired to have the poison mercuric sublimate administered to Overbury in his cell. It was a foolhardy plot, for while Overbury might be imprisoned for the moment in order to stop his tongue, he was known to be one of the king's homosexual lovers. The king would be furious if the poisoning were discovered. Nevertheless, the plot went ahead. Overbury died on September 15, 1613, after enduring five months of agony.

It looked as though the murder would go undetected, but—in another unexpected twist—the chemist's assistant was struck down with a fatal illness and made a deathbed confession. Elwes and three other men involved in the plot were put on trial and executed in late 1615, while Carr and Howard were tried the following year and also sentenced to death. However, possibly due to the king's lingering affection for Carr,

the penalty was waived, and the pair were instead confined in the Tower. After six years of imprisonment, they were allowed to return to their homes in the country. After all that had happened, their passion had turned to mutual hatred. Howard died of a disease of the womb when she was 39; Carr lived on. It is said that a while later, King James held his former lover and sobbed uncontrollably on his shoulder.

Gus Huberman

What must be one of the strangest cases in the history of crime began as a simple extramarital affair and ended with a husband shot dead. In between, Gus Huberman's older mistress literally treated him like a pet. Imprisoned in the attic, he was fed, watered, and played with as the mood took her.

Gus Huberman attracted Dotty Walburger's attention when he was just 16 years old. While her husband Bert was wealthy and successful, he was much given to the pleasures of the table and had grown so obese that he could no longer climb the stairs. For a woman who had her own appetites, which had nothing to do with food, the young and energetic boy who worked for a local paint company was a stark contrast to the man she had married. It was not long before the teenager and Dotty were conducting a passionate affair,

Noticing the difference in his wife and suspicious of the relationship with her new young friend, Bert Walburger hired a private detective to trail them and it didn't take long for the truth to be revealed. Faced with proof, Dotty confessed her infidelity and asked for a divorce, but Walburger refused, fearing that the court would award Dotty—and thus her lover—with a large portion of his fortune.

Unable to get rid of her husband and forced to promise that she would give her young lover up, Dotty took desperate measures. She knew that Bert was in no condition to reach the top parts of the house and her solution, while bizarre, was elegantly simple: she smuggled Huberman into the attic. Now she could indulge herself whenever she pleased while never appearing to leave the house. Whenever the Walburgers'

moved home—which they did often as Bert's business flourished—Huberman secretly came with them. Dotty was careful to always insist on a tall house with a large attic space.

The situation might have continued indefinitely, but for a violent argument that broke out between Bert Walburger and his wife on August 29, 1922. Hearing it from the attic and fearing for his mistress's safety, Huberman crept down the stairs carrying a revolver that he would later tell a court he always kept handy in case of burglars. He arrived just in time to see Dotty punched to the floor. As his wife fell, Walburger looked up to find himself being watched by his wife's lover, who he had believed to have been long gone. In a fresh rage, Walburger attacked Huberman and during the fight the gun went off. Walburger lay dead. Dotty later claimed the whole incident had happened while she hid in a wardrobe.

Gus Huberman's trial lasted five weeks, during which the press began calling him "The Phantom in the Attic." While the details of the case were undeniably shocking, Huberman's plight roused enormous sympathy. He was just a young boy who had been seduced and then kept like an animal by a woman more than old enough to know better. Finally though, it was a moving speech by Huberman's lawyer that saved him from the charge of murder. Earl Wakeman, defending the lad, told the court that his client was an orphan who had known misery all his life.

Huberman was found guilty, but not of murder but the lesser charge of manslaughter and sentenced to three years in prison. However, he had served longer than this while awaiting trial and was allowed to go free at once. By the time Dotty Walburger was put on trial separately, Huberman had found himself a wife. Dotty was also acquitted when the legal system felt Huberman had been through enough and did not deserve to appear at a court again.

Lila Jimerson and Nancy Bowen

When artist Henri Marchand had a casual fling with Native-American Lila Jimerson, he said it was of no great consequence to him; just another brief sexual encounter in a long line. It was a fling that would end in murder, however. But though the woman who actually committed the deed was easy to find, the case proved so difficult to untangle that we will probably never know who really plotted to kill Clothilde Marchand. Nevertheless, it is interesting to note that before the jury reached their final verdict, Marchand had taken a new, young wife.

On March 6, 1930, Nancy Bowen, a 66-year-old Cayuga Indian from the nearby Cattaraugus Reservation walked into the home of Henri Marchand, artist for Buffalo's Natural History Museum. Inside the house, Bowen confronted Marchand's wife Clothilde and asked her, "Are you a witch?" Taken aback by the question, Mrs Marchand jokingly replied yes. On hearing the answer, Bowen beat Clothilde with a hammer, stuffed chloroform-soaked paper down her throat, and left her for dead.

When the Marchands' youngest son Henri came home from school he found his mother sprawled across the first floor landing and ran to the nearby museum, bringing home his father and two brothers. At first it was thought that Clothilde had died from falling down the stairs, but the medical examiner soon found bloody gashes, the odor of chloroform, and signs of a furious struggle on the body of the tiny Frenchwoman. The police were brought in and after questioning Henri Marchand and an associate who boarded with him, began looking for 39-year-old Lila "Red Lilac" Jimerson.

She was arrested alongside Bowen, who had retained broken pieces from Clothilde's glasses and scraps of her bloodstained clothing. But what appeared a straightforward murder for revenge would prove anything but. The court would have to sift through strange accusations, denials, and counter accusations to try and make some sense of the case. Throughout the trial there was also a strong smell of racism, with District Attorney Guy Moore at one point referring to Jimerson as a "filthy Indian."

The prosecution alleged that Lila Jimerson— determined to exact revenge for her callous treatment at Marchand's hands—had fixed upon Clothilde's reputation as a white witch as a means of getting back at him. The French woman, like many of her nation, enjoyed picking and eating wild mushrooms and her love of these "strange hellish vegetables" was considered evidence among some of the Native-American community that she practiced magic. So Jimerson convinced Nancy Bowen, whose husband Charley had recently died, that Clothilde had used her dark powers to cause his death. Bowen was thus primed to exact Jimerson's revenge for her by killing her faithless lover's wife.

During the first trial, Marchand admitted the affair, but told the court it had come about as a matter of professional necessity between artist and model. He added that he had had more affairs than he could remember, dismissing Jimerson as a minor fling. The rest of the trial did not proceed well. Jimerson, who suffered from tuberculosis, collapsed. The federal government also attempted to meddle with the proceedings by enlisting the help of a top-flight lawyer, Richard Harkness Templeton, to defend Jimerson, leaving District Attorney Moore incensed and shouting in court for Templeton to be removed. At the end of the turbulent hearing no verdict was reached.

By the time a second trial came to court, 53-year-old Marchand was remarried to an 18-year old girl and, with the financial support of the Seneca and Cayuga tribes, Jimerson had hired an excellent attorney. Jimerson continued to deny the charge and accused Marchand of the killing, saying that he had told her he wanted to hire assassins to kill his wife. Then in a dramatic reversal— and from a hospital bed—she changed her plea to guilty for second degree murder. Soon she retracted that plea, then admitted first degree murder, then again changed it back to a plea of second degree murder. Now she admitted the killing, but insisted she had simply been a pawn in Marchand's plot to kill his wife and said that she had done everything out of love for him.

After months of confusion, Jimerson was acquitted on February 28, 1931. Nancy Bowen, the women who had actually committed the fatal attack, pleaded guilty to reduced charges of first degree manslaughter and on March 13, 1931, was sentenced to a one to ten-year prison sentence. Because she already had been detained in jail for longer than the amount of the minimum sentence, she was allowed to go free.

Winnie Ruth Judd.

Sharing an apartment with friends is often difficult, especially if they begin helping themselves to your belongings. However, as Agnes Ann LeRoi and Helwig Samuelson found out, if your roommate should decide that you are stealing their boyfriends then the payback can be horrifying.

When Winnie Ruth Judd, Agnes Ann LeRoi, and Helwig Samuelson—three unmarried girls—decided to share an apartment in Phoenix, Arizona, in 1931, everything went well at first. Like many young women living with friends, they enjoyed each other's company, borrowed clothes, and swapped gossip. Sadly, the easy-going atmosphere wasn't to last. Winnie was somewhat promiscuous and brought a stream of men back to the apartment. Agnes and Helwig objected. The three women had fierce arguments, and Winnie began to believe that her friends were putting obstacles in her way because they wanted her boyfriends for themselves. As her rage and jealousy mounted, she became more and more convinced that Agnes and Helwig were sleeping with the men that rightfully belonged to her.

On October 16, 1931, she snapped, and furiously demanded why the pair kept ruining her relationships. In the circumstances her roommates did the worst thing they possibly could have: they laughed at Winnie. She then shot them both dead.

Working with remarkable presence of mind for a young woman who had just committed a double murder, Winnie immediately put a bullet through her own hand in order to be able to claim self-defense should she be caught. Then she set about disposing of the bodies. Her plan was to dump them into the ocean in her home state of California, and she packed the corpses of her friends into a large trunk for transport, then booked a ticket on a train. When a porter came to collect it he complained it was too heavy and demanded that she instead put "the medical books"—as she described the contents—into smaller cases. Winnie solved the problem by sawing the bodies into pieces.

Incredibly, the cases got as far as California without incident and remained at the station while Winnie fetched her brother to help her with them, telling him brazenly, "There are two bodies in these trunks and the less you know about it, the better off you are." Winnie's plan now began to unravel. A baggage clerk smelled the distinctive odor of rotting flesh coming from the cases, and suspected Winnie and her brother of being meat smugglers. He asked them to open the cases, but Winnie told him she didn't have the keys. Fearing that she was moments from discovery, she grabbed her brother's arm and walked away briskly. As the pair drove away, the clerk made a note of the car registration plate. Then he called the police, still thinking that the worst crime that had been committed was the transport of contraband meat. His mistake was soon corrected in the most horrific manner imaginable. Detectives broke into the cases to find the putrid rotting corpses of two young women.

The hunt was on for a murderer, and Winnie couldn't keep ahead of the law for long. The police traced her brother's car and, meanwhile, the wound in Winnie's hand had become infected. She was forced to attend a hospital and, her cover blown, was arrested.

In court, Winnie maintained her painfully concocted story of self-defense, telling the jury that Helwig had shot her first and that she had then wrestled the gun away from her assailant. The fact that Winnie was now armed hadn't deterred her roommates, and Agnes and Helwig both attacked her again. In fear for her life, Winnie had shot them both.

No one believed her. Winnie Judd was found guilty

BELOW: Winnie Ruth Judd (centre), being returned to prison after one of her many escapes.

of the murders of Agnes Ann Le Roi and Helwig Samuelson and sentenced to death. But still she tried to evade justice. While in prison awaiting execution, Winnie's behavior convinced doctors that she was actually insane and not responsible for her crimes. At mental hearing, she put on a fine performance; pretending to hear voices, mumbling incoherently, and pulling at her hair and clothes. The death sentence was commuted to a life of imprisonment in the Arizona state mental institution. Winnie proved sane enough to manage to escape from the secure hospital several times, at one time staying on the run for seven years during which time she worked as a housekeeper. Winnie was finally released on December 22, 1971, 40 years after her deadly fit of jealousy.

Thomas Andrew Keir

The tale of Australian Thomas Andrew Keir is a confusing one, for while awaiting trial for the murder of his second wife, Rosalina Canonizado, police unearthed the remains of his first wife Jean beneath his home in New South Wales. While he was found not guilty of murdering Rosalina, his first wife came back to haunt him and, after various appeals, he would eventually serve time for her killing.

Keir married his first wife Jean in August 1984 when he was 26 and Jean was 18. Four years later, Keir claimed that his wife had run off with another man, leaving their three-year-old son behind. A few weeks after reporting his wife's disappearance, Keir met Rosalina Canonizado while in Sydney attending a family wedding. He divorced Jean on the grounds of desertion and married Rosalina in the Philippines in 1989. Then, on April 13, 1991, Rosalina was found murdered in the same house where Jean had once lived. She had been strangled with a lamp cord and then set on fire. Keir was charged with murder, the prosecution giving a substantial life insurance policy as his motive. But, believing Keir's claims that he was out shopping at the time of the murder, a jury found him not guilty on April 6, 1993. However, while Keir was awaiting trial in prison in 1991, police received information which led to them digging beneath Keir's house where they found fragments of human bone. DNA testing revealed them to belong to Jean Keir.

On September 17, 1999, Thomas Keir was found guilty of Jean Keir's murder in the New South Wales Supreme Court and sentenced to 24 years imprisonment comprising a minimum term of 18 years and an additional term of six years. The court was told Keir killed his 22-year-old wife in a jealous rage after discovering her infidelity. However, the trial judge did not mention Rosalina Canonizado's case during Keir's sentencing. Subsequently, on February 28, 2002, the New South Wales Criminal Court of Appeal revoked Keir's conviction on the grounds that the judge had misdirected the jury regarding the DNA evidence. At this first appeal the judge reduced Keir's sentence by two years to 22 years imprisonment with a non-parole period of 16 years.

A new trial commenced in July 2002 and on October 17 of that year, Keir was again found guilty of Jean's murder. He successfully appealed a second time because of misconduct on the part of members of the jury, but was once again found guilty of Jean's murder at a third trial in December 2004, and the previous sentence was upheld. The court heard that over a period of years Keir had threatened Jean that he would kill her if she left him or "messed around with somebody else." The day after killing his first wife, Keir "apparently coolly and calmly commenced an extensive course of deception designed to conceal the murder." He later dug up her remains and hid them elsewhere, but seven of Jean's bones were left behind and uncovered when police excavated the yard in 1991.

Keir has been decreed to be eligible for parole in

2014 because of time already served. His later conviction for the murder of his first wife would seem to cast doubt on the verdict of not guilty for the murder of Rosalina Canonizado, but perhaps it could be said that Jean had reached out from beyond the grave and exacted the justice owed to both of Thomas Keir's dead wives.

Ralph Klassen

Ralph Klassen's killing of his second wife caused outrage in Canada in the 1990s, not least because he received such a light sentence. The controversy that followed his trial would see a petition presented to the Canadian parliament in which 15,000 people demanded the provocation defense be abolished.

The 13-year marriage of Ralph and Susan Klassen had long been a stormy one. They had already separated several times, and then reconciled, when they agreed to part for yet another trial separation of six months in October, 1995. Klassen left their Whitehorse home and moved to Alberta while his wife began finding an independent life for herself. In fact, she was relieved to be rid of her husband. His temper and jealousy had become increasingly difficult to live with and Susan found herself enjoying her newly peaceful life and freedom. So much so that when her husband began calling her later that month asking that they reconcile immediately rather than wait for the six months to end, she refused.

Suspecting that his wife was now involved with another man, Ralph Klassen returned to Whitehorse on November 1, and arrived at his old home demanding again that Susan take him back. Again, she refused him.

In the early morning hours of November 2, 1995, Ralph Klassen strangled his 36-year-old wife in the bed of their home, applying so much pressure to her neck that he sprained both his thumbs. He then took a pillowcase and tied it around Susan's neck, permanently cutting off the oxygen flow to her brain. There were no signs of a struggle.

When he was sure she was dead, Klassen wrote a brief note for his wife's supposed lover. It said, "I'm sorry I went into a jealous fit of rage. The image of you and my wife together made me insane." He then drove his car into a truck in a suicide attempt, but survived against the odds. When police arrived on the scene he confessed to killing his wife.

Klassen was charged with second degree murder, but used the Canadian provocation defense to have it dropped to manslaughter. The jury found him guilty on January 17, 1997. For the killing of his wife Ralph Klassen received a sentence of just five years imprisonment. The term was greeted with shock by the public. However, it was also established that he would be eligible for an early release in May, 2000, when only two-thirds of the light sentence had been served.

There was an immediate outcry. A week later more than 300 people marched through Whitehorse to protest and, also spurred on by the sentence, Klassen's first wife also came forward to tell how Klassen had repeatedly assaulted her during their marriage, on one occasion choking her. In response to the outrage on May 27, the Federal Justice Crown appealed against the lenient sentence arguing that it was "inadequate, given the aggravating factors of spousal violence and breach of trust." A month later three judges dismissed the appeal, saying that the five-year sentence was in line with those imposed in similar cases.

While the controversy raged on, and eventually culminated in an appeal to parliament that the law be revised so that others couldn't use the same defense in the future, Ralph Klassen's sentence remained unchanged. As suggested at his trial he was released from the William Head Institution, a medium-security federal penitentiary on Vancouver Island, in 2000.

Ada Le Bouef & Dr. Thomas Dreher

James Le Bouef was allowed to live only so long as he turned a blind eye to his wife's passionate liaison with his best friend. When he began to raise objections that threatened to end the affair his fate was sealed.

In the 1920s, Morgan City in Louisiana's was a simply community of simply country folk. Set in the bayou country of swamps and creeks fed by the waters of the mighty Mississippi River, many Morgan City people lived by trading as frog catchers, trappers, moonshiner's, and alligator hunters. But James and Ada Le Boeuf were a cut above most folk in the area. In a time when electricity was moving from a luxury to a necessity for

BELOW: Lake Palourde, the beauty spot in southern Louisiana where Ada Le Bouef, Thomas Dreher and Jim Beadle dumped the body of Ada's husband.

every home, he was superintendent of the Morgan City Light and Power Company and a man of some standing in the small town.

The Le Bouefs had been long married, with five children, when Ada began suffering from terrible headaches that confined her to bed. Her worried husband immediately called his good friend Dr. Thomas Dreher to ease her pain. At first Le Bouef thought that Dreher was simply attending Ada so frequently out of concern for his wife, but as Ada's headaches began to strike more regularly with Dreher in attendance each time, it became obvious that it wasn't a dose of medicine the doctor was giving her. Nevertheless, Le Bouef didn't have the courage to face the scandal that would follow a confrontation of that kind in such a small town. He discreetly allowed them to continue with their liaison in the hope that it would fizzle out and things could get back to normal.

However, the affair couldn't escape the attention of others for long in such a small community, and the neighborhood was soon abuzz with rumors of adultery taking place at the Le Bouef house and anywhere else Ada and the Dreher could find to meet. An anonymous letter was sent to Dreher's wife, telling her, "Two nights ago there was a lady and a man in that empty shack in the bayou. One of them was Ada Le Boeuf and the other was your husband!" Someone else spread a story that Dreher and Ada had been spotted swimming naked together in the bayou.

James Le Boeuf had been prepared to keep quiet in order to keep his humiliation from becoming public knowledge, but now the secret was out he demanded that the affair stop straight away. But he underestimated the strength of the lovers' passion, and the steps they were prepared to take to preserve it" Le Boeuf's body was pulled out of the bayou in July 1927. He had been shot twice in the head.

The identity of his murderers was obvious, and the police swiftly arrested Ada and her lover. Soon after, they also brought a trapper of dubious reputation named Jim Beadle into custody. He was known to have held a grudge against James Le Boeuf.

All three were tried together at Franklin, Louisiana. Dreher's story was that Ada sent him a note asking him to get rid of her husband. It said that she would be rowing on the local lake with him on July 1, and that would be the time to strike. Dreher called on Beadle and they rowed out together. Dreher claimed it was Beadle who fired the two shots, but the trapper denied it, telling the court that the doctor shot James Le Boeuf, after which he had "slit open Le Boeuf's stomach" so that the corpse would sink to the bottom and be hidden forever.

All three were found guilty of murder and conspiracy to commit murder. Dr. Thomas Dreher and Ada La Bouef were given death sentences and were hanged side by side on February 1, 1929. Jim Beadle was jailed for life for his part in the killing.

Thomas Ley

For some, a crime of passion is committed in a burst of terrible anger or jealousy, while for others the jealousy grows in their minds until it drives them literally insane. It was unfortunate for John McMain Mudie that he crossed the path of a man who was completely possessed by his own fevered suspicions.

The body of John Mudie was found in a chalk pit in Surrey, England, on November 30, 1946. He had been beaten and hanged with a dirty rag stuffed in his mouth, then trussed and dumped. He had been a decent man in life; popular and jovial, he had served his coun-try well during World War II and in peacetime had become a barman. His only crime was to take lodgings in a London house that was also shared by Maggie Brook, the long-term mistress of Thomas John Ley, a former Minister of Justice in New Zealand.

The police hunted down the killer quickly and efficiently. The identity card in Mudie's pocket led them straight to his lodgings, and their questions soon revealed a likely suspect, for Ley's terrifying jealousy was well known. And when one of the men who had helped him murder his victim turned Queen's Evidence, the whole story unraveled.

Despite the fact that Maggie Brook was a respectable woman, her lover was obsessed with his suspicions over her conduct. At some point or another he had accused her of sleeping with virtually every man she knew, including those who lodged at the same house. For some inexplicable reason though, he had come to focus his jealousy on Maudie, perhaps simply because Maudie's simple, likeable character was so different from his own dark nature.

Twisted by his suspicions, Ley hatched a plot to remove his rival and recruited carpenter Lawrence Smith and chauffeur John Buckingham to help. A woman friend, Lilian Bruce, was paid to play the role of

RIGHT: A 1947 photograph of murderer Thomas John Ley, a former Minister of Justice in New Zealand.

BELOW: The chalkpit at Woldingham in Surrey where the body of barman John Mudie was discovered in 1946.

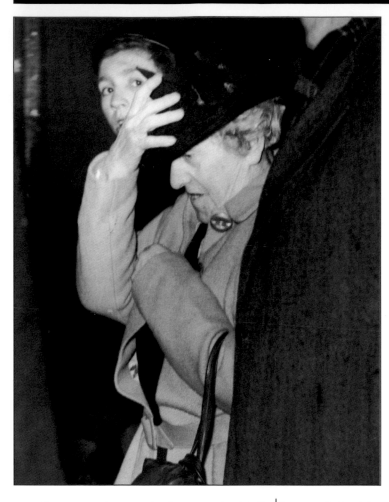

LEFT: Mrs Emily Ley, the wife Thomas John Ley, arriving at Waterloo Station from Australia, to attend her husband's trial.

RIGHT: John Buckingham being helped into his car by his son (left) after giving evidence at the Old Bailey, London, in the trial of Thomas John Ley

When Buckingham heard about the discovery of John Mudie's body he went straight to the police. He had stayed outside with the car and had no knowledge that he had been part of a murder. All charges against him were dropped, and he later testified against Ley and Smith. Police also learned that the two men had been paid in one pound notes, the exact amount and denomination that had been withdrawn from Ley's bank that very day.

The four-day trial started on March 19, 1947, with both Ley and Smith pleading not guilty. Nevertheless, the case against them was unanswerable, and so dreadful was the crime against an innocent man that the death sentence was passed. Before he was hanged though, a wealthy woman who seemed to be attracted to Mudie and so lure him back to her home in a chauffer-driven car—with Buckingham at the wheel. The house they arrived at, however, was not hers, but Ley's. Once inside, Mudie was attacked by Ley and Smith, severely beaten, and hanged with a cord. Ley then handed Smith and Buckingham £200 cash each for their efforts—and for their silence.

Ley was declared insane and given a reprieve. That presented a legal dilemma; if the man who organized such a brutal murder was not going to be executed, how could the man who had been paid to help face the death sentence? Smith was reprieved too and sentenced to life imprisonment. Within four months of his arrival at the top security mental institute of Broadmoor in Berkshire, Ley died of a brain haemorrhage.

Ann Marie Linscott

Fortunately for the wife of her lover, Ann Marie Linscott's plot to assassinate her was discovered before it could do any harm. Nevertheless, it is an interesting case and one that shows how crimes of passion might adapt to the digital age.

The age of the internet has resulted in many curious affairs. Many people who would never otherwise have met have developed intense passions for each other in cyberspace and in numerous cases a liaison conducted in virtual reality has had a disastrous effect on real-life relationships. One such affair began in 2004 when Ann Marie Linscott met a man whose identity has never been revealed in an internet chat room. Ann Marie was 49, a wife, and mother to two teenage children, but thoughts of her family were far from her mind

as the online lovers tapped out messages of lust on their keyboards.

Eventually, they managed to contrive a meeting. In 2005, the man involved was sent to a conference in Reno, Nevada. Ann Marie joined him there and at last their passion became physical. The brief sexual encounter only served to deepen their intimacy, and the pair continued the relationship by phone and email, the enforced separation serving only to fan the flames of passion, for Ann Marie especially. Although she and her lover managed to meet again, it was not enough for Ann Marie and she hatched a plot to make the man she adored single. It proved to be as stupid as it was potentially deadly.

In November 2007, three California residents were separately searching the website craigslist.com for job opportunities when they came across an advert that looked interesting. The job was described only as a "freelance" position and each of them asked for more information. They began exchanging emails with Ann Marie Linscott, who used an alias, and it soon became apparent that the freelance position was a crude code for a contract killer.

Linscott asked each of the three job applicants to "eradicate" a woman living in Butte County, California, and provided a description of the victim, her age, and the address where she worked. On two occasions she offered payment of $5,000 upon completion of the task. Realizing that she was deadly serious, all three of the jobseekers reported the mystery employer to the police.

Californian detectives quickly established the identity of the intended victim and discovered that she was married. Under questioning, the details of her husband's infidelity were revealed, and the trail finally led them to Ann Marie. Background checks on her revealed a list of irregularities: She had once taken out a restraining order on one of her colleagues, and he had responded in kind, claiming that she had made unwanted advances. She had also given false information on her resume, saying that she had worked as a massage therapist at a hospital that had never heard of her.

Linscott was arrested at her home in January 2008 and charged with perpetrating a murder-for-hire scheme. On February 4, 2009, she was found guilty and sentenced to 12 years and seven months in prison. The judge hearing the case condemned Linscott for showing no remorse and said the heavy sentence was to protect the public from people like her, and to deter anyone else who might be considering using the internet to recruit a killer. Strangely, her husband, John, supported her throughout.

Denise Labbe & Jacques Algarron

This crime of passion is unusual, and more sickening than most. It was not committed out of revenge or in the heat of the moment, but against a complete innocent whose mother had the misfortune to come under the spell of a philosophy student whose beliefs were nothing short of insane. He abused her love for him by asking her to prove it in the most vile way imaginable.

Denise Labbe's life had often been a struggle, but she had worked hard to better herself. She was the daughter of a poor postman and after being orphaned at 13 had educated herself to the point where she was able to land a job as a secretary. She also allowed herself a little fun along the way, usually with the male students of her home town of Rennes, France, and by the time she reached 25, she had a toddler daughter called Catherine. Nevertheless, she was coping well with life's demands until she met a charismatic graduate of philosophy named Jacques Algarron. He was three years her junior and seduced her with the line he always used on women: "I offer you fervor." She was immediately bewitched by the complex and well-read young man and began a passionate affair with him.

Algarron was a great admirer philosophy that suggested the existence of "super humans" and told his new girlfriend that he believed they were a super couple. Unfortunately, his demented ideas quickly grew into an obsession. He needed Denise to prove that she was superior to other women and worthy of his love. The scheme Algarron hit upon should have told Denise

that he was an extremely dangerous individual, but she was head over heels in love and couldn't bear the idea that she might lose him. Algarron read Denise a story in which a mother kills her child by another man to please her lover and told her how beautiful it was. She had to suffer, too, he said. The deluded Denise agreed, convinced by what she saw as Algarron's high intellect and advanced philosophy.

Her first attempt to kill Catherine wasn't successful. Appalled by the enormity of what she was about to do and disturbed by the appearance of a neighbor, Denise found that she could not drop her daughter from a window as planned. Her second went little

ABOVE: Jacques Algarron, being escorted in a police car on the second day of his trial in Blois, France.

better. Denise threw Catherine into a canal, only to be overwhelmed by her maternal instinct to protect her child. She summoned help, and the little girl was pulled out of the water by a passerby.

By now Algarron was becoming impatient and threatened to leave her if she did not carry out his orders. So, on November 8, 1954, she drowned Catherine in a washtub then telegraphed Algarron to tell him that she had done as asked. He later told a friend, "It takes courage to kill your own daughter."

The child's disappearance soon aroused suspicions among Denise's neighbors, and police were called in to question her. She confessed to the horrific crime, but told them that Algarron was to blame.

The thunder and lightning that accompanied the opening of the trial of Denise Labbe and Jacques Algarron was seen as a sign of their demonic possession. Both were found guilty of murder with Denise sentenced to life imprisonment and Algarron to 20 years. Algarron, however, had a final statement to the court and pompously stood to deliver it. "Certain monsters," he told the stunned people in the room, "are sacred because often the same qualities are found in a monster and in a saint." Like the horrendous crime he had incited Denise to commit, it was beyond anyone's comprehension.

Adolph Luetgert

The trial of Adolph Luetgert for the murder of his wife Louise in 1897 became one of the first in the United States to be carried out under the full glare of the media and with the nation eagerly awaiting every grisly new revelation. It was hardly surprising as the case had all the elements of a penny dreadful story: infidelity, violence, murder, and a particularly grisly method for deposing of the body.

The trial of Adolph Luetgert for the murder of his wife Louise in 1897 became one of the first in the United States to be carried out under the full glare of the media and with the nation eagerly awaiting every grisly new revelation. It was hardly surprising as the case had all the elements of a penny dreadful story: infidelity, violence, murder, and a particularly grisly method for deposing of the body.

Like many of the marriages within these pages, Adolph and Louise Luetgerts' was not a happy one. He was the owner of a sausage factory and she was his second wife, but the fact that he was married did not stop him conducting numerous affairs and during their frequent arguments, during which Louise would implore her husband to stop sleeping with other women, Luetgert often became violent. In fact, neighbors once reported seeing Luetgert trying to strangle his wife, stopping only when he realized he was being watched.

On May 1, 1897, when her brother came looking for her, Luetgert admitted that Louise had disappeared. He claimed that she had left him and that he didn't know where she had gone, but her brother was suspicious. He informed the police who took Luetgert in for questioning, asking him why he had not reported her missing when the year before he had come to them for help when his dog disappeared. Luetgert maintained that he had hired a private detective to find his wife, fearing a scandal if his marital problems became public.

No one believed him and after a witness came forward to say they had seen Luetgert leading his wife into a back alley by his factory on April 24, a search for her body began. At first a nearby river was trawled, but when that proved fruitless the police turned their attentions to the factory itself and soon uncovered some gruesome evidence: fragments of human bone and a wedding ring with the initials "LL" in one of the vats. They also found a night watchman, who had unwittingly helped with the boiling up of Louise Luetgert and had been curious about the strange slime he had been asked to dispose of. He later testified that Luetgert had told him, "Don't say a word and I'll see you have a good job as long as you live."

The press went wild. Newspapers fought one another for scoops, people across the country claimed to have seen the missing woman alive, and each new clue led to fresh rounds of speculation about the crime. Meanwhile, sausage sales plummeted nationwide as rumors circulated that Luetgert had destroyed his wife's body in one of his factory's meat grinders.

In fact, the rest of her body was never found and it is impossible to say what went on in the factory.

At Luetgert's trial, witnesses came forward to speak of his violent tendencies and letters from his various mistresses were read out. They suggested that Luetgert had promised to marry other women and share his fortune, though he was actually on the verge of bankruptcy. Through it all, Luetgert maintained his innocence, telling the jury that one day Louise would return to him. Despite his protestations, the evidence against him was overwhelming. Adolph Luetgert was found guilty of the murder of his wife and sentenced to life. He died in the Joliet State Penitentiary in 1899.

BELOW: Joliet State Penitentiary, in Illinois, where Adolph Luetgert served his life sentence for the murder of his wife.

Madame de Montespan

While love, passion, and jealousy have prompted human beings to some unspeakable acts over the centuries, the cruelty of Françoise-Athénaïs de Rochechouart de Mortemart—better remembered as Madame de Montespan—mistress of the French "Sun King," Louis XIV, was truly vile. In fact, the investigation into her conduct uncovered a nest of black magic so depraved that dozens of trials were held in strict secrecy, and the papers relating to them then burned.

For all that we now dismiss as old tales of witches, it is undeniable that throughout history there have been many who believe in magic. During the 17th century, the underground practice of witchcraft had become hugely popular in Europe. For those involved, the spells, potions, lotions, and bizarre rituals promised success in just about everything ranging from curing impotency to poisoning unwanted husbands and wives. And the practice of sorcery reached right into the very highest circle of all, the court of King Louis XIV.

Madame de Montespan had been Louis' mistress of for ten years, but it seemed that her time in favor was coming to an end. The king had taken another lover—Louise de la Valliere—and Madame de Montespan was determined to kill her rival. In order to secure the king's affections only for herself, she also decided to despatch the queen, too. Madame de Montespan had already been deeply involved in dark magical circles, and it was an obvious choice to take advice on how best to accomplish her task from a witch.

Her request was a terrible, deadly undertaking, and Madame de Montespan was swiftly passed up the magical hierarchy to the high priest of devil worship, a man called Abbé Étiene Guibourg. At his

RIGHT: A 1660 painting of Madame de Montespan, whose desire to retain her position as the mistress of King Louis XIV led her to commit a heinous crime.

insistence, the king's lover then took part in a horrific, despicable ritual: Madame de Montespan lay naked on a bed, her feet dangling on the floor, and with a sacred chalice balanced on her loins. A human baby was then brought out and its throat cut. As the child died, its blood was drained into the chalice, and its entrails drawn out, to be used in making the poisoned potion.

But before Madame de Montespan could administer the poison she was betrayed. When King Louis learned of his mistress's evil plot and the extent to which witchcraft had been involved, he ordered an immediate, remorseless investigation. Dozens of arrests followed. Perhaps fearful of the outcry should it be revealed how close to the throne witchcraft had come, he ordered that all trials should be held in the strictest secrecy. They

began in April 1679 and lasted right through until July 1683. During that time, 104 defendants were charged with various acts of black magic and murder. Those accused included a number of Catholic priests. By the end of the trial, 36 death sentences, four life sentences, and 34 other sentences ranging from banishment to heavy fines had been given. Strangely, the name Madame de Montespan was not mentioned once throughout the whole affair. In fact, her fate remains a mystery.

In 1709, Louis ordered every document relating to the hearings destroyed. One was overlooked, the minute book of the clerk of the court, which re-emerged at the end of the 19th century and finally revealed the shocking details.

Madame Fahmi

The 1923 sensational murder trial of the French-born, Egyptian Princess Madame Marguerite Fahmi divided East and West. Although she was clearly guilty of killing her husband, Marguerite's defense lawyer raised every cultural slur and stereotype he could in order to paint her as more sinned against than sinning. Even now many Egyptians are still irate that a prejudiced jury allowed her to get away with the murder of a member of their royal family.

Marguerite Laurent was a divorced woman in her early 30s when she met Prince Ali Kamel Fahmi Bek in Cairo. Ten years her junior, of royal blood, and the master of an almost mythical fortune, he wasted no time in pursuing the beautiful Marguerite. She would later say, "As Fahmi Bek's love for me grew stronger and stronger, I began to see before me a life I had only read about in A Thousand and One Nights and I heard passionate words of love and promises of what happiness his vast wealth could bring us."

The prince was used to getting everything he wanted. Sure enough Marguerite became his wife on December 27, 1922, and, as the marriage contract stipulated, she also converted to Islam two weeks later. However, converting to her husband's notions of a dutiful wife was to be more difficult than a simple change of religion for the fiery, passionate Frenchwoman. From

the beginning the royal couple had a tempestuous marriage, which came to a head in a furious—and very public—argument in the dining room of London's Savoy Hotel on September 1, 1923. During the row, Madame Fahmi told the bandleader that her husband had threatened to kill her.

Eventually, the couple retired to their luxury suite. A little while later Prince Fahmi opened the door to let their small dog run up and down the corridor. After whistling for it to come back, he closed the door. Moments later, three shots rang out. A passing porter rushed to the room to see Madame Fahmi throwing down a pistol. Her husband was lying on the floor bleeding. He died shortly afterwards.

Marguerite's trial for murder began on September 11, and lasted five days. The prosecution believed they had an open-and-shut case that could be concluded

without attracting much attention. They could not have been more mistaken. Only two days into the trial, the tiny courtroom became swelled with eager spectators and a long queue outside waited hopefully for seats to become available.

From the start, the trial illustrated the line written by Rudyard Kipling, a famous poet living at the time: "East is East and West is West, and never shall the twain meet." Sir Marshall Hall, heading the three member defense team, made every effort to sway the jury by playing on Western distrust of Eastern culture. As one Egyptian commentator later noted, "It was Hall who turned an ordinary criminal case into a trial of oriental customs, transforming it into a "public opinion" issue which had the French and British siding with Marguerite as the victim of oriental "backwardness" and "barbarity", and the Arabs rallying to the defence of their customs and traditions."

To a sympathetic jury, Hall painted a picture of an oppressed wife suffering at the hands of a bullying

ABOVE: The Savoy Hotel in London, where Marguerite Fahmi shot her husband, Prince Ali Kamel Fahmi Bek.

Egyptian Prince who made unnatural sexual demands upon her. He made a point of referring to Fahmi as "that Western woman" and described how Marguerite was found cowering after the pistol had gone off by accident on that fatal evening. The fact the pistol had gone off "accidentally" three times seems to have been forgotten. The reserved British jury was also disgusted, rather than impressed, at the Prince's many excesses. These, they heard, included spending half a million pounds on women, drink, and cars over just four years and giving costly gifts to the chief policemen in every city where he took up residence. The latter smacked of bribery and corruption.

The outcome was inevitable: Madame Fahmi was found not guilty of murder and not guilty of manslaughter. No doubt encouraged by her acting skills in court, she went on to become a film star.

Tony Mancini

In one of the most macabre murder cases of the early 20th century, petty criminal Toni Mancini was accused of killing his lover, Violet Kaye. But despite her decomposing remains being found in a chest that he had been using as a coffee table, Mancini was still acquitted. While there may be strong suspicions that the jury reached the wrong verdict in many other cases, in this one it is certain that they did. Years later, Mancini later made a deathbed confession.

The 42-year-old Violet and her 25-year-old lover inhabited a shady underworld of drugs, drink, and petty crime in Brighton, on Britain's south coast. She was a prostitute, and he worked occasionally as a waiter or at the door of a nightclub. Fuelled by their debilitating addictions and the difference in their ages, the couple's relationship was stormy, and jealousy boiled over on May 10, 1934. Violet had seen Mancini flirting with a teenage waitress at the Skylark Café, and witnesses later testified that an argument was already in progress by the time they returned to their lodgings.

That was the last time Violet would be seen alive. For nearly two months her body stayed in a trunk at the bottom of Mancini's bed. Although it smelled repulsive and fluids soon began to leak from it, Mancini simply threw a cloth over it and used it as a coffee table.

Meanwhile, he tried to cover his tracks by telling those who knew Violet that she had gone away for a while. He also sent a telegram to Violet's sister telling her the same. However, Violet's many prostitute friends became suspicious and reported her missing to the police. They immediately questioned Mancini, who panicked and went on the run. This was enough to prompt a police search and on July 18, they entered his lodgings. The first thing that hit them was the

LEFT: Violet Kaye, seen in a photograph from 1933, a year before her death.

smell, which led them straight to the grisly "coffee table" at the end of Mancini's bed.

The police eventually caught up with Mancini in London. He was arrested and faced a jury in December, 1934. Over the course of the five day trial the prosecution focused on the fact that Kaye had died from a fatal blow to the head and the gruesome coffee table Mancini kept at his lodgings. Who else but a murderer could live with a decaying body, they asked the jury. A handwriting expert was also brought in and confirmed the handwriting on the form for the telegram sent to Violet's sister matched that on menus Mancini had written at the Skylark Café. One witness, Doris Saville, said Mancini had asked her to provide a false alibi. Others—former friends of Mancini—claimed he boasted in the days after the murder of giving his "missus" the "biggest hiding of her life."

When the turn came for the case for the defense to be made, Mancini's counsel told the court of Violet's dubious drunken character, her jealousy, and—most crucially—her work as a prostitute. It was argued that Mancini had discovered her body at her flat and assumed she had been killed by a client. On the witness stand Mancini said he had panicked. He thought that because of his past criminal record the police would not believe his story and had put her body in a trunk then taken it with him when he moved to new lodgings.

Slowly, the prosecution case began to fall apart.

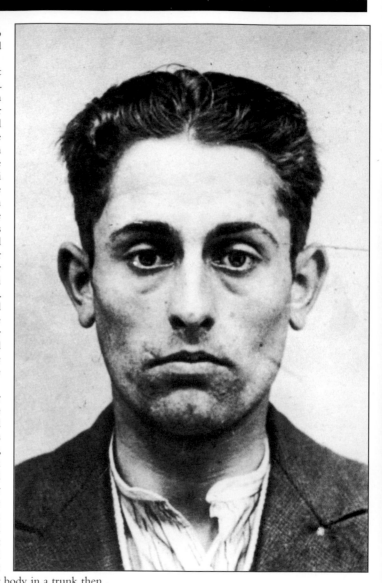

ABOVE: Toni Mancini, the petty criminal who only admitted to murder on his deathbed.

ABOVE: Tony Mancini leaving Lee Road Police Station, London, in a police car on the day of his arrest for the murder of Violet Kaye.

Blood-stained clothing that had been shown as evidence was proved to have been bought after Violet's death and the defense also told the jury that her body contained morphine. It was possible, they argued, that she had had fallen over while high on drugs and hit her head. In spite of their reputation as an argumentative couple, a number of witnesses also confirmed that Mancini and Violet had seemed contented. Mancini told the court he had loved his Violet even though she was a "loose woman."

After deliberating for two and quarter hours, the jury returned a verdict of not guilty and Tony Mancini walked free. For the next 42 years though, his conscience plagued him, and in 1976, shortly before

he died Mancini told a Sunday newspaper how Violet had died. During a blazing row she had attacked him with the hammer he used to break coal for the fire. He had wrestled it from her, but when she had demanded it back, he threw it at her, hitting her on the left temple and killing her.

Marie-Madeleine-Marguerite, Marquise de Brinvilliers

The eldest of five children, Marie-Madeleine-Marguerite was born into an aristocratic French family. Despite her nobility and good breeding, passion turned her into a monster; a serial murderer whose exploits would later inspired poet Robert Browning (The Poisoner) and several authors, including Alexandre Dumas (The Marquise de Brinvilliers) and Arthur Conan Doyle (The Leather Funnel).

The daughter of Viscount Antoine Dreux d'Aubray, a civil lieutenant of Paris, Marie-Madeleine-Marguerite submitted to an arranged marriage in 1651 at the age of 21. This was normal among the French aristocracy at the time, and the bride's her feelings on the matter were seldom taken into account. Unsurprisingly, Marie soon became deeply dissatisfied with her new husband, Antoine Gobelin de Brinvilliers. In addition to being a womanizer and gambler, de Brinvilliers all but ignored his wife, leaving her at the whim of temptation. It was close at hand: Chevalier Jean-Baptiste de Sainte-Croix was an army captain and friend of her father. The pair were soon locked in a passionate affair.

While her husband's illicit liaisons were well known in certain circles, her father was furious upon discovering his daughter was also having an affair. The fact that her lover was a family friend enraged him even further. Marie was forbidden to see her lover again, and in 1663 her father had Sainte-Croix thrown into to the Bastille prison in Paris.

Wrenched apart from the one man who had cared for her, Marie's passion turned to bitter hatred and a lust for revenge. When Sainte-Croix was eventually released, she ignored her father's order and was reunited with her lover. As chance would have it, he had learned the art of poisoning during his imprisonment. It was a skill the couple intended to make full use of as they plotted to take revenge on his lover's father, while at the same time ensuring Marie's inheritance. With the assistance of one of the royal apothecaries to the court of King Louis XIV, Sainte-Croix obtained tasteless but lethal potions, which Marie fed to her father. In 1666, he became her first victim.

Having killed once, it seems that Marie found it easy to do so again. Having quickly spent her way through her portion of her father's wealth, she turned her murderous attentions to the rest of her family. Her elder brother died in 1670, followed by her younger brother, and then her sister and sister-in-law. Of course, she also attempted to rid herself of an unwanted husband, but he proved stubbornly difficult to kill, though from now on he would be prone to mysterious illnesses.

Perhaps in an effort to find a potion that would finish him off, Marie worked to perfect her poison techniques on sick people in a local hospital. While visiting them under the pretext of being charitable, she killed as many as 50.

Her crimes were discovered in 1672. When Sainte-

Croix died that year, his wife opened a box that he had told her was to be delivered, to his mistress. Inside were poisons and papers that made it clear the pair had been on a murder spree.

Marie immediately went on the run, but was arrested in Liege. Under interrogation, she threatened, "Half the people of quality are involved in this sort of thing, and I could ruin them if I were to talk." But whatever secrets she knew, Marie took them to her grave. The once haughty aristocrat was brutally tortured, her jailers mainly employing what was known as "the water cure," in which she was forced to drink 16 pints of water. But no further information was forthcoming. Tried in Paris in 1676, Marie was found guilty and executed, her body and severed head being thrown onto a fire.

RIGHT: Alexandre Dumas, whose The Marquise de Brinvilliers was inspired by the exploits of Marie-Madeleine-Marguerite.

Francesco Matta

First loves are notoriously difficult to forget. Those days of innocent youth coupled with the first stirrings of sexual excitement leave indelible memories and, sometimes, every relationship that comes after is compared to the one left behind. When Susan Matta stumbled across her first boyfriend on the internet site Friends Reunited all those old memories came flooding back and she again fell deeply in love. But the happiness she though she had found came at a price her husband was unwilling to pay.

Having been divorced, Susan thought she had finally found the man of her dreams when she met Italian Francesco Matta, who ran a successful restaurant in Devon, England, in 1999. Matta's own marriage had also been annulled, and the two wed in 2003, after which they moved to Matta's home town of Caligari,

Sardinia, to begin a new life running a business leasing villas to vacationers.

All was going well until Susan posted adverts for the couple's villas on the Friends Reunited site in 2004. They caught the eye of Stephen Keen who had been Susan's first boyfriend 35 years before when she was 14 and he was 16. He was now a flight lieutenant with the RAF and married with two children, but immediately contacted her. She was delighted to hear from her old flame and as email after email arrived in their inboxes they rediscovered their old bonds. When Keen's wife Doreen discovered what had been going on she wrote to Susan, demanding that she leave her husband alone, but it was too late: the couple had fallen in love.

In February 2006, Susan traveled back to Britain to see her long-lost love and by the end of the trip both were certain that they wanted to make up for all the lost years and live together on a permanent basis. In April that year, Susan wrote a letter to Matta telling him about Stephen. Her distraught husband called to beg her to return, but she simply kept repeating the words, "I'm so sorry."

Matta couldn't let go of the woman he loved though. As Susan and Keen set up home together in Tiverton, Devon, he sent a stream of text messages telling Susan how much he loved her and begging her to end the affair. And when his wife refused he eventually tracked down her new address.

On July 6, 2006, Matta arrived in Devon in a hired van. When Keen answered the door his lover's husband stormed in shouting, "I thought you were an officer and a gentleman." He then said he had a hired a mafia hit man to kill Keen, and that the couple would have to pay £50,000 for him to call him off. As Keen picked up the phone to call the police, Matta lunged at him with a knife, stabbing him four times in the throat. Susan cradled her lover as he lay dying on the floor. When the

BELOW: The Friends Reunited website where Susan Matta got back in touch with her first love, Stephen Keen.

police arrived Matta told them calmly, "I came here to kill the man. I have done what I had to do." Turning to Susan, he continued, "My life is over. Now you will suffer as I am suffering." And as he was led away, he told his wife "I love you."

Francesco Matta was tried for murder at Exeter Crown Court in October 2007. He pleaded not guilty. The jury heard that while he accepted that he had killed Stephen Keen, he felt he should be convicted of manslaughter on the grounds of diminished responsibility. After several days of deliberation, the jury failed to reach a majority verdict and a retrial was ordered. On April 18, 2008, the jury at a second trial had no such difficulties. They found him guilty of murder, and Matta was sentenced to serve a minimum of 11 years before being eligible for parole.

Florence Maybrick

The marriage of Virginian beauty Florence Elizabeth Chandler to British cotton broker James Maybrick would later become littered with betrayals and despair, but at first they seemed happy. Despite the 23 year difference in their ages—Maybrick was 42, Florence just 19—they married in London in July 1881, soon after meeting on the White Star liner Baltic during an Atlantic crossing.

The newlyweds split their time between homes in Virginia and the grand Battlecrease House in the Liverpool suburb of Airbrush and appeared to lead a happy life. The marriage was quickly blessed with a son, James, and after the couple settled permanently in Liverpool a daughter, Gladys Evelyn, followed. Meanwhile Maybrick and his vivacious young wife enjoyed a swirl of social engagements and mixed in the best society. Theirs seemed a perfect life.

But as is so often the case, behind closed doors the reality of their relationship was very different. Maybrick was a hypochondriac and had begun regularly taking the poison arsenic, the one cure he felt would relieve his imagined illnesses. And the trappings of wealth were not all they seemed, either. The couple had lived beyond their means and financial disaster loomed. In an effort to stave it off, Maybrick quietly made attempts to save money. Florence was given a small allowance on which she not only had to survive herself, but from which she was expected to pay the wages of five servants and all the household bills.

The marriage began to crack, but further humiliations were in store for Florence. The young wife, so pretty and spirited, now found out that her husband had been keeping a string of mistresses, one of whom had borne him five children. In those Victorian times there was little Florence could do except keep up the lie that all was well for friends and associates while fuming in private. Her perfect life of love and wealth lay in tatters.

The emotional strain must have been torture, as Florence tried to cope with an arsenic-addled, unstable, philandering husband under the threat of financial ruin. It is perhaps no great surprise then that when temptation arrived, Florence gave in quickly, seeking solace—and revenge—first in the arms of one her husband's brothers and then with a man named Alfred Brierley. The latter had been a guest at one of the Maybrick's popular dance evenings, which they continued to hold in order to keep up appearances. Florence became quickly besotted with him. Young, attractive, and healthy, Brierley was everything her husband was not.

Sad at home, and thinking herself deeply in love, Florence threw caution to the wind and booked a room at Flatman's Hotel in London under the name of Mr and Mrs Thomas Maybrick for herself and her new lover. Telling her husband that she was visiting a sick aunt for a few days, Florence joined Brierley at the hotel, and together they enjoyed several days of illicit pleasure. For the unfortunate Florence though, even this tryst was to be tainted with disaster and betrayal. Before they parted,

Brierly confessed that he had fallen for another woman. As she later recalled, "He said he could not marry me and that rather than face the disgrace of discovery he would blow his brains out. I then had such revulsion of feeling I said we must end our intimacy at once."

Meanwhile, in her eagerness to be with Brierly, Florence had forgotten that the hotel was a regular haunt of her husband's cotton-trading associates. It didn't take long for news of his wife's adultery to reach Maybrick's ears, and in those hypocritical times his fury wasn't lessened by guilt over his own frequent betrayals.

It seems that Florence soon got over her problem with Brierley. Soon after Maybrick saw his wife talking to her lover at the 1889 Grand National horse race at the Aintree course near Liverpool. And the romantic pair displayed every sign of be a happy couple. Humiliated and enraged, Maybrick tore into his wife when the couple returned home to Battlecrease House and a loud and violent row ensued. Maybrick punched his wife and ripped her dress. As she staggered away, he threatened divorce before storming out of the house— presumably into the arms of one of his mistresses.

Servants later reported that after the argument Florence appeared unusually calm. Serene even. One maid also recollected that it was at this time she had noticed that Mrs Maybrick had begun soaking large quantities of flypapers in arsenic in her room. These she had purchased during two visits to the local chemists. Florence assured the maid that she had heard that the resulting mixture made an excellent treatment for the skin and ensured a pale complexion.

BELOW: Liverpool cotton merchant James Maybrick, who died from arsenic poisoning.

ABOVE: Florence Maybrick making her statement to the Liverpool Court during her trial for the murder of her husband James Maybrick.

If Florence's mental state was already crumbling, the next calamity to befall her may have finally pushed her over the edge. She visited Brierley again, hoping to win back his affections after their tender moments at Aintree, but the young man told her that their affair was over for good.

James Maybrick became ill—quite genuinely this time—on the morning of April 27th – just over a month after his row with Florence. A Dr. Humphreys was quickly called to Battlecrease House, but could find no obvious cause for his patient's symptoms of vomiting, numbness in his limbs, and shivering. Vexed by Florence's revelation that her husband had been taking arsenic and strychnine and Maybrick's fevered

denials, the doctor diagnosed chronic dyspepsia and left, hoping that this was just another instance of Maybrick's hypochondria.

Maybrick did not recover. Two days after the doctor's first visit Florence again bought flypapers at the local chemist, and soon after her husband's condition deteriorated. Still perplexed, Dr. Humphreys prescribed the Victorian cure-all tincture of white arsenic and carbonate of potash.

The previously popular Mrs Maybrick had by now become the subject of scandalous gossip. Word of the couple's sexually tangled lives had leaked out and it had become common knowledge that Florence was desperately unhappy in her marriage. The ever-fickle Brierley now also reappeared on the scene and, with neither he nor Florence making much effort at secrecy,

ABOVE: Portraits of Florence and James Maybrick taken from an 1889 edition of the British illustrated newspaper The Graphic.

it soon became widely believed that Florence was poisoning Maybrick in order to marry her young lover. Suspicions were further aroused when the Maybrick's nanny, Alice, intercepted a letter from Florence to her reinstated lover. Dated May 8, it read, "Dearest, since my return I have been nursing my M day and night. He is sick unto death."

The nanny passed the letter to Maybrick's brother Edwin, who in turn showed it to another brother, Michael. Together they rushed to Battlecrease House and promptly gave orders that Florence was not to be left alone in her husband's room. Nevertheless, her suspicious behavior continued. One servant later told police that Florence had been seen replacing the medicine in her husband's bottle with a different liquid, while another overheard Maybrick gasping out an accusation of poisoning to his wife.

James Maybrick died on May 11. The circumstances of his death were found to be suspicious and an immediate postmortem was called for. It revealed that Maybrick had been swallowing a particularly toxic irritant such as arsenic. On hearing the results, Florence fainted away and was taken to her own bed, where she would remain for several days, listening as the police searched her home for evidence of a crime.

They found letters from Brierley and enough arsenic to kill as many as 50 people. But what appeared to be an open and shut case was complicated by other evidence. Maybrick had been buying an arsenic-based tonic on a regular basis for 18 months and appeared to be long-term user. Nevertheless, Florence was arrested on suspicion of murder.

On July 31, 1889, she appeared at Liverpool Crown Court before Justice James Fitzjames Stephen charged with murder. Her defence put forward the argument that Maybrick's addiction to arsenic and other similar drugs meant that large traces of the poisons would be found in his body. Regular intake would have a cumulative affect, Florence's lawyers argued. Further, though Florence's marriage had been all but over, she had little motive for murdering her husband. The financial provision Maybrick had made for her and the children in his will was small, and Florence would have been better off legally separated from him.

It was undoubtedly a strong case, and perhaps that was just as Florence planned. However, it was not strong enough to convince the jury. In the end, it was Florence's last letter to her lover that condemned her.

She had hinted that Maybrick would not live through his latest attack of illness, and it looked as though she was predicting his death with certain knowledge that it would soon arrive. It is also likely that Florence's adultery played a part in setting the disapproving Victorian jury against her.

Without her husband or her lover, who had fled to escape the scandal, Florence Maybrick was found guilty of murder on August 7, 1889, after the jury had deliberated for just 38 minutes. She was sentenced to death, and an execution set for August 26. However, many people in both Britain and America believed that the evidence against Florence was too slight to warrant capital punishment, and petitions flooded in. Just three days before Florence schedule's execution, news came from the Home Office that her sentence should be changed to life imprisonment. Her life may have been saved, but it was much less than a full pardon. The Home Secretary declared, "The evidence clearly establishes that Mrs Maybrick administered poison to her husband with intent to murder, but there is ground for reasonable doubt whether the arsenic so administered was in fact the cause of his death." His was to be the last word. No court of appeal existed at that time, and Florence Maybrick was taken down to serve 14 years in prison.

She was released in 1904 and returned to America where she wrote a book, My Fifteen Lost Years, and then became a recluse living in a remote cabin. She never saw her children again and died alone on October 23, 1941. Among her few possessions was a family Bible. Pressed between its pages was a scrap of paper bearing directions in faded ink of how soaking flypapers in certain substances made a useful beauty treatment.

Ruby McCollum

The murder of senator-elect Dr LeRoy Adams by African-American Ruby McCollum is not notable for being an out of the ordinary crime of passion. What makes it stomach-turning is the treatment that Ruby received purely because she was black.

Senator-elect Dr LeRoy Adams of Live Oak, Florida, was not a pleasant man. Although married, he kept a mistress and would later be revealed as a thief and fraudster. But one lover wasn't enough for him. Adams also forced his sexual attentions on Ruby McCollum, who was already a wife and mother.

Theirs was not so much an affair as an exercise of his power over her, and time and again she submitted to his sexual demands, eventually giving birth to a child she insisted was the doctor's.

When she fell pregnant for a second time, it tipped her over the edge. She asked Adams to arrange a termination, and he refused, telling her to keep the baby though offering no financial support. On the morning of August 3, 1952, Ruby shot and killed Adams at his office.

The jury at Ruby's trial was made up of white men and from the start it was obvious that she was not going to get a fair hearing. The court simply did not want to know about an African-American woman having an affair with a powerful married white man. Neither were they interested in the fact that she had begged him to arrange the abortion of their second child and been turned down. They also turned a deaf ear to the fact that Adams had another mistress. As far as they were concerned a black woman who killed a white man deserved the full penalty of the law, and the circumstances were irrelevant. Ruby was duly convicted of first degree murder on December 20, 1952, and sentenced to death.

Fortunately for her, the judge had made a significant mistake. He had not been present during the jury's inspection of the crime scene, and on July 20, 1954, the Florida Supreme Court declared the trial invalid and overturned Ruby's sentence.

At a retrial, Ruby pleaded insanity. Court-appointed physicians declared her mentally incompetent and she was incarcerated for 20 years in the Florida State Hospital for mental patients at Chattahoochee. She served the full term.

After her first conviction, Ruby's plight was followed in a series of articles written for the Pittsburgh Courier by journalist Zora Neale Hurston. Entitled *The Life Story of Ruby McCollum*, the pieces ran during the early months of 1953. They put forward the case that Ruby's trial sounded the death knell for "paramour rights" in the south of the United States. The presumed right of a white man to take a black woman as his concubine was finally at an end.

Ruby, the tragic victim of pre-civil rights America, died of a stroke on May 23, 1992, at the New Horizon Rehabilitation Center. She was 82.

Charlotte McHugh

Dull-witted, lazy, and promiscuous, Charlotte had the good fortune to marry a man who worked hard to keep her and their children. Sadly, she saw her hard-working husband only as a meal ticket and—when she fell in love with a romantic gypsy—the husband became an obstacle.

Charlotte McHugh was born in Ireland in the early 20th century and by the time she had grown in to a young woman it was obvious that she enjoyed flirting and tempting men far more than working. Nevertheless, her sexual allure snared her a husband; a soldier named Frederick Bryant. They married when he was 25, and she 19, and moved to the rural English county of Somerset in the early 1920s. There, Charlotte would eventually give birth to five children, though there were always doubts about how many Bryant had fathered. Even so, he did his best to house and feed his idle, cheating wife and the growing number of children that filled the house. In 1925, Bryant was given a job as a farm laborer in Over Compton, near Yeovil, Dorset. Along with a small wage, Bryant was also given use of a cottage as part of his earnings.

While her husband worked hard, Charlotte existed only for pleasure. Numerous men were only too pleased to satisfy her sexual cravings, and some of them were even tempted into her marital bed while Bryant was out in the fields. Among her lovers was a gypsy horse-dealer named Leonard Parsons to whom Charlotte was particularly attracted. On the pretext of earning a little extra money for the family, she installed him in the house as a lodger in 1933 and when he wasn't out on the open road or with his own wife and four children, the affair flourished.

Having gotten away with so much for so long, and now deeply infatuated with her gypsy lover, Charlotte threw caution to the winds. She now paraded Parsons around the local village on her arm as if he were her husband and not Bryant, and made no secret at all of her passionate, and carnal, love for him.

The conservative rural community was shocked. Charlotte's behavior cost her husband his job, and the couple were forced to leave their cottage and move to Coombe, near Sherbourne. Charlotte did not give up Parsons, however. She was determined to have him at any cost, and the best solution she could think of was to remove her husband from the scene permanently.

In May of 1935, Bryant became ill with stomach pains. The doctor did not suspect poison and diagnosed gastroenteritis and he recovered, only to fall ill again on December 11. He was obviously a sturdy man for once again he survived the poisoning. Eleven days later though his mysterious stomach pains returned, and this time Charlotte had upped the dose. Bryant became violently ill and died within hours. When his body was examined, four grains of undissolved arsenic were found in his stomach.

The police searched the Bryant's home where the ever-lazy Charlotte hadn't even bothered to conceal her crime properly. A tin that had contained arsenical weed killer was found in a pile of rubbish and traces of arsenic were discovered on shelves in the house and in one of her coat pockets.

Charlotte Bryant was arrested on February 10, 1936, and charged with the murder of her husband. Her trial opened at Dorset Assizes, Dorchester, in front of Mr Justice MacNaghten, on Wednesday May 27, 1936, and it was reported that the unintelligent Charlotte seemed barely able to follow the proceedings. During her defense she protested that she had been on very good terms with her husband, but numerous witnesses drew a more accurate picture of her marriage for the jury and on May 30, 1936, Charlotte was found guilty of murder and sentenced to hang. She was executed, aged just 33, at Exeter Prison on July 15.

Candy Montgomery

Candy Montgomery's savage axe attack on the wife of her former sex partner left two children motherless. There was no question that someone else might have committed the terrible crime; Candy admitted it, but the jury was convinced by her claims of a psychological disorder and, amazingly, she was allowed to walk free.

Unlike many people who find themselves caught up in extramarital affairs, Candy Montgomery was not swept off her feet in raw passion but deliberately set out to find a lover. The Texas housewife was bored with her husband of seven years and wanted some excitement. In her own words, she said she was looking for "fireworks'. The man she chose was computer software engineer Allan Gore whom Candy met at a church volleyball game. Soon afterward, she pulled Gore aside and asked him straight out if he was interested in having an affair. It would be dangerous as both Candy and Gore's families attended the same Methodist church , but the two reached an agreement: they would sleep with each other, but make sure not to fall in love. On December 12, 1978, Candy and Gore met for their first sexual encounter. It did not produce the fireworks that she had been hoping for and Gore, too, was unenthusiastic. They tried again on numerous occasions, but after 10 months the affair fizzled out.

On June 13, 1980, Gore kissed his wife Betty goodbye and left home for a business trip to Minnesota. Betty had their baby daughter, Bethany, at home, and their other child—six-year-old Alisa—stayed with the Montgomerys, with whose daughter, Jenny, she had become good friends. Gore spoke to Betty again just before his flight departed, but he became concerned when she failed to answer his frequent phone calls later that afternoon. He began phoning friends and neighbors, asking whether they had heard from Betty. One of them, Richard Parker, went to the door and called for Betty, but saw nothing. He told Gore that he had found nothing amiss.

Next, Gore called the Montgomery home to check on Alisa. Candy said she had visited the Gore's house at 10am during a quick break from Bible School. Betty was fine, Candy insisted. But by the evening, with his calls still going unanswered, Gore was becoming increasingly frantic. From his hotel room in St. Paul, he called neighbors again and pressed them to go inside.

Parker returned to the house with two other men. The front door was unlocked and, this time, they went inside. Parker immediately heard whimpers. He followed the sound and found little Bethany in a bedroom. The men then noticed crimson smears on an upright freezer in a utility room adjacent to the garage. They peeked around the corner, and there on the vinyl floor lay the body of Betty Gore. Her yellow top and pink shorts were soaked red, and blood had pooled and

congealed beneath her body. The men's attention was drawn to the right side of her face, which had been disfigured by what appeared to be a large gunshot exit wound. Her left eye stared blankly into the distance.

Almost immediately, the telephone began ringing. It was Gore. Parker gave him the bad news, saying, "The baby is fine. But Betty's dead. She's been shot. It looks a like a suicide."

It wasn't suicide, and it wasn't a gunshot wound either, as the police discovered. Under questioning, Gore at first denied ever cheating on his wife. Then he admitted his affair with Candy Montgomery, whose bloody fingerprint had been left at the murder scene. Candy was taken in and soon crumbled during interrogation. In her version of events Candy told detectives that Betty Gore had confronted her about her affair and on learning the truth had come at Candy with an axe. Candy was hit but not badly. She grabbed the axe from her friend's hands and in a blind frenzy swung it at Betty's face, not once but dozens of times.

During the trial, Candy's defense team told the jury that she suffered psychological problems that stemmed from a troubled childhood. It was also said that she had an aversion to blood, the sight of which brought on violent feelings. The defense's final argument was that Candy acted in self-defense when Betty attacked her. It was enough for the jury, if not for observers at the court. A verdict of not guilty was pronounced, and Candy was set free with cries of "murderer" ringing in her ears. A newspaper summed up popular feeling with the headline, "Woman Hacked 41 Times in Self-Defense, Jury Rules."

Alice & Thomas Morsby

Although she adopted the surname of her lover, Alice Morsby was actually the wife of Thomas Ardern, the mayor of Faversham, in the English county of Kent. In 1550, Arden was murdered by Alice who wanted to inherit his fortune and begin a new life with the man she adored.

The household arrangements of Thomas Ardern and his wife were more than a little unconventional for their time in Tudor England. That fact that Ardern had married Alice for her connections and money rather than love was not so remarkable, but he appears to have been either an unusually understanding man or totally in thrall to his tempestuous wife. He did not object when Alice took Thomas Morsby, a young tailor, to her bed and even appears to have been on excellent terms with his wife's lover. The mayor often invited Morsby to stay at the family home while he was away on business and enjoyed Morsby's company at the gaming table when he was at home. The official record of the case says that Alice "did not only keep Moresby carnally in her own house, but also fed him with delicate meats and sumptuous apparel, all which things Ardern did know well and willfully did permit."

Although she enjoyed the almost constant attentions of her lover, Alice was still dissatisfied. She objected to being one man's wife and another man's mistress. In 1550, after years of a dull marriage and desperate to be free of the husband whose very existence prevented her from marrying Moresby, Alice decided Ardern had to die. The first attempts of the fledgling murderess involved a poisoned crucifix and poisoned pictures. These weapons failed.

Next, Alice appealed to her lover for help. While Morsby refused to initiate the murder himself he gave in to Alice's demands and together they plotted Ardern's demise. Others were taken into their confidence: their servants Michael Saunderson and Elizabeth Stafford, Moresby's sister Cecily, and two men of the town, John Green and George Bradshaw. The latter was dispatched

to Calais, France, with a mission to find willing assassins. He returned with two cut-throats called Loosebagg and Black Will.

As was their custom, Mayor Ardern and Thomas Morsby were sitting at the gaming table when the murderers struck. Black Will had been hidden in the house by Alice. The hired killer rushed into the room, threw a handkerchief around Ardern's neck, and strangled him. As the mayor's life faded, Morsby took up an iron and crushed his skull then brutally cut his love rival's throat.

The murderers, Moresby's sister, and the servants dragged the body to a nearby field. Black Will was paid the sum of eight pounds and immediately disappeared with his accomplice, Loosebagg. But the inept killers had failed to notice it was snowing and did not even bury the body. The next day Ardern's corpse was discovered, and investigators had no difficulty tracing footprints and bloodstains across the field back to the house. Everyone involved in the murder, with the exception of Loosebagg, who was never found, and John Green, were arrested, tried, and found guilty. Alice and her maid Elizabeth were burned alive at Canterbury on March 14, 1551. Morsby and his sister were hanged at Smithfield in London. George Bradshaw was hung in chains at Faversham. Black Will was burned on a scaffold. John Green was later apprehended in Cornwall and was returned to Faversham where he was also hanged in chains.

Augusta Nack and Martin Thorn

The 36-year-old Augusta Nack was an unlicensed midwife who also ran a boarding house—appropriately in Hell's Kitchen, New York City. A married woman, her husband had long since tired of her and after he departed Augusta took numerous lovers. The latest and most regular was German masseur Willie Guldensuppe, though when he went away on a trip, she could not resist the opportunity to introduce a little variety in her bed. Augusta decided that one of her lodgers, the youthful Martin Thorn, would suit her just fine.

Unfortunately for the couple, Guldensuppe returned unexpectedly in the middle of Augusta's seduction scene. Driven to a mad rage by seeing his lover in a state

of undress and in the arms of another man, the German furiously attacked Thorn. Beaten half to death, the barber was hospitalized.

While he slowly recovered, Thorn's thoughts turned to revenge: On June 26, 1897, parts of Willie Guldensuppe began bobbing to the surface of New York's East River wrapped in distinctive red and gold oilcloth decorated

BELOW: William Randolph Hearst, the press magnate whose reporters helped to reveal the sordid details of the murder of Willie Guldensupper.

with flowers. His upper torso and arms were found in one part of the river, his lower torso in another, and his legs in yet another. The head, which—as the court later heard—had been coated in plaster, was missing. But as the coroners worked to piece the body together, they noticed another small part wasn't there: a four-inch square of skin had been cut from the corpse's chest. It would play a crucial part in identifying the body for investigations eventually led to the Turkish baths where Guldensuppe had worked, and his colleagues were able to identify the body from an abscess on one finger as well as telling investigators that the German had had a tattoo in exactly the place the flesh was missing.

Meanwhile, the press were covering the case avidly. Sensing a sensational story, the newspaper magnate William Randolph Hearst assigned a large group of reporters from his Journal newspaper to the case, and soon they were making breakthroughs. First, they found Augusta, who oozed guilt when the pack of reporters quizzed her. She had withdrawn a large amount of cash from her bank account and had made enquiries about leaving for Europe on a steamship. The journalists also discovered where the oilskin had been bought, and by whom. Thorn was arrested soon afterward as he tried to slip across the border into Canada.

While Thorn denied everything, Augusta confessed under questioning. She told police that she had become tired of her German lover's numerous affairs while demanding that she remain faithful and that she had lured Guldensuppe to a farm cottage on the promise of sex. It was there that Thorn had taken his own bloody revenge.

Hearst's reporters soon tracked down the Long Island farm where the owner said a couple matching Thorn and Augusta's description had rented a cabin.

The farmer said he had noticed how all his ducks had suddenly turned pink while they had stayed there! They had been bathing in wastewater flowing from a pipe connected to the cottage. It was later discovered that Thorn had shot Guldensuppe, stabbed him, and cut him up in the bathtub.

So graphic were the details of the murder that during the trial a sensitive juror fainted. Augusta and her young lover were both convicted of murder, but while Augusta was sentenced to 15 years (serving nine) in Auburn Prison, Thorn met his death in the electric chair on August 1, 1898, at Sing Sing.

Fernado Ortega

A short and simple story, the case of Fernado Ortega perfectly captures the despair that accompanies humiliation and rejection. His was a sad, but typical, crime of passion.

Garage owner Fernado Ortega of Guadalajara, Mexico, knew he could never have the woman he desired. She was beautiful, while he was hunchbacked and ugly. They met in 1972 when Maria Pineda became Ortega's nurse, administering injections and generally caring for her patient who suffered from chronic tuberculosis alongside his physical deformity. And as the weeks passed Ortega's attraction to the pretty woman grew into an love.

That Maria did not return his feelings was obvious, but still he tried to explain how he felt. When she rejected him, Ortega's love turned to despair and desolation at his own physical shortcomings. Perhaps we could have felt pity for him, but for the fact that

Ortega decided that if he could not have Maria then he could not bear for her to be happy with anyone else. At knifepoint he forced her to drink deadly cyanide and laid her expiring body on his bed. As she lay dying, Ortega then he drank from the bottle himself and lay down beside her to await death.

The horrific scene was discovered by Francisco Pineda, a car mechanic who worked for Ortega and who—tragically—was also Maria's stepfather. His first thought was that Ortega had overpowered her so that he might rape her, but though Maria's skirt had slipped up to her thighs, Ortega had not wanted to violate the woman he loved. There was no sign that he had sexually abused her at all.

Pauline Yvonne Parker
& Juliet Marion Hulme

The case of two teenage lesbian lovers who murdered one of their parents shocked New Zealand in the mid-1950s. The two girls were so desperate not to be parted from one another that they were prepared to kill to stop it happening.

ABOVE: Juliet Marion Hulme (left) and her friend Pauline Yvonne Parker after being remanded in custody charged with the murder of Pauline's mother Honara Mary Parker.

Pauline Parker and Ju... came from different... Pauline's father managed a fi... while her mother, Honora Parker, took in lodgers to make e... meet; Juliet's father was a famo... British physicist and her mother a... marriage counselor. Nevertheless, the two young girls were drawn to each other, perhaps due to their similarities in temperament. Pauline's education had not been of the highest standard, but she was a gifted and imaginative writer, and Juliet was deeply sensitive to the point of being psychologically fragile.

Over time, what started out as a friendship became much, much more. The two adolescent girls—Pauline was 15, Juliet 16—began to explore their sexuality with one another and quickly became passionate lovers. As Juliet would later say, when they were together it was "better than heaven." Unfortunately, events were conspiring to bring their relationship to an end. Juliet's marriage-counselor mother divorced her father, and the young girl was deeply traumatized when she caught her mother in bed with a new man. Soon after, her father announced that he was returning to Britain to take up a new post, and Juliet would be sent to live with relatives in South Africa where it was hoped her health would improve.

Both girls were devastated at the idea of being separated, but Honora Parker made no secret of her relief. She had grown suspicious of their friendship and the strange hold Juliet had over her daughter, so when Pauline begged to be allowed to go to South Africa too, she refused. In doing so she became the focus of the girls' frustration

If Pauline was orphaned, they reasoned, there ~~e~~ no-one to stop her joining Juliet in South ~~~~ As Pauline wrote in her diary on February 13, ~~,~~ "Why could mother not die? Dozens of people ~~~~ dying, thousands are dying every day. So why not ~~~~other and father too?" It would be one of the many diary entries that eventually helped convict her.

On June 22, not long before Juliet was due to leave, Honora Parker took the two girls to Victoria Park for tea and cakes. After the treat, the three strolled in the park and when they reached a secluded spot, Mrs Parker bent over to pick up a stone that had attracted her attention. As she did a stocking loaded with a brick crashed into her skull. Over and over, the teenage girls took it in turns to beat Pauline's mother to death. And when they were sure that she was gone, they ran back to the tea kiosk, screaming for help and crying, "Mummy's been hurt."

Police found the stocking and brick close by Honora Parker's body and the two girls were arrested. Both admitted that they had they had helped in the grisly task of killing Mrs Parker, and both were found equally responsible. After a sensational trial unlike any New Zealand had ever seen, the two girls were found guilty of murder on August 29, 1954, and—in view of their ages—sentenced to five years in prison each with the added condition that when they were released they could never see each other again.

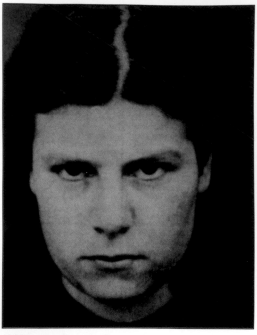

ABOVE: A New Zealand police mug shot of Pauline Parker, who was convicted with her best friend Juliet Hulme for the murder of her mother in 1954.

Alpna Patel

When Alpna Patel was married to a man she hardly knew, she didn't realize that along with a husband she would be getting a father-in-law who wanted to control every detail of her life. When she was forced to sleep in his basement while her new husband worked 500 miles away, she became desperate to get out of her appalling situation.

Alpna was 29 and her soon-to-be husband 26 when their marriage was arranged for them in 1998. Although they were both American, their families stuck rigidly to the rules of their homeland's culture and during the "courtship" the couple were strictly chaperoned during meetings and the brief dates they were allowed. The traditional wedding was an extravagant affair and afterward the couple, finally alone together, went to Disneyworld to enjoy a honeymoon during which they could get to know each other. As Viresh Patel would

now begin to discover, his new wife had a reputation for being "moody" and "temperamental."

It didn't take long for the marriage to begin to disintegrate. Back home from their brief vacation, Alpna found that her new father-in-law had strong ideas about how the young couple's lives should be run and as head of the family he was determined to implement them. Alpna was allowed to continue her work as a dentist at a local hospital in Buffalo, New York, but was told she had to live in the basement of her in-laws house and now needed to submit to her father-in-law's will in all aspects of her life. She even needed to seek his permission before going out with friends. Her husband, meanwhile, was to continue as a surgical resident in Baltimore, where he had an apartment that would become their married home on the occasions they spent time together.

For Alpna, the situation was intolerable and in March 1999, it came to a head. When her husband made a brief appearance at his parents' house, Alpna confronted him and a vicious argument was overheard by Viresh's sister. A day later a scowling Alpna argued with him again in the driveway. On March 23, 1999, Alpna Patel dropped another sister-in-law, Beena, off at school. As a court would later hear she seemed in a good mood and was even "giggly." She made no mentions of her plans for the rest of the day, but after Beena was delivered to school, she drove to the airport and took a plane to Baltimore.

When Baltimore police arrived at the Patels' one bedroom apartment the next day, they found Alpna sitting at the kitchen table—she was covered in blood. In the bedroom was the body of her husband, his jugular and carotid artery slashed with a knife that had been part of a set given to the couple as a wedding gift.

In court Alpna Patel claimed the killing had been self defense, stating that she and her husband had discussed the problems with their marriage, after which they had decided to sleep on it. She had awoken two hours later to find Viresh straddling her and pointing a black-handled steak knife at her chest. She told the court that she had managed to knock him off her and in the ensuing struggle for the knife, her husband was killed.

Alpna was acquitted of first degree murder at her first trial and the jury could not agree on the charge of second degree murder. At a second trial, in September 2000 she was given a three-year sentence for manslaughter. She served 13 months and was given credit for three more spent in custody during the trial. She was released in February 2002.

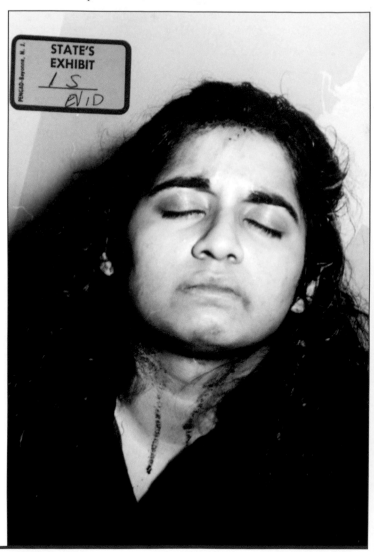

BELOW: A photo of Alpna Patel, 26, taken by Baltimore police after she was brought to the police station for questioning in connection with the murder of her husband.

STATE'S EXHIBIT 1S EVID

PENGAD-Bayonne, N. J.

ABOVE: Alpna Patel (right) with assistant attorney Lynn Williamson walking from court in Baltimore, during her trial.

Nan Patterson

Sex, adultery, and blackmail—the sensational 1905 murder trials of the beautiful young dancer and performer Nan Patterson had it all. And though the evidence against her was overwhelming, still she walked free, saved from the death penalty by her looks and an air of innocence that came easily to a professional actress.

The wealthy bookmaker **Caesar Young** died of a gunshot wound in the back of a horse-drawn hansom cab on the way to meet his wife at the New York docks where the couple were due to take a ship, bound for an extended tour of Europe. With him was another passenger; Nan Patterson, a young actress with whom Young had been conducting an illicit two-year affair. The lovers had met to say their farewells before Young's departure. They had also marked the occasion with a drinking spree.

As the only other person in the cab, Nan was arrested immediately, and it looked to prosecutors like an open and shut case. But when the case came to court and the details of the affair began trickling out, the press went wild and public support quickly surged around the actress. Nan Patterson, it was reported, had met Young two years earlier on a train to California. Despite her youth she was already married, as was he, but Nan was dazzled by the rich older man and the pair embarked on a passionate affair. As time went on Young gave Nan the money to divorce her husband, promising that he, too, would soon split from his wife. While she waited, he lavished his young mistress with expensive gifts and money. As is so often the case though, Young's divorce never materialized, and documentary evidence was produced that showed Nan had recently begun trying to blackmail her sugar daddy. Matters had come to a head in the back of the cab, and ended with Young slumped dead in his seat.

Nan denied all charges, testifying that Young had killed himself because she had ended their relationship, but the evidence continued to mount. The jury heard that on the day of Young's death, Nan's brother had pawned jewelry and used the cash to buy a gun. Still, the actress protested her innocence. The trial ended with a hung jury.

A second trial was convened with the press again feeding an insatiable public hunger for every tiny detail. The sheer volume of sympathetic, colorful newspaper articles meant that the public remained staunchly on the side of the accused. Nan maintained her plea of not guilty and she and her defense team played on her youth and saintly appearance for all it was worth. Her lawyer at one point declared, "What is there against this girl? She went on the stage, but it was to make an honest living. She met Young when she was but 19 years old. Who was the stronger of the pair?" When the trial ended, the New York Times reported that the closing scenes were "arousing public interest to a degree almost unprecedented in the history of criminal cases in New York."

The trial ended on June 3, 1905, with another hung jury unable to agree a verdict. Nan Patterson spent nearly a year in jail while legal discussions rambled on and talk of a third trial fizzled out. In the end it was felt that in another trial, any jury would base its decision on newspaper reports even though the evidence against her was so strong. Eventually, a court set her free. Nan walked out of the building to be welcomed by a cheering throng of supporters.

Queen Elizabeth I & Sir Robert Dudley

Queen Elizabeth I never married and is remembered by history as the Virgin Queen—the root of the name Virginia, which was named in her honor. However, the reality was very different. Although it remains unproven, the Queen is thought to have taken Sir Robert Dudley as a lover and conspired with him to murder his wife. The evidence against them is circumstantial but compelling.

Queen Elizabeth I never married and is remembered by history as the Virgin Queen—the root of the name Virginia, which was named in her honor. However, the reality was very different. Although it remains unproven, the Queen is thought to have taken Sir Robert Dudley as a lover and conspired with him to murder his wife. The evidence against them is circumstantial but compelling.

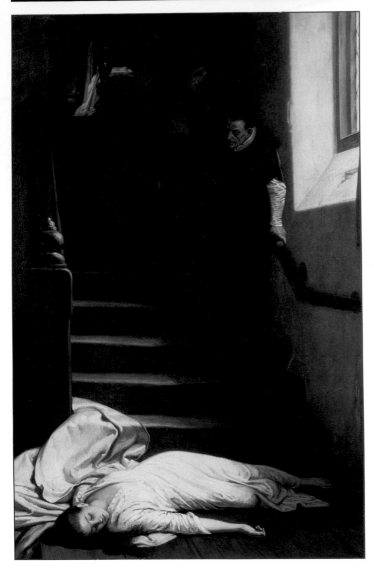

ABOVE: An 1879 painting by William Frederick Yeames depicting the death of Amy Robsart.

It is beyond doubt that Sir Robert Dudley was a philanderer and fiercely ambitious, yet his love for Queen Elizabeth appears to have been genuine. He was her constant companion and confidant for more than 30 years. After the death of his wife, Amy Robsart, he turned down numerous offers of marriage, including to a number of foreign princesses and one to Mary, Queen of Scots, which could have placed him on the thrones of both England and Scotland. All this he sacrificed in order to remain by his queen's side. For her part, Elizabeth heaped honors and riches upon her favorite companion. Indeed, the court of the day was inflamed with gossip regarding the pair, and it was widely believed that there was an love affair between them and that they would be married if and when Amy died.

Amy was the fly in the ointment of the Dudley's love for the queen. Although theirs appears to have been a love match, made when Amy was just 18, Dudley and his wife had been leading separate lives since Elizabeth I had come to the throne, and Dudley began to spend more time at court.

On September 4, 1560, the Queen had a strange—and rather suspicious—conversation with the Spanish ambassador during which she said that Amy Robsart was "dead or nearly so." In fact, it was widely known that Amy had a "malady in one of her breasts," which was possibly cancer. Nevertheless, it is suspicious that only four days later Amy was indeed dead. On September 8, she allowed

all her servants to take the day off to go to Abingdon Fair in Oxfordshire. When they returned, they found her at the foot of the stairs with a fractured skull.

While her death was officially deemed to have been a tragic accident, whispers soon circulated. There was a belief that Dudley and the Queen had organized Amy's murder between them; a belief that was strengthened when one of Dudley's staff was reported to have been part of the plot. It is possible, however, that such rumors were started for political reasons. There were some members of the royal court whose interests would have damaged by a marriage between Dudley and the queen. If so, the rumor-mongers won the day. Perhaps fearing to further inflame the scandal, Elizabeth and Dudley never married.

LEFT: A painting of Queen Elizabeth I of England by Flemish artist Steven van der Meulen.

RIGHT: A picture of Robert Dudley, Earl of Leicester, from around the time of Amy Robsart's suspicious death.

James Stewart Ramage

Fearing a violent reaction from a husband who had a history of lashing out when crossed, Julie Ramage made a careful plan to leave him as gently as possible, but she was only delaying the inevitable. Fourteen months later he took her body out to Australia's Kings Lake National Park and buried it.

To all appearances **James and Julie Ramage** had a perfectly normal middle-class family life. They owned a beautiful home in Melbourne, Australia, as well as a holiday house and the three cars in the garage, and had a very healthy bank balance. But Julie lived in fear of her 43-year-old husband and told friends that he might "lose it" one day. Nevertheless, keen to provide a stable family environment for their children, she endured his temper and occasional outbursts of violence for 20 years before finally deciding to leave.

In order to let him down gently Julie enlisted the help of friends and family. Avoiding a face-to-face confrontation, she left the family home while he was on a business trip abroad, leaving him with a letter that suggested they might get back together after a while. As she explained to friends, he was not ready to face the truth. The letter was a moving appeal for peace between them. She wrote, "If you do care for me, please let me go without a horrible fight, for the kids' sake. Let's prove to them that we are better than all the other separated couples that we know. I could hate you so much for some of the things you have done and said to me over the years, but I also understand that you are a good person and that you work hard and, most importantly, that you love our kids very much."

However, Julie had no intention of ever going back to her husband and before long had met a new man, Laurence Webb. Meanwhile, James Ramage seethed with anger at the desertion. On July 21, 2003, the violent confrontation that Julie had worked so hard to avoid exploded. Having regained her confidence and made furious during and argument, Julie told her husband that sex with him had repulsed her and that she should have left him 10 years earlier.

Ramage's response was terrible. He strangled his wife then put her body in his car, packed a change of clothes, and gathered up Julie's handbag and mobile. He then drove out to Kings Lake National Park and on the way called his wife's work and mobile numbers as if he were looking for her. At the park Ramage dug a hole and put Julie's body in it, then covered the newly turned soil with branches and bracken. A few meters away he dug a second hole, where he buried incriminating evidence, including the bedding that he had used to wrap her body.

Julie's disappearance didn't go unnoticed for long, and Ramage's long history of violence and the calls he had made after killing his wife immediately brought him under suspicion. Nevertheless, at his trial—which began on December 9, 2004, at Victoria's Supreme Court—he made full use of Julie's own outburst of temper to claim that he had been provoked. Although the prosecution argued that she would have been too afraid of Ramage to actually speak to him in that way, after 20 years of taking his verbal and physical abuse, Julie's alleged final snap of anger at her husband saved him from a murder charge. The jury found that he should be convicted of manslaughter. The judge, however, did not appear to be quite so convinced. Sentencing Ramage to a maximum 11 years in prison, Justice Robert Osborn said, "The killing was done with murderous intent and savage brutality and where, although the jury has accepted the reasonable possibility of provocation, it is apparent that such provocation was not objectively extreme."

Julie Ramage's mother, Patricia Garrett, perhaps summed it up best. Describing her son-in-law's prison sentence as pathetic, she said, "Any woman that's in a relationship where she feels threatened, I tell her not to stay for the sake of the children. Get out. My daughter stayed for the children, and she's paid the ultimate price. She's dead."

Dr. Buck Ruxton

The murder of Isabella Ruxton at the hands of her common-law husband was a classic crime of passion. Incensed at her cheating on him, Ruxton strangled and stabbed his wife to death, then turned his killing fury on a maid who had the misfortune to walk in and witness the act. The only thing missing was Isabella's guilt, for she was a faithful wife and completely innocent of the accusations he made against her.

A doctor of Persian ancestry, Buck Ruxton's jealousy of his wife was common knowledge among their circle of friend and acquaintances in Lancaster, England. In fact, he had become so suspicious of Isabella that when she took a trip to Edinburgh with some friends he secretly followed her, certain

ABOVE: Dr Buck Ruxton, who was convicted of the murder of his wife, Isabella Ruxton, and his housemaid, Mary Jane Rogerson at his home in Lancaster.

passion that violence took possession of him. He grabbed at his wife, strangled her into unconsciousness, and then stabbed her to death. During the struggle a maid, Mary Rogerson, heard Isabella's screams for help and she rushed to help, only to find Ruxton standing over the body of his wife. He immediately knew that if he were to escape punishment then Mary would have to die too and he quickly dispatched her in the same way. Then, Dr Ruxton set about concealing his crime. First he had to deal with the bodies. On September 15, 1935, two severed heads and assorted dismembered limbs were found wrapped up in copies of the Sunday Graphic newspaper.

When Mary Rogerson's parents asked after her, Ruxton told them that their rather plain and single daughter had fallen pregnant and his wife had taken her away to have an abortion. They didn't believe him and reported her missing. Meanwhile, friends and neighbors had also begun to question why Isabella Ruxton had suddenly vanished. Ruxton was well known for his temper and jealousy and the rumor that he was responsible for the killings spread like wildfire. In desperation, and eager to throw detectives off his scent, Ruxton presented himself at the police station and begged for their help in finding his wife.

Unfortunately for Ruxton, he was already the prime suspect. The new forensic sciences of fingerprinting and super-imposure (where a photograph of a victim is matched to a skull) had allowed police to identify the victims, now all they needed was the evidence to convict Ruxton. They found it in the testimony of Ruxton's cleaner, who told them that on the day the two women went missing she had arrived at the house to find it in disarray with blood-stained carpets.

Ruxton was arrested on October 13, 1935, and tried at Manchester Assizes in March 1936. The jury took just over an hour to find him guilty of murder. Although a petition to have his sentence commuted was signed by 10,000 people it failed and he was hanged at Strangeways Prison in Manchester, on May 12, 1936. A few days later his signed confession was published. It read, "I killed Mrs. Ruxton in a fit of temper because I thought she had been with a man. I was mad at the time. Mary Rogerson was present at the time. I had to kill her."

that she was having an affair with a man called Robert Edmonson who was among the group. But while his snooping didn't turn up a single scrap of evidence against her, the facts did nothing to quench the fury that was boiling within him as he followed his wife from one hotel to another, sure that she was sharing Edmonson's bed.

Isabella returned home to find her husband waiting for her. By now he had worked himself into such a

Harmohinder Kaur Sanghera

When Sair Ali got married to his 17-year-old cousin, he didn't bother to trouble his existing lover with the news. But when she finally found out that he had been cheating on her with a new wife, Harmohinder's jealousy and anger drove her to a terrible revenge.

When Sair Ali got married to his 17-year-old cousin, he didn't bother to trouble his existing lover with the news. But when she finally found out that he had been cheating on her with a new wife, Harmohinder's jealousy and anger drove her to a terrible revenge.

Harmohinder Kaur Sanghera and Sair Ali met in 2005 when she was 23, and he 25. Instantly attracted to one another they began a passionate affair, kept secret to avoid scandal among their respective communities—Harmohinder was a Sikh, Ali came from a strict Muslim family. However, completely unbeknown to Harmohinder, her lover was already betrothed to his cousin Sana, and when they were married in Pakistan Ali still did not confess.

Nevertheless, Harmohinder's suspicions were aroused when Ali's passion for seemed to cool. They no longer met so often and when they did, he seemed distant. The reason, she was later to discover, was not only did Ali have a wife but she was already four month's pregnant.

Furious that the man she loved could keep such an enormous secret from her, Harmohinder decided that if her own happiness was to be destroyed, then Ali's would be too. She told a friend that the following day she intended to confront Sana with the truth about her husband's adulterous affair and then end the relationship with him for good. But over the next 24 hours she appears to have changed her plan.

Harmohinder drove to the couple's home in Bury, Lancashire, armed with a knife and stabbed Sana to death in a frenzied attack as she lay in her bedroom. Examiners would later find 43 knife wounds on the body, among which was a deep abdomen wound that had obviously been intended to destroy the 11-week foetus of Sana's baby boy. Harmohinder then calmly climbed through a kitchen window, secured the house, and drove back to her home in Birmingham.

Like many first-time murderers, Harmohinder was quickly discovered. Her footprints were found at the scene, and proof that she had travelled to Birmingham that day was easily gathered from CCTV cameras that lined the roads she had used. She was found guilty of murder in November 2007 and sentenced to life, to serve a minimum of 14 years.

Nevertheless, Harmohinder's revenge had found its target. The cheating Sair Ali lost both his wife and child. Although no one could ever deserve the punishment that Harmohinder meted out, Ali must have known that if his own behavior had been different the crime might well have been averted. As he later said, "No one can sleep. We all have nightmares. We cannot stay in the house now. No one can go into Sana's bedroom; the door is always closed. Her clothes still hang in her wardrobe. We can't face it yet and don't feel we ever can."

Larissa Schuster

Since dubbed the "Mad Chem Chick" by the press at the time of her arrest Larissa Schuster seemed the least likely of murderers. Stout, bottle blonde, and 42 years old, she was a successful businesswoman and devoted mother. The method she chose to despatch her husband was so sickening that it shocked the United States. Her story is a complex one but perfectly illustrates what can happen when love turns to ashes.

Larissa Schuster's background gave no hints that one day she would become a murderer. She was born on a farm in Missouri and raised by parents who taught her strong Christian values. She was, as a court was to hear many years later, a "happy and normal child" with a love of animals and people.

At college, Schuster appears to have been a popular A-grade student and a star baseball player. After learning to drive she became a volunteer hospital worker. If there was a flaw in her character it was that she had expectations of others that sometimes could not be fulfilled, expectations that saw her first serious relationship end disastrously.

BELOW: Larissa Schuster listening to evidence being given at a hearing in a Los Angeles County courthouse during her trial for the murder of her husband.

Despite the painful break-up with her first boyfriend, Larissa pulled herself together and while still at college fell in love again, this time with a young man called Tim Schuster, who she met and married shortly before graduating with honors. The couple set out on a married life that was full of promise. He was a registered nurse, she a bright graduate quickly taken on to perform research for the pesticide industry by ABC Laboratories in Columbia, Missouri. In 1985, they were blessed with a daughter, Kristin, and four years later Larissa was offered the job of laboratory manager for the Pan Am airline in California. The family moved to Fresno, California, and in 1990 Larissa gave birth to their son, Tyler.

To the outside world Tim and Larissa's family life looked like the fulfilment of the American dream; they were comfortably off and regular churchgoers with a wide circle of friends. If Larissa had suffered from a lack of self-confidence in her younger years, success at work had given her a new poise. But behind closed doors, as is so often the case, the relationship was not all it seemed. Over the years, Tim Schuster had gradually begun treating his wife with more and more contempt. He belittled her efforts at her job and constantly reminded her of her poor, rural upbringing. The couple bickered and argued often, and though beneath it all Larissa still loved her husband, their house had a constant atmosphere of tension and mistrust. In court, she would later describe her home life thus: "Everything seemed fine on the surface; trying to do good and admirable things, but the problem was the interior of the marriage. It was surviving but still had problems."

In fact, the marriage was breaking down fast. The Schusters' sex life had dwindled and, unhappy at home, Larissa threw herself into work. Often tired and irritable as well as suffering

S

ABOVE: Shirley Schuster, mother of murder victim Timothy Schuster, hugging Clovis Police detective Larry Kirkhart, outside superior court, before a verdict was read in James Fagone's trial for the murder of her son.

from the constant strain of a difficult marriage, she tried to maintain some kind of order in the house by being a strict disciplinarian with the children. In turn, they developed behavior problems, something Larissa had to deal with on her own. Kristin was sent off to live with her grandparents in Missouri in a bid to give her a more settled home life.

Amazingly, in this pressured environment the Schuster's marriage struggled on for another 12 years, during which time Larissa invested much of her emotional energies into work. Eventually, she opened her own business, Central California Research Laboratories, and came to be respected as one of the top chemists in the country. Nevertheless, the unhealthy marriage had become increasingly poisonous. By now the Schusters could not even look at each other, and Larissa confided in a friend that she genuinely hated her husband. Something had to give, and Larissa finally asked Tim for a divorce.

To her surprise, he refused to even acknowledge the request, let alone move out of the family home, and the marriage limped on until Larissa noticed that her husband had started keeping a journal. Her curiosity was aroused and she sneaked a look one night to find that Tim had been writing damning entries about her emotional state and inability to care for the children or her business. He had also noted actions that could be interpreted as signs of mental problems. Larissa jumped

to the obvious conclusion—her business was doing well and Tim was preparing to wage a bitter divorce battle to take the children and as much money as possible.

After more angry scenes, Tim finally left the family home in July 2002. He was awarded custody of their son and took away every stick of furniture and every possession while Larissa was away visiting her parents and Kristin. By now, her mental state had begun to unravel. All the love she had once felt turned to a bitter loathing. She began making vicious, angry calls to her husband, up to eight times a day, calling him names, mocking his sexual performance, and telling him that he was a terrible father to their children.

The divorce dragged on. A year later the couple were still fighting over their share in Larissa's business, with Tim wanting a million dollars as a settlement. The emotional turmoil was also taking a toll on their children. In an attempt to find a little peace for them and herself, she took Tyler to visit his sister and grandparents in Missouri. Tim Schuster retaliated by calling the police and accusing his wife of kidnapping their son.

In the middle of all this confusion Larissa had found a friend and confidante. James Fagone was a young laboratory assistant. Lazy, lacking in ambition, and with a variety of personal problems of his own, it is probably a sign of her state of mind that Larissa didn't recognize immediately that he was a deeply disturbed individual. Nevertheless, he proved useful and was often at her house clearing the yard, walking the family dog, and generally helping out. Larissa found that she could talk to the young man and often, of course, their conversations revolved around her problems with the divorce and

her hatred of her husband. Fagone assured her of his own disgust at Tim Schuster and promised to help whatever the circumstances.

What finally caused Larissa to snap was a fairly trivial incident by the standards of her acrimonious marriage and divorce. She wanted to take Tyler to Disneyland and then on a visit to Missouri. Tim scuppered it. It proved to be the final straw. Now, Larissa just wanted her husband dead.

In the early hours of July 10, 2003, Fagone and Larissa went to Tim's home and fired a stun gun at him as he opened the door. They then dragged him through the house, held a chloroform-soaked rag to his mouth, and tied him up before loading him into a truck and driving him to Larissa's house. What happened next outraged the court and the American public. While

ABOVE: Judge Wayne Ellison speaking during the murder trial of Larissa Schuster in a Los Angeles County courthouse.

still alive, Tim Schuster was shoved head-first into a 55-gallon plastic barrel, then Larissa and her accomplice poured hydrochloric acid over him and sealed the barrel.

Two days later Fagone and Larissa drove the barrel to her Fresno business premises. She poured in more acid, but had trouble resealing the lid so she used a handsaw to cut off her husband's feet. However, Larissa knew that the incriminating barrel couldn't remain somewhere so obvious. She organized a storage unit and called her friend to ask him to remove it, but by that time even the deranged Fagone had had enough by now and fled the area.

Police were alerted to Tim Schuster's disappearance

when the normally obsessively punctual man failed to turn up for appointments. A search of his home quickly established that something was amiss. There was no sign of Tim, but his wallet and mobile phone remained in the house. Further enquiries led to interviews with staff at Larissa's laboratory. Investigators heard of the hatred between the couple, their multi-million dollar divorce, the custody battle, and how Larissa had often been heard to say that she wished her husband was dead. Larissa immediately became the prime suspect.

While it was already obvious to the police that they had found their killer, investigations continued. At the laboratory, staff told of how Larissa had joked that her husband's body might fit into the 55-gallon barrel. And when they went to show it to officers were surprised to find it had vanished. Another employee told them that Larissa had asked him to rent a truck and a storage unit in his name so that she might hide some property from her husband until the divorce was final. When she had returned the truck, the employee noticed blood on one of Larissa's shoes.

Over the next couple of days, police searched Larissa Schuster's home, her offices and laboratory, and the self-storage unit. They unearthed several items including blond wigs and bloody tennis shoes from Schuster's home; and Fagone's time sheets, chemical order invoices, saws, and a mop and bucket from the business. And when they opened the self-storage unit they found what remained of Tim Schuster. Partially dismembered and decomposing, the corpse was later described as "intact from only the belt buckle down."

Police arrested Fagone on July 15, 2003, and Schuster the next day. Three days later, detectives searched Fagone's home and seized receipts for a stun gun and a 14-inch cable tie, bank statements, folding buck knife, and computer equipment.

Under questioning, it immediately became apparent that Larissa's mental state was completely breaking down. One moment she expressed sickness at the atrocity she had committed on the man she once loved, the next she was desperate not to let Tyler down by missing the promised trip to Disneyland.

Fagone and Schuster first appeared in court on September 29, 2003. Then followed another hearing at Fresno County Court where the couple pleaded innocent to charges of murder with special circumstances—torture, murder during a kidnapping, lying in wait to commit murder, and murder for financial gain. The Fresno County District Attorney's Office later added a fifth special circumstance—that the pair murdered Timothy Schuster during a burglary. If convicted of the murder and any of the special circumstances, the law could impose the death penalty.

While the killers awaited trial in jail, the police and lawyers took almost three years to carefully compile their evidence and prepare for court. The case of James Fagone, by now aged 25, finally came before a judge on November 25, 2006, at Fresno County Court. The prosecution had prepared well and a judgement was reached quickly. His guilty verdict was read out on December 11. Fagone was given life imprisonment with no chance of parole on February 20, 2007. On hearing the sentence he muttered, "I humbly ask the court for your forgiveness."

The trial of Larissa Schuster began at Los Angeles County Court on October 15, 2007. Roger Nuttall, her defense lawyer, attempted to paint Larissa as a victim of circumstances, a woman who had tried her best to maintain order amid terrible emotional stress, and eventually failed. He described her as "a very committed mother, talented individual, and a very lovely human being." The prosecution, however, argued that Schuster was a domineering woman who repeatedly made threats against her husband and that Fagone had only become her accomplice because she intimidated him. Nuttall responded by repeatedly questioning the validity of Fagone's evidence.

Schuster's case lasted longer than that of her accomplice. Nevertheless, she was finally found guilty in December 2007 and, like Fagone, was sentenced to life without parole on May 16, 2008. Judge Wayne Ellison told her that her attorneys were to be thanked for saving her life. He commented, "This is the kind of case in which the jury may have imposed the death penalty, and this court might have upheld the imposition of that penalty. In the light of everything Mr Nuttall has said, it is true to say, he saved your life."

O. J. Simpson

It was the trial of the century, possibly the most famous and widely followed courtroom drama ever witnessed. And at first it seemed an open and shut case: the celebrity suspect had been watched on televisions around the world apparently fleeing justice, motive was clear, and crucial evidence had been found in the shape of an incriminating glove. All the elements of an obvious crime of passion were in place. And yet the former football star, O. J. Simpson was acquitted of the charge of murdering his ex-wife Nicole Brown Simpson and her friend Ronald Goldman. He walked free in 1995 after the longest trial in Californian history.

The drama began at 11.40pm on June 12, 1994. The barking of Nicole Simpson's pet dog alerted neighbors that something was amiss and the police were called to her Brentwood, Los Angeles, home. What they found there was truly shocking. While her two young children— Sydney, 8, and Justin, 5—slept upstairs, Nicole and her friend Ronald Goldman had been brutally slain. Nicole had been stabbed many times through the throat; the wounds so ferocious she was almost decapitated. Goldman had minor wounds to his body as well as fatal slashes, suggesting the murderer had played with his or her victim before finally despatching him. The police put the time of the double murder at between 10.15 and 10.40pm.

It did not take long for investigators to name Nicole's ex-husband, the football star O. J. Simpson, as the prime suspect, and an appeal went out for him to turn himself in while a huge crowd of reporters gathered at the police station. Instead, Simpson responded by sending a letter, which his lawyer read out. It said, "First everyone understand I had nothing to do with Nicole's murder… Don't feel sorry for me. I've had a great life." It followed by naming Simpson's partner at the time Playboy Playmate Traci Adell as an alibi.

The hunt was on. Police tracked calls from a cell phone in Simpson's van in Orange County and, later, a patrol car spotted a white Ford Bronco being driven by Simpson's friend, Al Cowlings, headed south on Interstate 405. Cowlings yelled that Simpson was pointing a gun at his own head. The officer kept his

RIGHT: O. J. Simpson accompanying his children, Sydney and Justin, at the funeral service for his ex-wife, Nicole Simpson.

distance, but followed the vehicle, which was traveling at just 35 miles an hour. For some time a Los Angeles KCBS News Service helicopter had exclusive coverage of the chase, and it was soon joined by nearly a dozen others. Already, the case had become a media circus.

One radio station contacted Simpson's former coach, John McKay, who went live on air to beg Simpson to give himself up. Meanwhile, thousands of curious spectators thronged overpass roads along the route waiting to catch a glimpse of the rolling crime scene. By this time, a staggering 95 million people around the world were watching on TV.

The 50-mile chase ended at 8.00pm outside Simpson's Brentwood home, and Simpson was allowed

Police cars pursuing the Ford Bronco (white, right) driven by Al Cowlings, carrying fugitive murder suspect O. J. Simpson.

to go inside before his attorney, Robert Shapiro, arrived and suggested Simpson turn himself in.

There was more drama to come, and it began to unfold rapidly. A grand jury, called to determine whether to indict Simpson for the two murders, was dismissed two days later when it was considered that the media frenzy would prejudice its decision. Then a man who might have been a key witness was dismissed after selling his story to the newspapers. Jose Camacho, a knife salesman at Ross Cutlery, claimed that had he sold Simpson a 15-inch German knife similar to the murder weapon three

Blood Trail at Bundy

LEFT: O. J. Simpson reacting as a coroner describes the autopsy report on Nicole Brown Simpson in court in 1095.

Los Angeles Police Detective Tom Lange (left) pointing to pictures of the trail of blood at Nicole Brown Simpson's condominium where she and her friend Ron Goldman were murdered, during testimony in the O. J. Simpson murder trial.

weeks before the fatal attacks. A female witness who claimed she saw Simpson driving away from Nicole's home on the night of the murders was forbidden to give evidence for the same reason. Nevertheless, after a week-long court hearing, a California Superior Court judge ruled on July 7, that there was ample evidence to try Simpson. At his second court appearance, on July 23, Simpson stated, "Absolutely, one hundred percent, not guilty."

Amid a welter of media attention, the trial began on January 25, 1995. Los Angeles County prosecutor Christopher Darden stated that Simpson had killed his ex-wife in a jealous rage and opened the case by

playing an emergency 911 call made by Nicole Brown Simpson on January 1, 1989. The jury heard Nicole crying out that Simpson was going to attack her, while her husband could be heard shouting threateningly at her in the background.

The prosecution continued to produce what seemed like damning evidence: Simpson had a history of violence toward his wife and dozens of expert witnesses testified that DNA, fingerprints, blood, and shoe prints clearly placed Simpson at the scene of the crime. All evidence, it was alleged, pointed to a murder during which Simpson had forced Nicole to the ground, grabbed her hair to pull her head back, put his foot on her back, and slit her throat as she lay face down on the ground. A trail of blood spots had been identified leading from Nicole's house to Simpson's Bronco and his own home on Rockingham Drive.

While this evidence alone looked convincing, even more was produced. Simpson had last been seen in public on the night of the murders at 9.36pm when he returned to his house with Brian "Kato" Kaelin, a bit-part actor, after which they had eaten at a nearby McDonald's. Simpson was not seen again until 10.54pm when he got into a limousine and went to LAX Airport to fly to Chicago. During the time the murders took place no alibi could be given. Simpson had also been spotted driving the Bronco to and from the scene during the time both prosecution and

defence agreed the murder had been committed. The driver of the limo the accused would later take to the airport reported that he had arrived at Simpson's home around 10.30pm and rung the doorbell, but got no answer. He then saw Simpson come home about 15 minutes' later. At first Simpson's excuse for not answering the bell was that he had overslept. Another witness, a neighbor, said he heard "three loud thumps" and went out to investigate. The two men both said they had seen Simpson outside, looking agitated. Further evidence showed that DNA samples from bloody footprints leading away from the bodies and from the back gate of

BELOW: Prosecutor Brain Kelberg points to a chart showing where wounds were inflicted on murder victim Ronald Goldman in the O. J. Simpson murder trial.

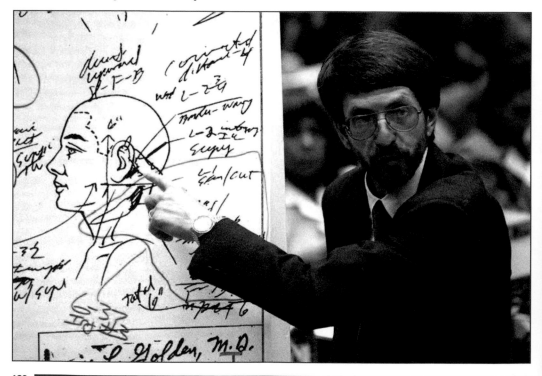

ABOVE: O. J. Simpson showing the jury a new pair of Aris extra-large gloves, similar to those found at the crime scene.

the condominium matched Simpson's blood.

Although no actual murder weapon had been found, and no further witnesses had come forward save those who had earlier been dismissed, the prosecution was confident of a conviction.

Now it was the turn of Simpson's top-flight defence team, which had been described by the press as a "Dream Team." It comprised lawyers F. Lee Bailey, Robert Shapiro, Alan Dershowitz, Robert Kardashian, Gerald Uelmen (a law professor at Santa Clara University), Carl E. Douglas, and Cochran, as well as Peter Neufeld and Barry Scheck, two attorneys specializing in DNA

evidence. They swiftly set out to destroy the evidence, alleging that Simpson was the victim of police fraud and that "sloppy internal procedures" had contaminated the DNA evidence.

Further to this, they claimed that Simpson had not left his house that evening, but had been busy packing for his trip to Chicago, save for a short break during which he had gone outside to hit golf balls into a children's sandpit in the front garden—hence the three loud thumps on the wall of the neighbor's bungalow. The Spanish-speaking housekeeper of another neighbor testified that she had seen Simpson's car parked outside his house at the time of the murders. When challenged, however, she said she could not be sure of the exact time she had seen the car. But adding weight to the defence was the evidence of an airport check-in clerk who said Simpson appeared perfectly normal at LAX airport on the night of the murders.

The defence also suggested that Simpson was not physically capable of carrying out the murders; Ronald Goldman was a fit young man who had put up a fierce struggle against his attacker while Simpson had chronic arthritis. To counter this, one of the prosecuting team, Marcia Clark, showed an exercise video that Simpson made two years earlier.

The most famous piece of evidence was till to come though: a glove carrying traces of Goldman's DNA that had been found at Simpson's house. Cochran goaded an assistant prosecutor into asking Simpson to put the glove on. It appeared too tight, prompting Gerald Uelman to

BELOW: O. J. Simpson reacting to the not guilty verdict at his criminal trial for the murders of his ex-wife and Ron Goldman.

tell the jury, "If it doesn't fit, you must acquit." Police had planted the glove in Simpson's house, they claimed. Prosecutor Darden would refute that Simpson was framed in his closing arguments, pointing out that police had visited his house eight times on domestic violence calls without arresting him before eventually citing him for abuse in 1989.

Ripples from the Simpson case were felt far and wide during the trial, and stirred racial tension between black communities in which many thought Simpson a victim of injustice and white communities where a majority believed he was guilty. It also caused a storm of argument over media coverage of trials.

Following a trial of over eight months the not guilty verdict was returned by a majority African American jury at 10.00am on October 3, 1995. After long months of hearing the evidence they deliberated over the decision for just four hours. In all, 150 witnesses had

ABOVE: Lou Brown (left) and Juditha Brown (right), the parents of Nicole Brown Simpson, with their attorney John Kelley (centre) outside the Santa Monica, California, courthouse, following the guilty verdicts in the O.J Simpson wrongful death civil trial.

given testimony and media coverage was unprecedented throughout. Simpson's defence was said to have cost between three and six million dollars.

Nevertheless, there were still more dramas and revelations to come. In post-trial interviews a few jurors said that they believed Simpson probably committed the murders, but that the prosecution had bungled the case. Three of them later published a book called Madam Foreman, in which they described how police errors, not race, led to their verdict, and that they considered prosecutor Darden to be a "token black" assigned to the case. A year later, both the Brown and Goldman families sued Simpson for damages in a civil trial. On February 5, 1997, the jury unanimously found there was sufficient evidence to find Simpson liable for damages in the wrongful death of Goldman and battery of Brown. In its conclusions, the jury effectively found Simpson liable for the death of his ex-wife and Ron Goldman, although the burden of proof is lower in civil cases than in criminal ones. Yet another indication that Simpson's acquittal may have been a miscarriage of justice came in September 2004, when porn star Jennifer Peace came forward claiming that she was Al Cowlings' girlfriend and that Cowlings—who had been in the car with Simpson during the famous chase— had told her that Simpson confessed his guilt. In 2008, Mike Gilbert released his book How I Helped O. J. Get Away with Murder, which told how Simpson had also confessed to him.

Yvonne Sleightholme

At first glance the killing of Jayne Smith by a former girlfriend of her husband appears to be a straightforward case of a murder committed by an unbalanced woman in a frenzy of jealousy. However, Yvonne Sleightholme has always maintained her innocence and after she was convicted evidence came to light that suggests there may be a shred of truth to her claims. Nevertheless, she served six years more in prison than the judge at her trial recommended.

Yvonne Sleightholme, a doctor's receptionist, met William Smith at a disco nightclub in Yorkshire 1979, and the two began a relationship soon after. But while they talked of weddings Smith began to have doubts about his girlfriend and, growing weary of her controlling nature, he eventually finished with her. Yvonne took it badly and lied that she was dying of leukemia. Out of sympathy Smith briefly took her back, but it soon became obvious that there was nothing physically wrong with Yvonne and meanwhile he had met Jayne, who he would later marry. The relationship with Yvonne ended once again.

On December 12, 1989, the body of Jayne Smith was found in the yard of the couple's farm at Salton in the Yorkshire Dales, England. It looked like an attempted rape gone wrong; her clothes were in disarray and her body scratched. She had died of a gunshot wound fired at point blank range into the back of her head. There was a strange irregularity about the killing though, and one that would lead straight back to Yvonne Sleightholme. Jayne's attacker had taken the trouble to remove her wedding ring. It spoke of a murder committed out of jealousy rather than lust.

At her trial in May 1991, Yvonne claimed she had been at the farm on the night of the murder, but had had nothing to do with it. Mr Justice Waite, prosecuting, argued that after her fiancé had broken off their engagement and later married another woman, the already unstable Sleightholme had been twisted by envy and "wrought upon the newly-married couple a terrible revenge." The jury was convinced. Yvonne was found guilty of murder and sentenced to life in prison, with a recommendation that she should serve at least ten years.

Several years later, Yvonne's supporters came up with new evidence that seemed to cast doubt on the court's decision. A bloody handprint had been found in her car, but it was too large to have been made by her. Nevertheless, Yvonne's hopes of taking her case back to the Court of Appeal were dashed when judges threw out the application. Still she protested that she was innocent and, in January 2002, gave an interview to the local evening paper from Styal Prison in Cheshire. She told the reporter that she would never admit to killing Jayne Smith, saying, "I value the truth more than anything… I didn't do it, and nothing—not even the chance of freedom—will make me lie and say I did it. I was not responsible for that terrible murder."

In March 2003, the Yorkshire Evening Post newspaper revealed it had obtained documents proving Sleightholme had been an exemplary prisoner, and that she was not, as had been claimed, likely to commit another violent act. The editor wrote to the parole board, asking for it to look again at the application, and Ryedale member of Parliament John Greenway passed the documents on to a government minister. The following month, the then Home Secretary David Blunkett referred the case back to the board for a fresh review. Following this, Sleightholme was transferred to an open prison, Askham Grange near York, finally being released in December 2005 after 16 years in prison.

BELOW: Yvonne Sleightholme being helped into Leeds Crown Court, to face charges for the murder of Jayne Smith.

Pam Smart and Billy Flynn

Pam Smart began a fling with one of the boys at the school where she worked in order to get back at her cheating husband and never expected to fall in love with a 16-year-old boy. When she did, she conspired with her lover to remove the man who stood in the way of their future together. She should have remembered that it is impossible to keep secrets in the classroom.

The marriage of Pam Smart and her insurance salesman husband Greg was already rocky by the time that he came back from a business trip and confessed that he had had a one-night stand while he was away. Pam was furious and determined to level the score with him. She was 21 and attractive, and had always had a certain sexual allure. It was obvious that William Flynn, one of the boys at the school where she worked, had long had a crush on her, so Pam set out to teach the young student a few things he would never have learned in the classroom while taking revenge on her cheating husband.

Pam and Flynn were soon having sex whenever they could and at some point Pam realized that what had started out as a casual thing had become much, much more. Now she constantly craved the attentions of her teenage lover and was deeply infatuated with him. She wanted Flynn so much more than she wanted Greg Smart, but instead of a lengthy divorce, her thoughts turned to getting Smart out of the way a little more speedily.

She confided in Flynn and at first the boy was shocked by her plan, but his older lover was persuasive and soon he had agreed to what looked like a foolproof murder plot. He recruited two of his best friends, Pete Randall and Vance Lattime, to help and another, Raymond Fowler, would go along with them just for the ride. On May 1, 1990, having been married for less than a

LEFT: Pamela Smart on the witness stand during her trial at Rockingham County Superior Court in Exeter, New Hampshire.

teacher was sleeping with one of the boys and she staged the whole thing." The caller mentioned all three boys involved in the killing by their first names. Flynn, Randall, and Lattime were arrested on June 11, 1990. Flynn was charged with first degree murder, the other two with being accomplices to first degree murder. Pam Smart was arrested at work on August 1, 1990 with the officer, Dan Pelletier telling her, "Well Pam, I've got good news and I've got bad news. The good news is we've solved the murder of your husband. The bad news is you're under arrest."

The trial of Pam Smart and the three boys began on March 5, 1991. With its ingredients of a young attractive

ABOVE: Vance Lattime giving evidence against Pam Smart in Rockingham County Superior Court in Exeter, New Hampshire.

BELOW: William Flynn appearing at Rockingham Superior Court in Brentwood, New Hampshire in 2008. Flynn, was seeking a sentence reduction.

year, Pam was at a school meeting, which gave her a perfect alibi. Greg Smart was at their home Derry, New Hampshire, when the boys entered the house, shot him in the head, and quickly made the scene look like a badly botched burglary. On returning home, Pam discovered the body and—pretending to be devastated—called in the police.

But teenage boys are never very discreet. Randall and Lattime were overheard talking about the killing and another pupil, Cecelia Pierce went to the police. She agreed to co-operate with them and made recorded phone calls in which she encouraged Pam to give details of the murder plot.

Hers was not the only accusation the police heard. Flynn told a friend that he shot Greg Smart because he beat his wife and gossip and rumor spread like wildfire in the schoolyard. The police department received an anonymous phone call informing them that "the school woman involved with the murder of her husband after seducing a teenage student, it attracted huge media attention. The jury went out on May 20 and deliberated for 13 hours before finding Pam guilty on three counts; conspiracy to commit murder, accomplice to a murder, and tampering with a witness. She was sentenced to life imprisonment. Flynn and Randall each received 40 years with a parole review in 2018. Lattime was sentenced to 30 years, but released in 2006. Fowler also received a prison sentence, later extended because of a parole violation. He was eventually released in 2005.

Madeleine Smith

The 19th century is notorious for its strictly enforced morality, particularly when it concerned the behavior of wealthy young women. The slightest sin could permanently ruin a girl's reputation, bring shame on the family, and wreck her hopes of a good marriage. And for a girl to lose her virginity out of wedlock was the ultimate crime, so for 19-year-old Madeleine Smith the threat of a previous sexual dalliance being revealed to her family and new fiancé was a peril worth killing to prevent.

Madeleine was the daughter of a prosperous Scottish architect and enjoyed all the trappings of her father's wealth; a busy social life in her native Glasgow as well as a large country home. Unfortunately, her carefree lifestyle would come to an abrupt end. It began when friends introduced her to a dashing young Frenchman in the street. Pierre Emile L'Angelier was an apprentice nurseryman staying in Glasgow and immediately caught Madeleine's eye. The young girl was overwhelmed by her new passion and began to meet L'Angelier in secret whenever it could be arranged, and when a meeting was impossible she poured out her feelings in letters, addressing them to "my own darling husband."

Their love was chaste for months, and could later have been explained away as a girlish crush had this continued. But that was to change during an unchaperoned visit to the family house in the country that Madeleine managed to arrange. In secret, L'Angelier followed his wealthy young love, and with her parents absent their desire for each other could be contained no longer. Afterward, she wrote another of her gushing letters to L'Angelier, telling him, "If we did wrong last night it was in the excitement of our love." The couple became unofficially engaged.

In those days when a young woman's conduct was watched carefully, it was inevitable that Madeleine would eventually be found out. Sure enough, her parents soon became aware of their daughter's illicit affair with a mere apprentice. Although Madeleine managed to keep from them the information about the loss of her virginity, they were shocked and instantly ordered an end to the affair. And it seems that Madeleine had become bored of her lover anyway, and certainly didn't waste any time pining for him. Soon after, she was introduced to a wealthy bachelor named William Harper Minnoch. There was an instant attraction between the two of them, and this time Madeleine was given her parents' blessing for what, after all, was a much better match. The only fly in Madeleine's ointment was her former beau.

L'Angelier had kept all of Madeleine's letters, which contained unmistakable references to the fact that she had surrendered her virginity to him. Knowing how devastating these would be if they ever became public knowledge, she wrote to him, begging that the letters be returned so that she could destroy them. The spurned L'Angelier had other ideas however. Instead, he threatened to reveal all to Madeleine's father unless she honored her promise to marry him.

Her response was to hatch a plot that would forever silence the man who had the power to ruin her reputation and with it her future happiness. Not long after, a woman was seen in a shop buying arsenic. She signed for the poison in the name of M. H. Smith. Meanwhile, Madeleine had continued writing to L'Angelier and lulled him with sweet words and protestations of undying love. Soon, she had managed to arrange another meeting, smuggling the young man into the basement of the family's Glasgow home. During the visit she kept up the appearance of a young girl still in love, while serving her blackmailer cocoa laced with arsenic.

Madeleine played her part so well that L'Angelier suspected nothing when he became ill soon after their meeting. As soon as he was able, he returned to Madeleine's basement. And a second cup of cocoa. This one would prove fatal. Within hours, L'Angelier fell gravely ill and in less than a day, he was dead. His doctor, mystified at L'Angelier's symptoms, ordered a postmortem that revealed 87 grains of arsenic still in his patient's stomach. It did not take the police long to discover a bundle of Madeleine's letters at L'Angelier's lodgings, and the tale they told gave investigating officers a prime suspect for the murder. Madeleine was arrested on March 31, 1857. She stood trial soon after.

Her defense told the jury that Madeleine had bought arsenic to use as rat poison and maintained that L'Angelier had often taken arsenic himself for health reasons. It was a flimsy argument and all evidence pointed to her having murdered her former lover. Nevertheless, it was deemed circumstantial, and not enough to convict her. Instead, a verdict of "not proven" was given, which in Scottish courts means that the jury does not believe the accused to be innocent, though the prosecution has failed to make a strong enough case. Fortunately for Madeleine what would have been a key witness—a person who had seen her together with a male companion on the night of the poisoning—was not allowed to

testify. They had come forward too late and the trial had already started. Madeleine walked free from the court, but was widely believed to be guilty of murder. Her engagement to William Minnoch came to an abrupt end, and instead she married George Wardle before leaving Scotland—and the scandal—behind for good.

BELOW: A contemporary illustration of Madeleine Smith, from around the time of her trial for the murder of her former lover Pierre Emile L'Anglier.

Susan Smith

However grisly and twisted the murder, most of us can understand how a thwarted love or systematic abuse might lead someone to a killing rage. Susan Smith's crime though, went far beyond that. It is one thing to murder a cheating lover, but to take the lives of your own children is on a level of horror all its own.

The crime of three-year-old Michael and his 14-month-old brother Alex was that they came between their mother and the man she wanted to be with. Recently divorced, struggling to cope, and becoming deeper in debt with every month that passed, 23-year-old Susan Smith was desperate for the security that her relationship with Tom Findlay might bring. He, however, was not ready to step into a ready-made family and wrote to tell her that though he cared deeply for her, he was just not ready for the responsibility. As he would later strenuously point out, at no point did he make any suggestion that Susan should somehow get rid of her children.

Nevertheless, that is exactly what Susan decided she needed to do. Although she might have given them over to the custody of their father, instead she strapped them into the back of her car, took the emergency brake off,

BELOW: Police mug shots of Susan Smith released by the South Carolina Department of Corrections after her arrest in 1994.

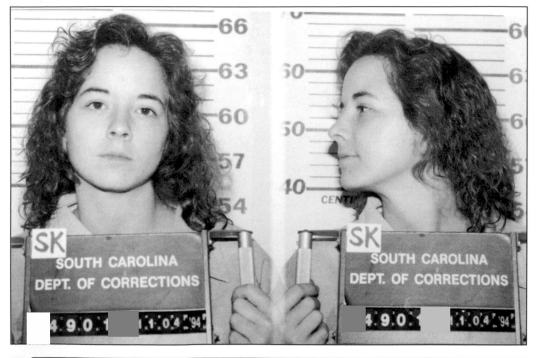

and let it roll downhill and into a lake where the two boys drowned.

At about 9.15pm on October 25, 1994, the police took a call from a hysterical woman. Smith told them that she had been driving her two children home in Union, South Carolina, when a young black man had forced his way into the car while she was stopped at a red light. At gunpoint, he demanded Smith drive off and then pushed her out of the car a few miles down the

ABOVE: A shrine at John D. Long Lake, South Carolina, featuring toys and pictures of Michael and Alex Smith, who were murdered by their mother Susan.

road, before driving away with her two boys still strapped into the back seat.

A huge manhunt immediately swept into operation and the eyes of America fastened on the devastated young woman. But the television appeals of Smith and her estranged husband David produced no results, and the search, too, was a failure. Puzzled by the lack of success, nine days after the boys had gone missing the police again questioned Smith to see if there might be some detail not yet mentioned which might help them. This time she broke down and confessed to her terrible crime. Police divers were sent to search the lake and quickly found her Mazda not far beneath the surface, with her sons dead in the back. Smith was charged with first degree murder.

The trial of Susan Smith began amid a whirl of media attention on July 18, 1995. It was to become one of the most avidly followed and harrowing court cases the United States has ever witnessed. From the start the prosecution were determined that the jury understood the severity of the crime, and the details heard in court were shocking. One diver recalled the moment that he had shone his flashlight at the car and through the murky water had seen "a small hand against the glass." Lawyers defending Smith argued that it was not murder, but a suicide attempt gone awry. Rejected by the man she had hoped might turn her life around, they told the jury that Smith had wanted to take her own life along with her sons'. They also painted a detailed picture of Susan's life up to that point—the alcoholic father who had committed suicide, the sexual abuse she had suffered as a child, and the desolation she carried with her every day.

It was a powerful defense and in her closing speech, Judge Judy Clarke asked the jury to show mercy toward Smith, telling them that she had made the decision "with a confused mind and a heart that has no hope." Nevertheless, the sheer horror of Smith's crime was more powerful. On July 28, 1995, she was found guilty of the murder of her two sons. Her sentence was life, with no possibility of parole until 2025.

Paul Snider

To marry a woman who turns heads whenever she walks into a room can be difficult for an insecure man. For Paul Snider, whose wife was Playmate of the Year in Playboy magazine, the attention she received was more than enough to turn him mad with jealousy, and when she divorced him and became involved with one of Hollywood's great directors, his envy became a killing rage.

Dorothy Stratten was plain Dorothy Hoogstratten when Paul Snider walked into the Dairy Queen in Vancouver, Canada, where she worked in 1977. She was stunningly beautiful and he was a man on the up. After seducing her, Snider began taking sexy photos of his lover and eventually managed to get them published in the men's magazine *Playboy*. Dorothy's sex appeal did not go unnoticed, and soon the couple were invited to join in the fun at *Playboy* founder Hugh Hefner's "Playboy Mansion." At first Snider was happy for Dorothy to indulge in sexual frolics with the other guests; it was good for her career—and for his bank balance. But Snider hadn't stopped to consider how attached he had become to Dorothy. As he realized that he had fallen in love with her so his jealousy grew.

The couple married in Las Vegas in June 1979. In August, Dorothy was Playmate of the Month. Dorothy was 20 and Snider, 29. At the time, Snider's new wife told friends that she couldn't imagine being with anyone but Paul. However, Snider was now obsessed with Dorothy's career and was increasingly controlling. He forbade her to drink coffee, because it would stain her teeth, and it is rumored that he also poisoned her pet dog because he was jealous of it. Dorothy couldn't ignore his erratic behavior for long, and the marriage crumbled. After a year if marriage they filed for divorce. Life in 1980 was good for Dorothy—she was Playmate of the Year. Free of the man who thought he had discovered her, she began seeing film director Peter Bogdanovich then moved into his Bel Air home.

Snider had lost both the woman he loved and the key to success and riches. He took a distinctly sinister turn. He hired a private investigator to follow Dorothy.

On the morning of August 14, 1980, Dorothy agreed to meet Snider at the apartment they once shared. She arrived with a large handbag containing $1,000 to pay off her ex-husband. It was around 11pm that the private investigator finally got an answer from the numerous phone calls he made to the apartment. He told one of the women who lodged with Snider that he had been trying the number all day and asked her to check on her landlord. When she did, she found Dorothy lying across Snider's waterbed, dead from a bullet would. She was missing the tip of her left index finger, blown off as she tried to protect her face.

Close by was the body of Snider. He had shot himself. Examination of the scene revealed that Dorothy had been sexually brutalized both before and after she died. She was cremated and buried on August 19, at Westwood Memorial Park.

BELOW: Playboy Playmate Dorothy Stratten in May 1980.

Dr. James Howard Snook

For three years the wealthy and successful Dr. James Snook met his young lover several times a week in the rooms he rented so that they might have a comfortable place to have sex. But somewhere their relationship went awry. What started out as a purely physical affair ended with Theora Hix laying dead in a patch of weeds, battered with a hammer and her throat slit.

Doctor Snook was successful and confident man to whom life had been kind. He was a professor of Veterinary Medicine at the Ohio State University in Columbus and a respected horse surgeon. He had also won two Olympic gold medals for pistol shooting and enjoyed the love of his devoted wife Helen and their baby daughter. And in June 1926, soon after giving 21-year-old medical student Theora Hix a lift to the university, he also had a fresh and attractive young sexual partner. After spending a day at work, Snook visited Theora in the rooms he rented. The couple would make love in the early evenings then the doctor would return home to his wife. As Snook would later testify, neither he nor Theora were in love, the relationship was purely sexual. For a relationship that was all about sex though, something was amiss. Theora taunted her older lover about his sexual performance and even went so far as to recommend books he might read to improve his technique.

Nevertheless, the relationship continued. On one occasion, after a break-in at her university room, Snook gave Theora a Remington Derringer pistol for protection, and the two began going to the New York Central Rifle Range on the outskirts of Columbus to practise. It was here that two 16-year-old boys discovered her body on June 16, 1929. She had been beaten around the head and her throat was cut. The body was soon identified; Theora's roommates had already reported her missing and when her photograph appeared in the local newspaper, Mrs Margaret Smalley recognized Theora as the young "wife" of a man called Howard Snook who rented the room from her.

When Snook was arrested, police found blood inside his car, on the clothing he wore the night of the murder, on his ball-peen hammer, and on his pocket knife. He had tried to clean everything, but enough traces remained to declare his guilt.

Exactly why Snook's passions were roused to the point where a previously law-abiding man would beat a young woman to death will never be known. The only testimony we have is Snook's, and he had good reason to construct a story that would help the jury see him as a victim of a jealous lover's threats. In fact at his trial, Snook testified that he and Theora had driven to a local country club to make love. Once they arrived, she had told him that she wanted to go "some place where I can scream," and Snook had taken her on to the New York Central shooting range.

Snook then told Theora that he then had to go as he was due to visit his mother. At this point, he said, Theora became angry shouting, "Damn your mother. I don't care about your mother. Damn Mrs Snook. I'm going to kill her and get her out of the way." Snook said she then continued to threaten his family, even saying she would kill his daughter. He went on to testify that she had grabbed open his trousers and began to bite and pull at him. In fear for his safety and for his family's lives, Snook said he grabbed the ball-peen hammer from his kit in the back of the car and hit her with it. Theora then screamed, "Damn you, I will kill you too." According to Snook, she began digging through her purse. Afraid that she was looking for the Derringer pistol, he hit her on the head with the hammer several times until she fell to the ground.

We should approach this tale with caution, for Snook's explanation of Theora's cut throat changed over time. At first he said he did not know how her neck had come to be cut open, but it was pointed out to him that it had been cut so precisely that only someone experienced in anatomy and surgery—such as a veterinarian—could have done it. He then said that he had cut her throat because he did not want to see her suffer from the head wounds.

On August 14, 1929, Snook was found guilty of first degree murder and sentenced to death in the Ohio Penitentiary's electric chair. Before the day of his execution arrived, his story changed again. Snook supposedly confessed to a warden that the murder had been premeditated. After several attempts to obtain a new trial or change the verdict to manslaughter or second degree murder, Snook was executed on February 28, 1930.

Ruth Snyder

Ruth Snyder led a double life: To her husband she was a doting wife and mother, and to her lover she was a domineering sexual mistress. But dissatisfaction, coupled with a good helping of greed, would lead her and her lover to try and make her double life a single life.

At the age of 20, in 1895, Ruth Sorensen was an attractive and charming young operator at a New York City telephone exchange where one bungled call changed her life and set in motion a train of events that would eventually lead to murder. The call was between a man named Albert Schneider, who was the art editor of a magazine called *Motor Boat*, and his client. Ruth was so sincere and appealing in her apology for having messed it up that Schneider offered her a job as a sec-

RIGHT: A photograph of Ruth Snyder taken in 1927, the year that she murdered her husband.

retary on the magazine. Before a year had passed they were married, and afterward changed their names to Snyder to avert some of the anti-German feeling that was then common.

Seemingly a perfect suburban couple, their home on Long Island soon welcomed the arrival of a baby, and Ruth sank all her energies into being as good a mother and wife she could be. And for a while she enjoyed it. Her husband, however, was not so happy. He was domineering, prone to outbursts of temper, and found domestic life boring. The two began to lead separate lives, neither questioning the other about where they were or with whom.

Young, attractive, and all but deserted by her husband, Ruth invited her mother to move into the house, and with a permanent babysitter on call, began a series of affairs, the most serious of which was with corset salesman Henry Judd Gray. Theirs was an unusual sexual relationship, with Ruth now taking on the dominant role and Gray enjoying subservience. The two would later be labelled by the press "Granite Woman and Putty Man."

The only thing that stood in the way of Ruth's total freedom was her husband and the money he brought in to support her and the baby. However, Ruth soon came up with a plan to solve both problems.

Back in her role as the concerned wife, Ruth persuaded her husband to purchase a life insurance policy and with the assistance of an agent (who was subsequently imprisoned for forgery) she signed an additional $48,000 policy that paid extra if an unexpected act of violence killed the victim. She then made a series of botched attempts to kill Snyder, all of which he survived.

But on March 20, 1927, with the help of Gray, Ruth finally succeeded. When Snyder was safely asleep in bed,

the couple sneaked into his room, smashed his head, garroted him, and stuffed his nose full of chloroform-soaked rags. They then made a hasty attempt to make it look like the Snyders had been victims of a burglary gone wrong. Ruth got Gray to tie up her ankles and wrists, but managed to "break free" to raise the alarm while her lover fled the scene.

It didn't take detectives long to unpick the lies. Ruth was betrayed by many small clues. The police wondered why when she had undone her wrists she had not untied her ankles as well. And whoever had attacked Albert had gone out of their way to kill him, which didn't fit into the pattern of a burglary. Finally, property that Ruth said had been stolen started turning up in odd places around the house. Then detectives came across a letter signed "J.G." Snyder tried to convince them the initials were those of a young woman that her husband had once dated, but a flip through Ruth's address book revealed the names of a total of 28 men. One was Judd Gray.

Eventually though it was Ruth who declared her guilt. When the police took her in for questioning and told her that they already had Gray in custody and that he had confessed everything. She crumbled and the whole story spilled out. In fact, it was a standard police trick. At that time they hadn't even caught up with Gray though he was arrested at a hotel in Syracuse later that night.

Both Judd Gray and Ruth Snyder were charged with murder, and the case went to trial on April 18, 1927. Each tried to blame the other for the murder, but the jury found both guilty and they were sentenced to death. They were executed on January 12, 1928. Ruth Snyder would later achieve a degree of grim fame after a reporter took a picture of her dying in the electric chair with a miniature camera strapped to his ankle.

George Stoner

A difference in age is no barrier to love, as Alma Rattenbury found out when she advertised for a boy to help around the home she shared with her husband. She would also find out that the young are just as prone as their elders to jealousy.

No stranger to scandal, 39-year-old Alma Rattenbury and her 67-year-old husband Francis had been forced to flee their home in Canada by wagging tongues. He had been married when he began his affair with Alma and, soon after, asked his wife for a divorce. When she refused, he simply moved his mistress into the family home until eventually his wife agreed to part. Inevitably, the details of this scheme to force an innocent woman into divorce became public knowledge and the criticism of Alma and Rattenbury was so great that they crossed the Atlantic to seek a quiet life in Bournemouth, England.

Unfortunately, a quiet life was not what they found. The couple bought a large house and moved in with Alma's thirteen-year-old son Christopher from an earlier marriage, and the couple's six-year-old son John. They soon found that a little extra help would be needed to run the house, and Alma placed a notice in the Bournemouth Echo advertising a position for a, "Daily willing lad, 14–18, for house-work; scout-trained preferred. Apply between 11–12, 8–9 at 5 Manor Road, Bournemouth."

The willing lad who answered was the handsome but shy George Stoner. In fact, Alma found him very willing indeed: as well as his household chores, Stoner soon found very pleasant extra duties in Alma's bed. He quickly became so indispensable that his part-time position was changed to full time and he was given

BELOW: A long queue of people forming outside the Old Bailey court for the trial of Alma Rattenbury and George Stoner, jointly charged with the murder of Francis Rattenbury.

ABOVE: Petitioners trying to persuade railway staff at Waterloo Station, London to add their names to the petition appealing to the Home Secretary to grant a reprieve George Stoner.

a room in the house. Francis Rattenbury was fully aware of his wife's infidelity, but now slipping into old age he had become impotent and turned a blind eye, much preferring to share his evenings with a bottle of whiskey and let his wife have her fun.

For a while the unorthodox situation appeared to work well, but as time progressed Stoner fell ever more deeply in love with his sophisticated older mistress, and grew jealous of her elderly husband. Greedy for every

moment with her, he became upset when she spent time with Rattenbury and flew into a rage when the husband and wife went away for a weekend together. Convinced that Rattenbury was finally trying to win his wife back, when they returned and Alma told him that they would also be away the following weekend, Stoner's jealousy finally got the better of him.

On the afternoon of March 24, 1935, Stoner borrowed a wooden mallet from his grandparents, telling them that he needed it to erect a screen in the garden. Later that evening, Francis Rattenbury was found seriously injured. He had been bludgeoned on the head from behind. Three days later he died from his injuries and what had previously been an assault case became a murder.

The police immediately questioned Alma, who appeared to be the worse for wear through drink or drugs. Perhaps she originally intended to take the blame, for over and over she kept repeating that she had "done him in." Nevertheless, soon after, Stoner confessed to another servant, Irene Riggs, that it was he who had dealt the killer blow that did for Rattenbury. She went to the police. Alma and Stoner were both arrested and charged with murder.

The lovers were tried together at the Old Bailey on May 27, 1935. Both pleaded not guilty with a now sober Alma passionately claiming she had nothing to do with her husband's death. Stoner was quiet in court, but his defense counsel suggested that though he had hit Rattenbury in a jealous rage, he had not intended to kill. The jury did not agree. Stoner was found guilty and sentenced to death. Alma was acquitted much to the consternation of the crowd waiting outside. In their eyes, a three-times married older woman had led an innocent young lad to kill.

A few days later, Alma took the train from Waterloo to Christchurch, not far from her Bournemouth home. She sat down on the banks of a river and wrote a handful of farewell notes. Then she plunged a knife several times into her heart, and died almost immediately. It is clear from the notes and from the words of a song she wrote while awaiting trial—subsequently published as Mrs Rattenbury's Prison Song—that she was deeply in love with Stoner, and took her own life out of grief for her loss and shame at what had happened. Stoner, when informed of her death, broke down and wept.

Alma was buried a few yards from her late husband, and during the ceremony signatures were collected for an appeal for mercy for George Stoner. Over the next few weeks an astonishing 320,000 people, including the local mayor and MP, signed the petition. It was handed to the Home Secretary, who commuted Stoner's sentence to penal servitude for life. A model prisoner, he was released seven years later in 1942. He died in Christchurch Hospital in 2000 aged 83 on the 65th anniversary of Francis's murder.

John Sweeney

Sweeney's crime of passion was a straightforward fit of selfish anger directed at a talented young actress who he had tried to love him despite the fact that he beat her. When she finished the relationship and refused to take him back, his rage was fatal.

Dominique Dunne was just 21 and a promising actress with a bright future when she met 25-year-old chef John Sweeney at a Hollywood party in 1981. She had been born locally, in Santa Monica, California, but after her parents divorced had moved to New York City, before returning to Los Angeles to try for a Hollywood acting career. Within two weeks she had won her first job and the following year would land her first major movie role as Dana Freeling in the 1982 horror classic Poltergeist.

But while Dominique's career was doing well, her relationship was causing problems. Sweeney was the eldest son of a troubled family and had emotional difficulties. At first these manifested themselves in jealousy and attempts to control Dominique. He was suspicious of everyone she met, dominating, and would often show up at film sets, rehearsals, and Dominique's acting classes to watch over her.

However, on August 27, 1982, the couple had their first major quarrel, and Dominique got her first taste of the violence that the man she loved was capable of. Sweeney grabbed her by her hair and slammed her head on the floor so roughly that he pulled out handfuls of her hair.

A month later they had another argument and this time Sweeney threw Dominique to the floor and began to choke her. Luckily a friend was present and intervened. The next day Dominique went to work on an episode of Hill Street Blues. Ironically her part was that of an abuse victim. Not all of her bruises were applied by the make-up artist's brush.

By now, the actress had had enough. She finished the relationship with Sweeney and changed the locks

Restaurant chef John Sweeney sitting in a courtroom in Beverly Hills, California, during his trial for the murder of actress Dominique Dunne.

on the doors of the house they once shared. Sweeney wasn't prepared to let his girlfriend go without a fight though. On October 30, 1982, Dominique was at the house rehearsing a scene for a television series with a fellow actor, David Parker, when her ex-boyfriend arrived. There was a fierce argument that ended with Sweeney strangling the young star, putting her in a coma. She died in hospital on November 4, aged just 22. Dominique had been working on a new TV series when she was attacked. On the credits of the second episode were the words "In loving memory of Dominique Dunne, her family and friends miss her."

John Thomas Sweeney was charged with murder and the case came to trial in August 1983 in Santa Monica. Incredibly, Sweeney's lawyer, Michael Adelson, argued that Dominique was to blame for her own death, saying that she had provoked the violent struggle because she refused to be reconciled with Sweeney. On the witness stand Sweeney himself said he "just exploded and lunged toward her" and added that he said he had no memory of what happened next. Adelson argued it was not a real crime, but an act of despair.

The police evidence, however, told a different story. According to the officers who arrested him Sweeney seemed to be quite calm and collected—and much more interested in his own fate than in Dominique's—when they arrived at the scene. They told how, during his first interrogation, Sweeney had showed no remorse for what he had done. Medical evidence also confirmed that the duration of the strangulation was at least three minutes. If it had been an explosion of anger, there was enough time for

RIGHT: John Sweeney being escorted from the courthouse during his murder trial.

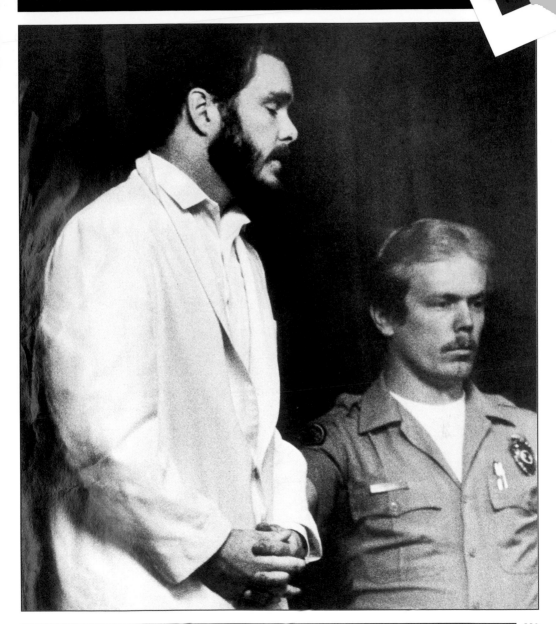

Sweeny to take control of himself. If he had stopped a few seconds earlier it may have saved Dominique's life.

Sweeney was convicted of the voluntary manslaughter of Dominique Dunne and only served two and a half years of a six and a half year prison sentence. Members of the jury later said they would have convicted Sweeney of murder had they been aware of his earlier history of violence against women.

Although the time he served did not seem to reflect the magnitude of his horrific crime, on his release Dominique's mother did not let him slip quietly back into Hollywood life. When Sweeney got another job as chef at a Los Angeles restaurant, Ellen Griffin founded a grievance support group called "Justice for Victims of Homicide." On the nights that John Sweeney worked, she and other group members would hand out slips of paper to the restaurant's customers that read, "The hands that will prepare your meal tonight also murdered Dominique Dunne." John Sweeney soon lost his job and was forced to move to the Pacific Northwest where he changed his name to John Maura.

John Tanner

The disappearance of Rachel McLean hit the headlines of the British press early in 1991, and for over a fortnight her killer fooled both the public and the police. Clever and calm, John Tanner hid his crime well and went on to make appeals for information about her whereabouts.

Bright and young, with a promising future ahead of her, Rachel McLean was studying English Literature at St. Hilda's in Oxford and was just 19 years old when her 22-year-old boyfriend, John Tanner, strangled her to death. He was a British-born New Zealander, studying in Nottingham. As their relationship was deteriorating Rachel complained that Tanner was controlling and possessive. She no longer wanted to see him and started dating other students. Nevertheless, when he said that he wished to visit her, she agreed.

On the evening of April 13, 1991, Rachel waited at Oxford station for Tanner to arrive and when his train was delayed she returned to her home. He followed on by taxi, arriving at around 7.30pm. Various people later reported seeing them together around Oxford the next day, but that would be the last time that Rachel was seen alive. That night, in a fit of jealous rage, Tanner killed his ex-girlfriend.

It took him several hours to find a suitable hiding spot for her body, but when he did it was a good one. There was a closet beneath the stairs and at the back, behind piles of household junk, Tanner discovered an eight inch gap that led to a space beneath the floorboards. He dragged his girlfriend's body into it and then crawled beneath the hallway pulling Rachel to a spot under her own bedroom. Then he covered the body with old carpet and made everything look just as he found it. Tanner then left the house and made his way back to Nottingham, pausing to pen Rachel a brief love letter in which he mentioned how lucky she was that the long-haired man they had met at Oxford station had offered her a lift home.

By April 19, Rachel's friends had begun to realize that something was amiss. She had been due at a meeting with her tutor and to sit an exam in the afternoon, but had missed both. One called her parents to find out if she was okay and was told that they hadn't seen her either and that she had been in Oxford the previous weekend. By April 22, Rachel's disappearance was headline news and a massive search for her was underway. Naturally, her boyfriend wanted to help all he could and spoke movingly of how he had kissed her goodbye at the station a few days earlier. He also mentioned the fictitious long-haired man again, saying that he had joined them for coffee, and that Rachel had seemed to know him.

Police searched Rachel's house and nearby scrubland, while divers dragged the River Cherwell and Rachel's parents made a nationwide appeal at a press conference on April 24th. Still there was no sign on her. A day later a photo-fit image of the man Tanner claimed to have met at the station was released, and by April 28th police had widened the search to include the sewers around her home.

On the 29th, Tanner agreed to appear in a television reconstruction and with a female police officer playing the part of Rachel, he was filmed at Oxford station, reliving the final coffee with his girlfriend and their final kiss. As the last person to see her alive, he was already under suspicion, but said, "I did not kill her. I don't know what happened to her. In my heart of hearts I know she is still alive."

However, by agreeing to take part in the reconstruction he helped seal his own fate. Two people came forward after seeing it. Both remembered Tanner at the station, but neither saw Rachel or a long-haired man. It became even more obvious that Tanner's tale was a lie when police finally discovered her body in the cavity beneath her floorboards. He was immediately arrested at a Nottingham pub, and taken into custody where he refused to answer police questions.

The evidence against him was continuing to mount up though, and Tanner finally broke down and confessed. On May 4, 1991, he was formally charged with the murder of Rachel McLean before magistrates. He was tried for his crime in early December, convicted, and sentenced to life imprisonment. Released 12 years later in 2003,

ABOVE: John Tanner, shown during a press conference making an appeal for information about the whereabouts of Rachel McLean.

John Tanner immediately returned to his home town of Wanganui, New Zealand.

Marie Tarnowska

The crime of Russian Countess Marie Tarnowska was to treat the men who adored her as puppets in her deadly games of intrigue and betrayal. Her cold appetites knew no limits and those who loved her were either ruined or died. Not by her hand, but always she was behind the scenes, pulling the strings.

Born in 1879, Marie was descended from one of the aristocratic houses of Ireland and the daughter of a man who had been made Count Nicholas O'Rke by the Tsar when he emigrated to Russia. At 17 years old, and outstandingly beautiful, she married the wealthy Count Tarnowska. Together they ruled over the glittering aristocratic society of Kiev and their union was blessed with three children. But as time passed, Marie grew bored of married life and developed a taste for exercising the power she had as a countess and as a woman of boundless sexual allure.

One of her early lovers, Alexis Borzlevski, invited her to shoot him through the hand to demonstrate his devotion to her. The incident didn't go unnoticed, and the count then challenged Borzlevski to a duel. Marie's lover was shot dead. Another of her bedmates, Vladimir Stahl, killed himself rather than confront the count at a dueling ground. Yet another was shot dead by the count at a dinner party when Marie deliberately kissed him to provoke her husband. The powerful count was acquitted of the murder on the grounds of his wife's provocation.

Not surprisingly, perhaps, after this spate of incidents the marriage ended, but not before Marie had woven her lethal spell over the lawyer dealing with her divorce. After she toyed with his emotions, Maximillian Prilukoff was prepared to give up his wife and family, career, and fortune to have her. He botched a suicide attempt when she rejected him and the proceeded to follow her around wherever she went, a 19th-century stalker.

Free of her husband's jealousy, Marie traveled to Venice, Italy, and her army of lovers increased. One was young and handsome Nicolas Naumoff, who deserted his wife and children to devote himself to her. She enjoyed torturing him during sex sessions, burning his body with cigarettes. Yet another of her victims

was Count Pavel Kamarovsky who insisted that she marry him. She agreed, but only after he insured his life for her benefit. He was dead within a month; shot

by Naumoff. Marie had led her masochistic lover to believe that Kamarovksy had insulted his virility and honor in various letters.

The fact that Kamarovksy had died so soon after insuring his life inevitably raised suspicion, and the Italian police arrested Marie, Naumoff, and Prilukoff (who had helped draft the fatal letters) in 1907. Their trial began on May 14, 1910, by which time the scandal of the killer countess had sparked outrage at every level of society. A lynch mob waited for her arrival at

the courthouse, and the gondola that brought Marie and her two lovers to the court was greeted by mobs shaking their fists and screaming. When she tried to step onto shore a group of women dragged Marie to the edge of the canal, shouting, "Drown her! Drown

ABOVE: Nicholas Naumoff, who was so infatuated with Marie Tarnowska that he deserted his wife and children to be with her.

RIGHT: Countess Tarnowska arriving at court in Venice under a police escort for her own safety.

her!" Guards from inside the courthouse were forced to rescue the accused!

At the hearing, Prilukoff and Naumoff blamed their actions on their infatuation with the countess, while Marie Tarnowska threw herself on the mercy of the court. She wept copiously and promised to devote the rest of her life to a convent and good works if the jury would just be lenient. The performance saved her life. Pronouncing the verdict, a spokesman for the jury said, "We reject the theory that she was mad. But we

find that her mental faculties were partially destroyed." Marie was sentenced to eight years in prison; Prilukoff to 10 years in solitary confinement; Naumoff to three years in prison because he was "suffering from a partial mental collapse." One newspaper reported of Marie, "She is not yet thirty but at least six men have ruined themselves for her; two of these met tragic deaths and four of them deserted wives and children."

For a time, the prison chaplain and jail keepers in Venice treated their prisoner kindly, smuggling in

cigarettes and good food for the aristocratic prisoner. But after the chaplain found an "extremely improper" novel in her cell she was transferred to a much harsher prison in Rome to serve the remainder of her sentence. Still she used her sexual power over men, and her besotted lawyers were able to have her sentence reduced: Marie was released after five years. She later committed suicide, but before she took her own life made an announcement that became legendary, saying "I am the most unfortunate woman in the world. I am a martyr to my own beauty. For any man to behold me is for him to love me. The whole pathway of my life is strewn with the bodies of those who have loved me most."

Michael Telling

Although there can be never be a good excuse for killing another human being, it is difficult not to feel a pang of sympathy for Michael Telling. Already of a fragile state of mind before he married for the second time, his vicious wife did everything in her power to send him over the edge. And when he inevitably snapped, she reaped the harvest of her bitter tongue.

All of Michael Telling's family wealth couldn't buy him a happy childhood. While he may have had everything he wanted in terms of material things, his violent alcoholic father and a cold, unloving mother left him emotionally scarred by the time he reached maturity. A failed marriage did nothing to help, but after he met Monika Zumsteg while on holiday in America and again fell in love his inner turmoil would reach boiling point.

He could not have picked a worse match than his second wife. Almost as soon as the wedding was over, Monika turned on her husband. Her days and nights were spent languishing around the couple's British country home in West Wycombe, Buckinghamshire, drunk and high on drugs, and for entertainment she taunted her husband. She told him that he was sexually inadequate, that she had only married him for his money, and that she had taken lovers both male and female: anything she could think of that might wound the man she had married.

For a brief period the couple seemed to realize just how destructive their problems were. Monika joined Alcoholics Anonymous, and Telling admitted himself to a psychiatric hospital, but it was to no avail. Back at home the pattern of their relationship quickly reasserted itself, and Telling was finally pushed to breaking point by the woman he both adored and detested. On March 29, 1983, as Monika sneered at him yet again, he grabbed a rifle and shot her. Telling left the body where it lay for two days before dragging it into a bedroom and then spent the next few days talking to his wife's corpse. Finally, some semblance of sanity returned and he was forced to deal with the situation. Friends were told that Monika had run off, and Telling made a long distance drive to the South West of England to dump the body after first having removed Monika's head in an attempt to stop the body being identified. Unfortunately for him, the expensive clothes that she was still wearing gave the police the vital clue they needed when the body was discovered and when they searched Telling's home Monika's decomposing head was found in the garage. "I just snapped" was all he could say.

At his trial the prosecution attempted to portray the killing as a cold-blooded, premeditated murder. They presented Telling's careful covering of his tracks as evidence that he was brutal, but sane. The case of his defense counsel, however, was stronger. Backed up by psychiatrists' reports and the testimonies of his friends and family, they showed that Telling was seriously disturbed. Even his mother took the stand to tell of her son's troubled childhood and suicide attempts and as the court heard of the verbal abuse that he had suffered from his wife, Telling gained some small measure of sympathy. When the time came to give their verdict, the jury acquitted Telling of murder but found him guilty of manslaughter on the grounds of diminished responsibility. He was sentenced to life imprisonment.

Harry Kendall Thaw

An obsessive, violent man of unrestrained appetites, Harry Kendall Thaw may have married the woman that he had relentlessly pursued, but he never forgave or forgot his former rival for her affections; the man who stole from her what he had wanted for himself—her virginity.

Thaw was the son of a wealthy Pittsburgh coal and railroad baron. While his mother later claimed that her son had been trouble from the day he was born, Thaw's father secured him places at private schools, the University of Pittsburgh, and, later, Harvard University. Nevertheless, Thaw squandered the advantages that came with the best education that money could buy. He preferred a wild life of gambling and chasing women and was eventually dismissed from university after chasing a taxi driver with a loaded gun.

Moving to New York City, Thaw began taking drugs and hanging out with chorus girls in Broadway shows. He also became friendly with the famous architect Stanford White with whom he shared a passion for showgirls. The friendship was short-lived though; it soured when Thaw discovered White had made sarcastic remarks about him and his ability to impress women. Thaw's hatred for the architect deepened when White showed an interest in Evelyn Nesbitt, a chorus girl from the show Florodora who had also caught Thaw's eye.

Although White warned the showgirl about his former friend, Thaw continued to pursue Evelyn, presenting himself as a considerate suitor. During an illness, Evelyn was hospitalized, and Thaw visited her regularly, also taking the opportunity to ingratiate himself with her mother. Meanwhile, White's interest in her waned, leaving the way clear for Thaw to woo Evelyn (and her mother) with promises of a luxury lifestyle. Eventually, the strategy paid off and Evelyn agreed to marry him. But it was a tainted victory for Thaw. When Evelyn accepted the proposal she also confessed that her virginity had been lost to Thaw's rival, Stanford White.

Thaw's reaction was extreme. He took Evelyn to an isolated castle in Germany, raped her, and beat her mercilessly. Astonishingly, the marriage still went ahead—possibly because by now Evelyn was too scared of her fiancé to break the engagement off. The newlyweds settled in Pittsburgh with Thaw's mother.

On June, 25, 1906, they made a visit to New York City. That evening they went to Café Martin to dine. Thaw immediately spotted Stanford White and soon learned that his wife's former lover was to attend the premiere of stage show Mam'zelle Champagne, a show the Thaws were also planning to see that night.

Following dinner, a seething Thaw took Evelyn back to their hotel and disappeared, returning just in time to pick her up and head to the show. Curiously, he wore a large black overcoat though it was a hot evening. At the rooftop theater of Madison Square Garden, the hat check girl tried to relieve Thaw of his heavy coat but he refused to take it off. The couple were shown to their table where Thaw appeared distracted. He could not sit still but wandered through the crowd during the show, approaching White's table several times only to back away again. Then, during the show's finale song, I Could Love A Million Girls, Thaw walked up to Stanford White and fired three shots at close range into his face, killing him instantly.

At first, the crowd first thought the shooting was part of the show, but as realization dawned that Stanford

White was actually dead, Thaw—holding the gun aloft—walked through the crowd and met Evelyn at the elevator. When she asked what he'd done, he replied that he had "probably saved your life."

Thaw stood trial for murder twice. At the first, from January to April 1907, the jury could not reach an agreement. At the second in January 1908, Thaw pleaded insanity. In an effort to protect her son, Thaw's mother set out to corrupt the trial. She offered Evelyn a million dollars plus a quick divorce to testify that White had abused her, and Thaw had simply been trying to protect his wife from an evil man. Evelyn did just as she was asked, perjuring herself in court with the skill of a professional actress.

Thaw was found not guilty by reason of insanity and thus escaped the death penalty, though he was incarcerated at the Mattawan State Hospital for the Criminally Insane in Fishkill, New York. Here, he enjoyed almost total freedom and in 1913 Thaw took the opportunity to escape, walking out of the asylum to a waiting car that drove him over the border to Canada. He was quickly extradited back to the United States and two years later a jury judged him sane. Thaw was released after serving just seven years in a comfortable institution. Nevertheless, he soon tangled with the law again. In 1916, he was accused of sexually assaulting and horsewhipping a teenage boy. Again declared insane, Thaw was sent to another asylum where he spent seven years before regaining his freedom once more in 1924.

Thaw died of a heart attack at the age of 76 in Miami, Florida, in February 1947. He left $10,000—less than one per cent of his wealth—to his former wife for whom he had once killed. Having trusted the Thaw family, Evelyn never did receive the million dollars she had been promised for her part in helping her violent husband evade justice.

Charles-Louis Theobald, Duc de Choiseul-Praslin

The scenario of a man growing weary of a wife and taking a younger lover is a familiar one. But while such stories usually involve heartbreak and emotional anguish, few end as tragically as that of the Duc de Choiseul-Praslin, Charles-Louis Theobald.

ABOVE: The Luxembourg Palace in Paris, where Charles-Louis Theobald committed suicide while awaiting trial for the murder of his wife.

The aristocratic **Duc de Choiseul-Praslin,** had married his wife Fanny when she was a dazzling young beauty of just 19. But as the years passed and Fanny gave birth to their 10 children one after another, she put on weight and her famous looks deserted her. Perhaps if her husband had loved her as he should, she would have entered a cheerful old age delighting in her family and not caring about her fading beauty, but the duke could not be content with his aging wife. He tormented her with a series of barely secret affairs. The latest in a line of young women to tumble into his bed was the family governess, and this time the duke was more in love than ever. Yearning to be free of the miserable Fanny, his thoughts turned not to divorce, but to murder.

On August 17, 1847, the Choiseul-Praslin family spent the night at their house in Paris. At 5am, servants heard screams from Fanny's room and rushed to her aid, believing burglars had broken in. They knocked at the locked door in vain. Now all was quiet. The servants ran to the garden in a bid to catch the intruder. When they returned, empty handed, Fanny's bedroom door had been opened. Inside was the duchess, dripping with blood and propped up on the bed. Her throat had been cut and her face beaten to a pulp with a blunt object.

Suspicion immediately settled on the duke, who had been nowhere to be seen during the commotion. Police searched the house and soon unearthed the blood-stained handle of a dagger, a blood-stained bathrobe that someone had tried to wash, and a leather sheath. Also discovered were pitiful letters from the duchess to her husband begging him to end his affair with Henrietta and listing his previous lovers. A loaded pistol was found by the duke's bedside. The evidence suggested that Choiseul-Praslin had first intended to shoot his wife but realizing this would be heard, attempted a silent death by cutting her throat instead. However, the incompetent killer failed to sever her windpipe with his first slash allowing Fanny to raise the alarm by screaming.

The duke's guilt was further proclaimed by blood stains found in his bedroom wash basin and bite marks on his leg that his wife had given him during her struggles. Staff also told police of the violent arguments between the couple and how, during one, she had threatened to leave her husband.

Pathetically, the duke protested that he had tried to defend his wife from the intruders, but his flimsy story fooled no one. After being held under house arrest, he was transferred to the Luxembourg Palace in Paris pending trial by the Court of Peers. However, on August 18, 1847, while in custody, he took advantage of a guard's absence to poison himself with arsenic. Even on his deathbed, the Duc de Choiseul-Praslin denied all accusations.

Norman Thorne

A plain woman, Elsie Emily Cameron was not used to receiving attention from men, so when Norman Thorne made advances toward her she quickly gave him her heart and her body. And when he decided that he didn't want to marry her after all, she was so distressed that she felt the only way to keep him was to lie.

Elsie Cameron and Norman Thorne met in 1920 while she was working as a typist in London and he was an electrical engineer. At only 18, he was nine years her junior, but he didn't seem to be put off by the difference in their ages and nor did he seem concerned about Elsie's spectacles or the fact that she wasn't a great beauty.

Flattered by his attentions, Elsie fell in love. Thorne had ambitions beyond being an engineer and wanted to run

RIGHT: Chicken farmer Norman Thorne standing amongst his birds at Crowborough, Sussex, on the exact spot where the remains of his missing fiancée Elsie Cameron were later found buried.

ABOVE: Norman Thorne boarding a train at Crowborough Station in Sussex, on his way to Brixton, London, for the enquiry into the murder his fiancée, Elsie Cameron.

his own business. Accordingly, he bought a small piece of land at Blackness, Crowborough, Sussex, and set up Wesley Poultry Farm, working hard to make it a success between rushed visits to Elsie. When he converted a farm shed into living accommodation, Elsie began traveling down to Sussex to see him and during the Christmas of 1922, Thorne proposed and was accepted.

Elsie's happiness wasn't to last though. Soon after they became engaged, Thorne's business began to fail and pleading financial difficulties he refused to set a wedding date. The situation was further complicated when he met a woman called Bessie and decided that he preferred his new lover to his fiancée. In October 1923, Elsie traveled down to Crowborough and, as

usual, stayed with neighbors. She spent a week with Thorne but her intuition told her that his feelings had changed. When she returned home to London, she wrote a letter telling her fiancé that she was pregnant in a bid to hurry the wedding. Thorne's reply was not what she expected. Cornered, he confessed that he tired of her and told her about Bessie.

Distraught, Elsie rushed to Thorne's farm and arrived unannounced on the morning of November 30, 1923.

To calm her, Thorne relented and said that he would marry her and she returned to London hoping that the future she had so longed for was still just around the corner. The following week, Thorne's father visited the farm that week to discuss his son's finances and offer some advice. He warned Thorne to be cautious over Elsie's claims of being pregnant and told him to write to her and discover the truth. When she received the letter, Elsie became even more desperate than before and on Friday December 5, 1923, she again caught the train to Crowborough station from where she walked to Thorne's farm.

Five days later Elsie's father sent a telegram to Thorne asking after his daughter. Thorne replied that he had not seen her. The next day Mr Cameron informed the police of his daughter's disappearance. They found that Elsie had been seen by two flower-growers while walking toward the farm at about 5.15 pm on the last day that anyone had seen her. Thorne, however, remained adamant that Elsie had not been to the farm. By the beginning of January there was still no sign of her, and police began questioning Thorne's neighbors, one of whom said she had seen Elsie entering the farm on the day she had vanished. Sussex police requested assistance from Scotland Yard and officers decided there

was enough evidence to arrest Thorne and search the farm. Elsie's watch, bracelet, and jewelry were found in a tin and the attaché case she had been carrying was later found buried near outbuildings.

Thorne denied murdering his unwanted fiancée, telling police interrogators that he and Elsie had argued over his relationship with Bessie. He had stormed off and later returned to find that Elsie had hanged herself from a beam with his washing line. Fearing that no one would believe his story, Thorne said he cut her down, chopped off her legs and head, and buried the parts under his chicken run. However, a postmortem showed no signs of rope marks and Thorne was charged with murder.

The case came before Lewes Assizes on March 4, 1925. Thorne's defence argued that the postmortem report was flawed, telling the jury that creases on Elsie's neck may have been made by a rope. The police countered this by testifying that there was no sign of a rope having been suspended from any of the farmhouse beams. Twelve days later the jury returned a guilty verdict. Thorne was hanged on April 22, 1925, the day that would have been Elsie's 27th birthday.

Jean-Pierre Vaquier

When British inn owner Mabel Jones took a vacation in Biarritz, France, in 1924, she wasn't the first married woman be carried away by the holiday atmosphere and the suave charm of French men. But what was for her a simple vacation romance turned into a dangerously obsessive love for the man she left behind.

Leaving her husband Alfred to run the Blue Anchor Inn in Byfleet, Surrey, Mabel Jones headed for the south of France and a well-deserved break. She booked into the Hotel Victoria and soon fell in with a dapper, bearded Frenchman called Jean-Pierre Vaquier who was working there. He was a skilled technician and delighted guests at the hotel by arranging the transmission of music concerts into the hotel's salon. The debonair Frenchman was also soon delighting Mabel in different

ways. The couple had a brief, but very passionate liaison.

All too soon it was time for Mabel to return home, and she bid her lover a fond farewell, thinking that would be the last of the matter. She was mistaken though. Back in England, Mabel received a telegram from Vaquier asking when it would be convenient for him to call on her. She ignored it and was startled when after she had been home a month Vaquier arrived at the inn. While she had finished the affair with no regrets

ABOVE: Mabel Jones, whose vacation affair would eventually lead to the death of her husband.

and just a few happy memories, Vaquier's love had blossomed into a driving obsession and now he wished to claim her for his own. Mabel was forced to have furtive meetings during which she tried to make it plain to the Frenchman that his attentions were unwanted, all the while looking over her shoulder to make sure her husband didn't notice Vaquier ardently attempting to woo her. Feeling guilty for the lengths he had gone to out of love for her, she didn't charge him for his stay, and it was explained to Alfred Jones that Vaquier was waiting for money to arrive to pay for his "business trip."

Vaquier's love was not to be so easily turned aside and he took it into his head that if Alfred was to be taken out of the picture, Mabel would return to his embraces once more. On March 1, 1924, Vaquier went to London and bought strychnine, signing the poison register "J. Wanker." Now familiar with Alfred Jones drinking habits and noticing the fact that he habitually took indigestion salts as a hangover cure in the morning, Vaquier spiked Alfred's bottle of medicine. On the morning of March 29th, he watched as Jones swigged from the bottle and then helped carry him to his bedroom when he became ill. Alfred Jones died in agony some hours later.

The sudden death prompted a postmortem during which Alfred's body was found to contain strychnine. Both Vaquier and Mabel were questioned and a photograph of the Frenchman was published in various newspapers. The chemist who had supplied Vaquier with the poison recognized his face, and the Frenchman was arrested at a hotel in Woking, Surrey, then charged with murder. Although he maintained his innocence throughout the trial at Guildford Assizes in July 1924, Jean-Pierre Vaquier was found guilty and hanged at Wandsworth Prison, London, on August 12, 1924.

ABOVE: Jean Pierre Vaquier, who in 1924 poisoned Alfred Jones, proprietor of the Blue Anchor Inn in Byfleet, Surrey.

Carolyn Warmus

A wealthy, if unhappy, family life gave Carolyn Warmus a sense of entitlement from an early age. Later, it would begin to show in bizarre behavior if one of her many affairs didn't go exactly as she expected; behavior that would come to a tragic climax when her latest married lover dumped her.

Carolyn Warmus was born in January 1964 and grew up in Birmingham, Michigan, a rich suburb of Detroit. Her parents divorced when she was just eight years old and by the time she began attending the University of Michigan it was obvious to those who came close to her that she had psychological problems. She seemed desperate for physical and emotional contact, but one by one all of her relationships broke down because of her possessiveness. Finally, one former boyfriend, Paul Laven, was forced to take out a restraining order to keep Carolyn away from him. The obsessive behavior continued when Carolyn moved to New York, where she hired a private detective to follow a married bartender who had also had the nerve to end their relationship.

Despite her emotional problems, Carolyn eventually earned a master's degree in elementary education from Columbia University and landed a job in September 1987, at the Greenville Elementary in Scarsdale, New York. There, she met Paul Solomon, a fifth grade teacher

RIGHT: The two-story Scarsdale apartment complex where murderer Carolyn Warmus allegedly shot her lover's wife before meeting him for sex in a parking lot.

BELOW: High school yearbook picture of future murderer Carolyn Warmus (center) who would kill her lover's wife eight years later.

who was soon to become yet another married lover. With no knowledge of Carolyn's previous behavior, Solomon badly misjudged her, introducing her to his wife Betty Jeanne and their daughter Kristan. Before long Carolyn was almost part of the family, becoming a big sister figure to Kristan whom she showered with expensive presents. Behind the scenes though, Carolyn was sleeping with Solomon and her resentment of his seemingly perfect, happy family life was growing.

During the early evening of January 15, 1989, a New York Telephone operator answered a call from a woman who was clearly in fear for her life. When it was suddenly disconnected, the operator immediately contacted the police. However, they were unable to trace the call, though it soon became apparent who had made it. When Paul Solomon returned home that night he discovered his wife's body. She had been beaten around the head with a gun and then shot nine times in her back and legs.

Detectives immediately suspected that Solomon had murdered his wife himself, but he was able to give credible alibis, including having spent part of the evening with Carolyn. The illicit relationship now came to an end. Solomon told Carolyn that he no longer wanted to see her and was soon involved with another woman, Barbara Ballor. It was this new relationship that pointed police in Carolyn's direction. She was soon back to her old ways, pursuing Solomon

and his new girlfriend and attempting to split them up. The increasingly suspicious police also learned that she had purchased a .25 caliber Beretta pistol just before Betty Jeanne had been murdered. Further investigations showed that on the day of the killing, a call had been made from Carolyn's home to a sports shop, where she later arrived to buy ammunition. With enough evidence to charge her for murder, the police moved quickly to arrest her.

The trial of Carolyn Warmus began on January 14, 1991, and from the outset she did little to court public sympathy. The tight outfits she wore accentuated her figure, and the New York press dubbed her Sex Tigress, A Woman Possessed, and the Black Widow. Nevertheless, the trial dragged on for months before the jury finally announced that it was unable to reach a unanimous verdict. On April 27, 1991, the judge announced a mistrial.

At the second trial, which began in January 1992, a new piece of evidence was presented: a blood-soaked woollen glove that had been found at the murder scene. It was shown to have belonged to Carolyn, and this time the jury was convinced of her guilt. On June 26, 1992, Judge John Carey told the court that Carolyn Warmus had committed "a hideous act, a most extreme, illegal, and wanton murder" and gave her a sentence that matched the severity of the crime: 25 years to life in prison.

Mary Eleanor Wheeler Pearcey

With an auburn-haired beauty so fine that even her hangman would remark that she was the most beautiful woman he had ever executed, Mary Eleanor Wheeler Pearcey, left a trail of broken hearts behind her. But when her own was shattered, she tried to mend it by killing the family of her lover.

Born in 1866, Mary Eleanor Wheeler was no stranger to unhappiness from an early age. Her father was a robber and murderer, and when he was hanged for his crimes Mary attempted suicide. She failed and soon after that her family moved to London where it seems

she tried to heal her emotional pain in the beds of a string of men.

The first was Charles Pearcey, whom Mary met when she was just 16. So smitten was Mary with him that she took his last name even though they never actually married. But despite the love that grew between them, Mary found it difficult not to flaunt her charms elsewhere, and Pearcey left her when he found out that she had been sleeping with married, self-made businessman Charles Creighton. For a while Creighton kept Mary as his mistress, but her wandering eye was soon caught by another—a young man named Frank Hogg who worked at his family's grocery store.

This time it looked as though one of Mary's relationships might last the distance. She fell deeply in love with Hogg, and he with her, but again the relationship was wrecked by infidelity. This time though it was not Mary who cheated. Hogg had been sleeping with a girl called Phoebe Styles. When she fell pregnant his family insisted he marry her. Mary was devastated, but when Hogg offered to move away to spare her feelings she told him that she would prefer he stayed close to her than suffer the pain of never seeing him again.

Unsurprisingly, Hogg's marriage did nothing to cool his and Mary's passion for one another and they were soon back in each other's arms, while Mary also began seeing Charles Creighton again. She also took an interest in her lover's new wife and tried to befriend Phoebe, though it appears that she was instinctively wary of Mary. On one occasion she refused Mary's invitation to visit a seaside house, explaining to her husband that "no one would think to look for me in a big, empty house."

On October 24, 1890, Mary sent an invitation by messenger boy to her lover's wife and 18-month-old baby Tiggie; this time to take tea with her. Phoebe accepted and wrote a brief note for Hogg so that he would not worry, simply saying, "Shall not be gone long." She then pushed the baby round to Mary's apartment in a pram.

The body of Phoebe Hogg was discovered on the heath at Hampstead in north London. The man who found her later confessed to stealing her wedding ring and selling it for food before finding a policeman. A doctor who examined the corpse noted that Phoebe's throat was slashed from left to right, and that the cut was so deep her head had been nearly severed from her body. Newspaper reports assumed the murderer was a man because of the force used.

The following day, Saturday, 26th October, baby Tiggie was found on waste ground. Her only wound was a scratch on her forehead most likely caused by being dumped, but she was also dead. The pram was found some miles away, blood soaked and missing a bolt. The medical examiner could not determine if the baby suffocated under the weight of its dead mother, or if it died from exposure.

During Mary's trial, the court was packed with middle-class ladies. Her story had captivated numerous wives and mistresses who felt sympathy toward a wronged woman even though an innocent woman and tiny child had been the victims of her terrible revenge. Despite their support and her claims of innocence, Mary was sentenced to hang. In a very odd twist of fate, her execution, on December 23, 1890, was carried out by a man called James Berry who was the assistant to the man who had hanged her father at St. Albans some 14 years earlier.

Mary Eleanor Wheeler Pearcey was buried at Newgate Prison in an unmarked grave. While never confessing to the murders and saying the evidence against her was false, she said the sentence was just. She also left a cryptic note with her solicitor that read, "MEWP. Did not betray. MEW." No one knows what it means, though it has been suggested it was a note meant for a husband from a secret marriage.

Elizabeth Workman

Like many women before and after her, Elizabeth Workman snapped after enduring years of abuse from her husband. What makes her case more notable is that despite public support and the wishes of the jury, she still went to her death.

Elizabeth and James Workman were among a wave of immigrants who landed in Canada in the mid-19th century looking for a better quality of life. They came from Scotland, and Elizabeth was in her 20s, about 30 years younger than her husband who also brought with them his daughter Mary from a previous marriage. Sadly, they did not find the better life that they had hoped for in a new country. Poverty forced the family to live in a two-room apartment, in which Elizabeth soon gave birth to their son.

Elizabeth's miseries were made worse by the realization that she had married a drunken bully. Although she refused to criticize her husband, she often ran to the neighbors to hide from his vicious tongue and fists. One of those who gave her shelter was Samuel Butler, a black man who owned a small barber shop. A charitable man, Butler tried to help the struggling family by offering Elizabeth a job doing his laundery and cleaning the shop.

Elizabeth and Butler's friendship was soon noted by the town gossips and rumors began to fly that the pair were having a love affair, a relationship that would have been taboo at that time. The tittle-tattle inevitably reached the ears of James Workman, and on October 24, 1872, while Elizabeth was scrubbing the floor at Butler's barber shop, her husband arrived with their little boy. Obviously the worse for drink, James demanded that his wife return home. When Elizabeth refused, Workman made to grab her, but Butler intervened. Elizabeth was so furious that she beat her husband with a mop handle. However, her anger was not to end there.

As the court would later hear, the next morning an upstairs neighbor saw Butler leaving the Workmans' rooms. James Workman was in bed recovering from the beating his wife had given him, but still he constantly berated and abused Elizabeth until—as she later confessed—she could take no more. She beat him on and off for two hours until one heavy blow rendered her husband unconscious—for good.

Later that day, Elizabeth called on another neighbor, David Patterson, as she was concerned about her husband. But it was too late for him. At first Patterson said Workman had died in his arms but then he changed his story to say he was dead when he got there, and that the body looked suspiciously as if it had been washed clean of blood.

The postmortem examination was conducted on the following Sunday morning. James Workman's body was recorded as being malnourished and—in the coroner's view—bruises and abrasions on his legs were consistent with having been bound with a rope. Other bruises suggested that he had received between 20 and 30 blows from a blunt object. The killing blow, however, had been made by a "sharp cutting instrument" near the left temple. Two butcher's tools were found in the home that could have caused it.

Elizabeth was quickly arrested but denied having anything to do with her husband's murder, saying he had died of natural causes. She also staunchly defended Samuel Butler, denying he had anything to do with the death. Her trial lasted just two days, during which she heard a flood of evidence against her, ranging from absurd and irrelevant accusations that she was "not very kind" to witnesses declaring that although James Workman had verbally abused his wife regularly, he had never actually been seen to hit her. The court also heard suggestions of an improper relationship between Elizabeth and Samuel Butler.

The judge finally swayed the verdict. Although the jury had sympathy for Elizabeth and did not want to convict her for murder, the judge's conclusion was that there was strong circumstantial evidence against her and he recommended that the jury decided accordingly. Sure enough the jury returned a guilty verdict against Elizabeth while Samuel Butler was acquitted through lack of evidence.

Elizabeth Workman spent three months in prison before her execution on June 19, 1873. The reprieve she waited for never came despite growing public support. She walked to the gallows clutching a bunch of flowers. She was the only woman ever to be executed by hanging in Canadian history. A later report noted, "The crucial reason that Elizabeth Workman was allowed to hang was that the judge's negative characterization was uncontested at the trial by the defense. Elizabeth Workman, a poor, marginalized, working-class woman was ill-served by a judicial system that accorded her little regard. Specifically, no real effort was made to defend her."

Anna Zwanziger

If the unfortunate Anna Zwanziger was tempted, it wasn't by one man in particular, but by the idea of love itself. And for her, a happy ending was something she was prepared to kill for.

Born in Nuremberg, Germany, in 1760, Anna Schoenleben was not well favored by fate. Described as "ugly, stunted, without attraction of face, figure, or speech; a misshapen woman whom some people likened to a toad," she yearned for love. And despite her lack of physical beauty she eventually managed to find it. Her first husband, Herr Zwanziger, was even quite a catch, or so it seemed at the time. He was a successful lawyer with whom Anna had two children.

For a time it looked as though she might have found what she had craved, but Anna's happiness proved to be short-lived. Zwanziger was a heavy drinker, and as time passed became an uncontrollable and violent alcoholic. His wealth soon disappeared on drink and his rages terrified his wife. The family became so poor that Anna was forced into prostitution to earn enough money to feed her children, though insisting to friends that she only slept with "gentlemen."

When Zwanziger's years of alcohol abuse eventually saw him into an early grave, his impoverished widow looked for work as a housekeeper and cook. However, it was not really a job she was after, but a way of introducing herself into a house where she might find what she really wanted—another man, a new husband who would make up for the failings of the first.

She was meticulous in plan, only advertising her services amongst the circle of judges in Bavaria. Sadly, the only employers—and would-be lovers—Anna could find were already married or engaged. Nevertheless, there was one promising candidate, a judge called Glaser who, though married, was separated from his wife. Anna tried to encourage his interest. However, even an estranged wife was still a wife, and Anna ruthlessly set out to remove her from the scene permanently. Pretending concern for her employer, she set up a reconciliation between the couple at the judge's home. Then Anna liberally laced Frau Glaser's tea with a fatal dose of arsenic.

She killed in vain. Even with his wife dead, Glaser wasn't interested in the ugly creature who kept house for him, and Anna was forced to give up and try her plan elsewhere. She took employment with another judge, named Grohmann and again tried to make the hapless man fall in love with her. Unlike her previous employer, Grohmann was happy to take advantage of the sexual favors that Anna was offering, but not happy enough to take her as his wife. When Anna heard he was planning to wed another woman, she once again turned to arsenic and put large amounts in Grohmann's soup. He died a horrific death in agony.

Still Anna was convinced that her plan would work, especially as she was now so practiced in removing any obstacles from her path with a dose of poison. Her third employer was yet another judge, a gentleman by the name of Gebhard. Soon after he took Anna on, his wife became sickly and claimed that her food tasted strange since the arrival of the new housekeeper. At first her husband did not believe her, but he began to take her tale seriously when he found a white sediment in his brandy glass. It was too late: his wife died in convulsions. Even that wasn't enough for Anna. So twisted had she become that she decided the judge must be hers and hers alone. She fed his small child a biscuit dipped in arsenic-laced milk and soon the infant, too, died. Judge Gebhard had their food analyzed and traces of arsenic were found. By the time he received the results, Anna had already fled.

Anna Zwanziger was arrested in October 1809 after police exhumed her many victims' bodies and discovered more traces of the poison. She had foolishly led them straight to her by writing letters to the Gebhard family to ask if she could have her old job back. She eventually confessed, admitting, "Yes, I killed them all and would have killed more if I had the chance." The woman who was so envious of others' beauty—and husbands—was beheaded in July 1811.

Picture Credits

Getty Images
Front Cover, main image
1, 2 Yvonne Hemsey/Getty Images, 13, 14, 17
David McNew/Getty Images, 21, 22 & 23 Topical
Press Agency/Hulton Archive/Getty Images, 25
Universal Pictures/Getty Images, 28 Dennis Kunkel
Microscopy, Inc/Getty Images, 29 Miller/Topical
Press Agency/Hulton Archive/Getty Images, 31,
33 Topical Press Agency/Hulton Archive/Getty
Images, 34, 35 Henry Guttmann/Getty Images, 39
Will F. Taylor/Edward Gooch/Hulton Archive/
Getty Images, 40, 41, 42 (top) J. DAVID AKE/AFP/
Getty Images, 43 POOL/AFP/Getty Images, 44
(top) J. DAVID AKE/AFP/Getty Images, 48 Justin
Sullivan/Getty Images, 54, 55, 58 David Goddard/
Getty Images, 60 & 61 & 62 & 63 Topical Press
Agency/Getty Images, 64, 65 Topical Press Agency/
Getty Images, 66 & 67 & 68 Keystone/Hulton
Archive/Getty Images, 70, 71, 72, 73, 74, 75, 77
Edward Gooch/Getty Images, 78, 79 Topical Press
Agency/Getty Images, 82 W. G. Phillips/Topical
Press Agency/Getty Images, 85 Roger Viollet/Getty
Images, 92, 93 Keystone/Getty Images, 94 Bentley
Archive/Popperfoto/Getty Images, 97 Evening
Standard/Getty Images, 114 FPG/Hulton Archive/
Getty Images, 118 Yvonne Hemsey/Getty Images,
119, 120, 128 Brian Miller/Time Life Pictures/
Getty Images, 130 & 131 & 132 & 133 Keystone/
Hulton Archive/Getty Images, 137 Chicago History
Museum/Getty Images, 138, 140 Topical Press
Agency/Getty Images, 141 & 142 Topical Press
Agency/Hulton Archive/Getty Images, 143 E. Dean/
Topical Press Agency/Hulton Archive/Getty Images,
144 General Photographic Agency/Hulton Archive/
Getty Images, 146, 147 Leon Neal/AFP/Getty
Images, 149, 150, 157, 159 Popperfoto/Getty Images,
160 Express Newspapers/Getty Images, 165 William
Frederick Yeames/Getty Images, 166 SOTHEBY'S
LONDON/AFP/Getty Images, 167, 169 Topical
Press Agency/Getty Images, 176 STF/AFP/Getty
Images, 177 MIKE NELSON/AFP/Getty Images,
178 POO/AFP/Getty Images, 179 Lori SHELPER/
AFP/Getty Images, 180 & 181 POO/AFP/Getty
Images, 182 MYUNG J. CHUN/AFP/Getty Images,
183 HECTOR MATA/AFP/Getty Images, 189,

191 William F. Campbell//Time Life Pictures/Getty
Images, 193 Fotos International/Getty Images, 195
Archive Photos/Getty Images, 197 Popperfoto/Getty
Images, 198 Fox Photos/Getty Images, 204, 205
Topical Press Agency/Getty Images, 206, 207, 210,
211, 213 Kirby/Topical Press Agency/Getty Images,
214 E. Bacon/Topical Press Agency/Getty Images,
216 Topical Press Agency/Hulton Archive/Getty
Images, 217 Firmin/Topical Press Agency/Hulton
Archive/Getty Images, 218 Michael Abramson/Time
Life Pictures/Getty Images, 219 Michael Abramson/
Time & Life Pictures/Getty Images
Back Cover top left & top right, bottom left Archive
Photos/Getty Images, bottom right Keystone/Hulton
Archive/Getty Images

iStock
iStockphoto.com/Renphoto
18 iStockphoto.com/Terraxplorer, 20 (right)
iStockphoto.com/davidmartyn

Press Association
7, 8, 9, 10, 11, 12, 20 (left), 26, 37 (both), 42
(bottom), 44 (bottom), 84 (both), 88, 89, 90, 96, 100,
102, 104, 108 (both), 110, 115, 125, 135, 161, 162,
163, 171, 172, 173, 174,185, 186, 187 (both), 190,
200, 201, 203,

TopFoto
46 The Granger Collection/TopFoto, 47

Every effort has been made to trace the ownership of
copyrighted material and to secure permission from
copyright holders. In the event of any question arising
as to the use of any material, we will be pleased to
make necessary corrections in future printings.